Discoveries of America is a collection of personal letters written by 18 of the thousands of British emigrants who came to North America in the 15 years preceding the onset of the American Revolution. These accounts are rare: Few letters sent by emigrants during the colonial period exist. The letters reveal the motivations, experiences, characteristics, and emotions of these people who populated America at a crucial time in its history, and provide new insights into the mechanisms of the British-American migration, especially the organization of personal networks of family and friends.

D0908020

DISCOVERIES OF AMERICA

DISCOVERIES OF AMERICA

Personal Accounts of British
Emigrants to North America
during the Revolutionary Era

Edited by
BARBARA De WOLFE
Harvard University

Foreword by Bernard Bailyn

CAMBRIDGE
UNIVERSITY PRESS

PUBLISHED BY THE PRESS SYNDICATE OF THE UNIVERSITY OF CAMBRIDGE
The Pitt Building, Trumpington Street, Cambridge CB2 1RP, United Kingdom

CAMBRIDGE UNIVERSITY PRESS
The Edinburgh Building, Cambridge CB2 2RU, United Kingdom
40 West 20th Street, New York, NY 10011–4211, USA
10 Stamford Road, Oakleigh, Melbourne 3166, Australia

First published 1997

Printed in the United States of America

Typeset in Adobe Caslon

Library of Congress Cataloging-in-Publication Data
Discoveries of America : personal accounts of British emigrants to
North America during the revolutionary era / [edited by] Barbara
DeWolfe.
p. cm.
ISBN 0–521–38542–3 (hardback). – ISBN 0–521–38694–2 (pbk.)
1. British Americans – Correspondence.   2. British – Nova Scotia –
Correspondence.   3. Immigrants – United States – Correspondence.
4. Immigrants – Nova Scotia – Correspondence.   5. United States –
Emigration and immigration – History – 18th century – Sources.
6. Nova Scotia – Emigration and immigration – History – 18th century –
Sources.   7. Great Britain – Emigration and immigration –
History – 18th century – Sources.   I. DeWolfe, Barbara.
E184.B7D57   1997
971.6'00421 – dc20   96–21690
                                                                                            CIP

*A catalog record for this book is available from
the British Library.*

ISBN 0 521 38542 3 hardback
ISBN 0 521 38694 2 paperback

For My Friends and Family

CONTENTS

FOREWORD

A MERICA is forever being discovered – revealed, unveiled, analyzed, criticized, and praised by those who come to it from outside. Its fascination, for those who would commit their lives to it, remains, after almost four centuries, undiminished, and those who lead the way continue to send back reports of the world they find, the people they encounter, the pluses and minuses of life in America which will shape the decisions of others. In the nineteenth century and after, these reports became voluminous. Migrant letters to prospective followers of that era abound and have been collected and anthologized, along with commentaries in artistic form: novels, poetry, and plays. And in the twentieth century, television and instantaneous worldwide news reporting have created a running commentary, sometimes perceptive, often grotesque, on the state of the nation and its people, flashed to every corner of the globe.

But reports from the founding years – the formative years when America was not a center but a periphery, a far boundary, a marchland of the metropolitan world, exotic and seemingly open – are rare, and they are especially revealing. For in the long history of America's lure for people throughout the world, the later eighteenth century, and especially the 15 years before the outbreak of the Revolution, has a special place. Not only were the numbers of British migrants especially large in those years, but the concern of British officials over this heightened exodus and its implication of growing self-confidence and demographic strength in the colonies led to investigations that probed deeply into the character of the movement as a whole, into the motivations of the migrants, their expectations, connections, abilities, and disabilities. The records of these investigations have survived, and are invaluable historical documents. They allow one to see the background from which the emigrants emerged, their personal and family connections, and the course of their fortunes. On this background the personal accounts that survive take on greater meaning. The inner states of mind revealed can be grasped in proper context, and can be assessed as expressions of particular worlds.

In *Voyagers to the West*, a volume in the "Peopling of America" project, of which the present book is a part, some of these personal accounts were used, but only selectively. Much could not be included, and subsequently other such reports were found in manuscript form. Now Barbara DeWolfe presents in full the best of these eyewitness assessments written for prospective emigrants, and in her Introduction and meticulous editing she provides an incisive commentary on the details these letters contain and their implications for a broad understanding of the migration process. In presenting these discoveries of America she rescues the very ordinary people who wrote them from obscurity, identifies them and their families, and explains the circumstances at home that led them to consider migration, and something of their fate thereafter. The details matter; the particulars of these lives in motion bring them alive. Filling in the record from a multitude of ancillary sources, Barbara DeWolfe illuminates the larger movement of people of which these writers and their kin and friends were a part.

These eighteenth-century discoveries of America are not restricted in their meaning to the immediate circumstances and to the few years in which they were written. The writers' chief concerns, their views of American opportunities and dangers, their hopes and fears and their warnings about what it takes to succeed – the close, precise calculus that gets the best results and yet the boldness, the reckless adventurism, that is required – all of that seems timeless. The writers' search for opportunity, security, independence, and prosperity; their curiosity and zest for experience; their inevitable disappointments and gradual adjustment and recovery; and their continuing confidence, so often challenged, in a better future – all of that would be said again and again in later generations. But these discoveries of America on the eve of the Revolution – some never published before, most not easily available in print – have a unique freshness. They evoke a time when America, for Europeans, though no longer a barbarous land, still seemed unformed, still wonderfully malleable, if one had the skill and courage to shape some part of it. It was all promise, and it was full of mysteries still to be explored. These were truly formative years, culturally as well as politically, and these British discoverers of America were true explorers. Their detailed accounts of what they found, their assessments of possibilities, their enthusiasms and cautions, their warnings and encouragements, add significantly to the literature of American history and to the history of America's relation to the rest of the world.

Bernard Bailyn

PREFACE

THIS book has evolved slowly. During the last 20 years, while doing research for the "Peopling of America" project, a population study of colonial America, I found many interesting letters and documents that I thought should be made more accessible to researchers in emigration history. Originally, I planned to edit a volume of emigration documents, including letters, ship lists, depositions, advertisements for land and servants, memos, receipts, newspaper extracts, land allotments, and so forth. But letters that were written by British emigrants who were part of the migration to America before the Revolution stood out as especially interesting and illuminating. With the encouragement of Bernard Bailyn, I published some of these letters in *Perspectives in American History*, New Series, 3(1987). For this book, I have added more writings, and an Introduction that ties together some of the more common themes found in the letters, and provides background information on this pre-Revolutionary migration.

In putting together this volume, I have had help from many people and institutions. The funding for the research for the "Peopling of America" project was granted by the Rockefeller Brothers Fund and the National Endowment for the Humanities. An editing institute sponsored by the National Historical Publications and Records Commission provided a necessary conduit for information and guidance about documentary editing. One of the tutors at that institute, Gaspare J. Saladino, was, and has continued to be, immensely helpful and encouraging, as well as knowledgeable about all aspects of selection and editing. I am greatly indebted to him for his assistance.

The staffs and archivists of a myriad of institutions have been the backbone of this research. Without their custody, preservation, and organization of manuscript collections, as well as their knowledge and assistance, a project such as this would be unthinkable. The institutions they represent include the Public Record Office, London; Scottish Record Office, Edinburgh; National Library of Scotland, Edinburgh; National Register of Archives (Scotland); Aberdeen University Library, King's College, Aberdeen, Scotland; Orkney Islands Area Archives, Orkney County Library, Kirkwall, Orkney, Scotland; the Public Record Office of Northern Ireland, Belfast; Provincial Archives of New Brunswick, Fredericton; Mt. Allison University Archives, Sackville, New Brunswick; Public Archives of Nova Scotia, Halifax; Houghton Library, Harvard University, Cambridge, Massachusetts; Vermont Historical Society, Montpelier; Princeton University Library, Princeton, New Jersey; Historical Society of Pennsylvania, Philadelphia; Huntington Library, San Marino, California; North Carolina Department of Archives and History, Raleigh; Southern Historical Collection, University of North Carolina Library, Chapel Hill; and William L. Clements Library, University of Michigan, Ann Arbor. In particular I would like to thank James D. Galbraith at the Scottish Record Office; Alison Fraser at the Orkney County Library; Ciaran Mee at the Public Record Office of Northern Ireland; Allan Robertson at the Public Archives of Nova Scotia; Donna Beal at the Mt. Allison University Archives; and Barney Bloom at the Vermont Historical Society. I would also like to acknowledge Alexander Murdoch for bringing the Alexander Campbell of Balole letter to my attention, and for the role of the Scottish Records Program of the North Carolina Colonial Records Project, which is partially funded by the National Endowment for the Humanities. Finally, Widener Library and practically every staff member in it have been the life support system of this project.

Fred Anderson and Drew McCoy read the entire manuscript, and for this and their support, I cannot thank them enough. In addition, a few people read certain sections; they gave me good advice and helped me move the project forward: Mary Keeler, Edward Hanson, Virginia DeJohn Anderson, and Sue Schneps. Ed Hanson wields a mean red pen, but his editorial comments and keen eye for detail were invaluable. I thank others for sharing their expertise and assistance in specific areas: Patricia Denault, T. M. Devine, George Hamell, David Hancock, Christopher Miller, Alexander Murdoch, Nancy and Rolly Simpson, Russell Snapp, and Helena Wall. I also appreciate the efforts of Laurel Thatcher Ulrich, who helped me see the few women in this book more clearly.

Frank Smith was the perfect editor. Helen Wheeler, my production editor, had to put up with my revisions and excuses, while she diligently and expertly gave the manuscript her careful attention. I could not have asked for better editors. I would also like to acknowledge Alan Gold and the rest of the staff of Cambridge University Press who assisted in the design and production of this book.

I owe a special gratitude to Bernard Bailyn. He encouraged me to get this project started, and prodded me from time to time to keep it going. He read the manuscript several times, and always had important suggestions, many of which, I'm afraid, I failed to address to his satisfaction. His exacting standards, though impossible to meet, have nevertheless made this book better than it otherwise would have been.

Finally, I offer my appreciation for those to whom I dedicate this book. Without such a network of friends and family, as the emigrants in this book would attest, nothing is possible.

A NOTE ON SELECTION

IN spite of the difficulty of finding colonial emigrant writings, 41 letters, one memoir, and two pamphlets have survived that fulfill certain criteria established for this collection. Accounts were selected if they were written by British emigrants who arrived in America between 1760 and 1775,[1] and if they contained significant information about what the emigrants had discovered in America. These were people who came to America with the intention of staying for an extended period, if not permanently. What they said in their letters reflected their commitment to live in America, and not the detachment of a casual sojourner. Finally, an attempt was made to find letters that represented a wide geographical range of British colonies in America. The New England colonies, with the exception of present-day Vermont, are noticeably absent, but relatively few British emigrants went to New England during this period.

In applying these criteria, certain kinds of personal accounts were excluded, even if they contained interesting details about America. These include letters or diaries from people who were not permanent emigrants, such as missionaries, military personnel, travel diarists, and visitors; letters and memoirs written in hindsight; letters by emigrants whose dates of immigration are unknown; letters that focused on the political differences or military conflict between Britain and America; and letters concerned primarily with religious matters. In some cases transcriptions of letters were found that fit the criteria, but originals could not be located, and thus the transcriptions could not be verified. Collections of published letters that are easily available elsewhere are also excluded.[2]

---

[1] The one exception to this is Alexander McAllister, who arrived in 1739. His letters are included here because McAllister was a central figure in the migration of his Scottish countrymen to America, and he reports about the new arrivals. See his letters, this volume.

[2] Transcriptions of three excellent letters written between 1766 and 1784 by the Irish immigrant Job Johnson are on deposit in the Public Record Office of Northern Ireland in Bel-

Most of the letters in this collection could in some sense be regarded as "promotional" in nature, in that they contained information that attracted the interest of prospective emigrants. But "promotional literature" per se was also not included, because it was generally written by people who often distorted what they knew of the truth, because either they had little or no firsthand knowledge of America, or they had ulterior motives.[3] The writer of the pamphlet *A True Account of the Colonies of Nova Scotia and Georgia* (Newcastle, 1774), for example, does not claim to have been to America, and, in fact his account seems to be a compilation of facts gleaned from other contemporary sources.[4] It does not reflect the truth as the author experienced it, and therefore the words "true account" in the title are intentionally misleading.

The two pamphlets included in this book would certainly be classified as promotional literature; they were printed, sold, and distributed as widely as possible with the specific purpose of convincing people to move to America. But they are included here because one was written by an emigrant who had lived in America for several years,[5] and the other was written by two prospective emigrants who had toured Nova Scotia, and were well acquainted

---

fast. However, the depositor of this collection could not be located, and therefore the originals could not be used. These letters have been printed in Alun C. Davies, " 'As Good a Country as Any Man Needs to Dwell in': Letters from a Scotch-Irish Immigrant in Pennsylvania, 1766, 1767, and 1784," *Pennsylvania History*, 50(1983), 313–322.

[3] See, for example, [William Smith], *Information to Emigrants* (Glasgow, [1773]). Smith wrote a glowing letter giving "Proposals, Informations and Directions . . . [that] may be useful to such as intend Emigrating to that province [New York]" and sent it to Glasgow to be published. Smith's interest in attracting emigrants was to seat them on his lands in New York; he owned about 40,000 acres in the Kayaderosseres patent and in several towns and parishes in the counties of Albany and Cumberland (pp. 3, 5). Many such promotional tracts exist for this period, and include not only pamphlets, but also broadsides, newspaper advertisements, and flyers that were posted in inns and taverns in Britain, circulated throughout neighborhoods by agents, or published in British newspapers. See, for example: "St. John's Island," May 9, 1772, a broadside that was circulated throughout the Highlands to promote settlement on St. John's Island in Canada (SP 54/46, Public Record Office, London); "Wanted Immediately," advertising for redemptioners (Pemberton Papers, vol. 22, p. 43, Historical Society of Pennsylvania, Philadelphia); "To all Farmers and Tradesmen, Who want good Settlements for themselves and Families," 1772, describing the province of New York, giving directions to prospective emigrants (Americana Collection, SM# Am 1772, Accession #960.F.19, Library Company of Philadelphia).

[4] Some passages are paraphrased from the pamphlet [Scotus Americanus], *Informations Concerning the Province of North Carolina . . .* (Glasgow, 1773), published a year earlier. For example, passages on p. 14 of *A True Account*, and p. 20 of *Informations* are almost identical.

[5] See Alexander Thomson, *News from America*, this volume.

with many of the Yorkshire people who had already settled there.[6] These particular pamphlet writers were "insiders" who wanted to dispel false reports about America and give accurate accounts to their friends, who were often confused about what and what not to believe. These pamphlets, to be sure, were "cleaned up" before publication – the grammar and spelling were undoubtedly corrected and stylized for the printer – but they contain rich and authentic details that answered questions emigrants often had about climate, seasons, game, commodities, soil, trees, produce, prices, and the availability of land.

[6] See John Robinson and Thomas Rispin, *A Journey Through Nova Scotia*, this volume.

EDITORIAL
PROCEDURES

THE letters are transcribed literally, with the following exceptions: Superscripts and interlineations are lowered to the line and marginal material is inserted silently where appropriate; dashes are shortened to en-dash length; strikeovers are deleted except where they appear significant; closings follow after the last sentence of the letter, and signatures appear on a separate line, regardless of placement in the original; postscripts follow immediately after the text of the letter; run-on words are separated; quotation marks, when used by the author, are standardized; and repeated words are silently corrected.

Brackets are used for all material that the editor has inserted in order to clarify the text. Illegible or missing portions of the text are represented by 2-em spaces enclosed in brackets ([   ]), and such bracketed text containing more than five words is noted as such. Words that have some missing or illegible letters are enclosed in brackets with elipses. Editorial conjectures are enclosed in brackets with a question mark.

DISCOVERIES OF AMERICA

INTRODUCTION

O N May 21, 1772, the Dixon family "arrive'd before Fort Cumberland,"
Nova Scotia, where "things at first Glance wore a gloomy aspect."
Charles Dixon, in trying to bolster his wife Susanna's spirits, "frequently told
her . . . not to be cast down." Exactly two years later, the Harrison family had
a similar reaction when they disembarked at the same place. Young Luke
quickly announced that he did not like Nova Scotia "at all," and, though he
and his family stayed in America, many others returned to England on the
same ship, finding the "country" not "in any respect equal to the favorable idea
they had formed of it."[1] James Whitelaw, on the other hand, enjoyed the "very
pleasant" view of the banks of the Delaware River, "particularly upon the Pensilvania side," as his ship sailed up the river toward Philadelphia in the spring
of 1773. He was greeted at the wharf, and during the next few days was much
encouraged by people who gave him "good hopes" of purchasing a large tract
of land. Likewise, Hester Wylly was impressed with her first view of Savannah
in the autumn of 1768. She was met with an "affectinate reception," and
adapted easily to Georgia, which agreed with her "as well as Ireland."

Such were the first impressions – varied, unanticipated – of some of the
British emigrants who came to the American colonies in the decade before
the American Revolution.[2] Eager to report to their friends back home, they
wrote candidly about their first reactions and subsequent discoveries. America was bountiful. The flora was abundant and luscious; the fauna unusual.
Lands were cheap, mosquitoes pesky, corn yields high, and mutton prices
low. However, lest their enthusiasm should be misleading, the new colonists
also warned that cheap lands were diminishing, opportunities were good in
some places and in some occupations, but not in others, and that "settling
in" took time, patience, and, above all, industry.

---

[1] *Scots Magazine*, 36 (September 1774), 502.
[2] Throughout this book the word "emigrant" will generally be used to mean both emigrant
(from Britain) and immigrant (to America).

The 44 letters or personal accounts contained in this book[3] are valuable not just because they are vivid firsthand accounts of the emigrant experience in pre-Revolutionary America, but also because so few colonial emigrant letters have survived. This scarcity is not only the result of a poor survival rate. Many eighteenth-century Britons could not write. One study of seventeenth- and eighteenth-century assize court deponents revealed an illiteracy level for English males of about 42% and for Scottish males of 32%. For women, the illiteracy level was approximately 81% in both countries.[4] The women who were the most literate were, understandably, in the higher socioeconomic classes, and, at all levels, literacy for women often meant the ability to read but not write. Normally, girls in eighteenth-century England and Scotland were taught "reading, sewing, and knitting," while their male counterparts were taught "reading, writing, and arithmetic." These different curricula were based on the assumption that "girls should not be given the same education as boys since they would not be able to understand it and would in any case lack any opportunities to use additional learning." Like females, boys from the poorer classes were frequently denied writing instruction.[5]

The letters in this collection, therefore, reflect the patterns of eighteenth-century literacy as well as the scarcity of available colonial writings. Most letters were written by males from the middle ranks of society. Two exceptions are Hester Wylly, the sister of well-to-do Georgia planters, and the servant Baikia Harvey. Here and there one can find seventeenth- and eighteenth-century accounts written by women, servants, convicts, and the poor, but their stories to a large degree must be teased out of others' writings, or sources such as court records, tax lists, and wills.

Nevertheless, in spite of the obvious drawbacks in confining any study to individuals who can write, much can be gained from looking at what these people had to say about America at such a critical time in their nation's history. The time span restricting the selection to the period 1760–1775 is

---

3 This selection includes 41 letters, a memoir, and two pamphlets, one of which is a letter in pamphlet form. They were written by 18 people who settled in nine of the British American colonies.

4 See R. A. Houston, *Scottish Literacy and the Scottish Identity: Illiteracy and Society in Scotland and Northern England, 1600–1800* (Cambridge, 1985), 57–58. This study of illiteracy for English males is for the years 1640–1760, and for Scottish males 1650–1770. These samples are aggregate and unweighted. The Rev. Lachlan Shaw observed in 1775 that " 'it was much to find in a [Highland] parish three persons that could read or write'." Henry G. Graham, *The Social Life in Scotland in the Eighteenth Century* (London, 1937), 423.

5 Houston, *Scottish Literacy*, 60, 66, 63.

significant, since the migration of British subjects to America in the years between the Peace of Paris in 1763 and the beginning of the American Revolution was a unique period of migration history. As the tension and conflict between Britain and America accelerated to a crisis in the early 1770s, so did Britain's concern about the emigration of its subjects to these rebellious colonies.[6] The loss of population was a critical issue at a time when Britain faced the loss of that part of the empire to which these people were migrating, and what these emigrants wrote had a decisive impact on the nature and intensity of that emigration. This short time span also allows intercolonial comparisons of patterns, connections, and experiences. Did they share the same grievances? Were opportunities better in one colony or another? Some of these letter writers knew each other; most did not. But they all had one thing in common: Their first impressions were as different from their expectations as they were from their subsequent discoveries.

BACKGROUND: EMIGRANTS BEFORE DEPARTURE

The migration of British subjects to America in the decade before the American Revolution was extraordinary, not simply because of the numbers of migrants – people had been leaving Britain for America in large numbers for over a century – but also as a result of changes in the pattern and intensity of migration in certain areas. No fewer than 125,000 people left Britain in the decade and a half before the Revolution. Many followed well-established migration patterns, but others, especially those living in the northern parts of Britain, formed new configurations. They linked themselves in groups and emigrated by shiploads, sometimes clearing out whole farms and glens.

This migration has been studied in detail by Bernard Bailyn.[7] His analysis reveals that this was not a uniform movement of people, but rather that it had two distinct modes. One was "metropolitan," centering on southern England and the Thames valley. Emigrants who left from these southern ports were mostly young unemployed tradesmen in their early 20s who bound themselves to four or more years of servitude in an American colony, typically Pennsylvania, Maryland, or Virginia. The few women who were a part of this group were also, on average, young, single, and indentured. The other

---

[6] Bernard Bailyn, *Voyagers to the West: A Passage in the Peopling of America on the Eve of the Revolution* (New York, 1986), chap. 2.

[7] Bailyn, *Voyagers to the West*. For emigration figures, see p. 26.

migration, which consisted of emigrants from northern England and Scotland, represented a "provincial" pattern. These were not individuals traveling as indentured servants, but families, many of whom had been tied in some way to the land. The adults tended to be older and more financially secure, or at least they had resources to cross the Atlantic as free people. They more often chose to settle in peripheral areas away from the coast, where it was possible for them to buy or lease land.

The pattern that characterized the "metropolitan" migration was one that went back to the beginning of the seventeenth century. Servants to the Chesapeake had always been a part of the trans-Atlantic labor market, with supply and demand being the primary determinant of their numbers. The sources for these servants were the pools of unemployed labor in London, Bristol, and the smaller market towns and villages scattered throughout Britain. Some were two-or-three-stage migrants who traveled to larger cities in search of work, and then, when unsuccessful, found they had little choice but to indent themselves in order to find work in America. The transfer of labor was handled for the most part by small operators – merchants or shipowners who occasionally sent groups of servants to their American clients. The migration from southern England in the 1760s and 1770s continued this pattern, and was therefore neither remarkable nor alarming, even when the numbers swelled.

On the other hand, the loss of people from the northern part of Britain – from northern England, Scotland, and Northern Ireland – sent shock waves throughout the kingdom. People had been leaving these areas, particularly Ireland, since the end of the seventeenth century, but after 1763 the pattern and intensity of the migration changed. In contrast to the southern migration, which was composed mainly of individuals acting autonomously, this "provincial" migration consisted primarily of people who had organized themselves into groups of 100 to 400 people. Many planned their departure themselves by arranging for their own shipping; others found a "leader," often a merchant, who made the necessary arrangements. A few groups of people formed "associations" that consisted of prospective emigrants who pooled their money by buying shares that could eventually be redeemed for land in America.[8] Sometimes whole neighborhoods of families and friends

---

[8] At least five such emigration associations were established in the early 1770s. In this volume, see for the Inchinnan Company and the United Company of Farmers, p. 88; and the "Carolina Scheme," pp. 29–30. In addition, the customs officers in Wigtown reported that an emigration association was forming there in early 1774: T1/500, Public Record Office, London (hereafter PRO); see also *South Carolina Gazette and Country Journal*, May 24, 1774, "Extract of a letter from West Galloway, March 1," about a meeting of this association. "The Emi-

would leave in groups or associations large enough to found their own wilderness communities.[9] Their determination frightened many like Thomas Miller, the Lord Justice Clerk of Scotland, who remarked that "[w]hile Individuals think and Act for themselves, there is no great danger, that many will leave their Countrey. But when they enter into associations, and goe off in bodys from the same place, with their Wifes, Children & kindred, this removes the natural tie to their Country, because they carry the chief object of that attachment with them."[10]

These sudden changes led to a crisis in the early 1770s that was described variously as a "madness," a "contagion," a "frenzy," and an "evil" that would have "ruinous" and "dreadful" consequences.[11] It was an event that spawned years of heated debate in the press, in Parliament, in churches, among wealthy landowners in London coffeehouses, and among peat farmers in remote island hamlets. Visitors and travelers remarked on it. Songs and poems were written about it. So frightening was the potential depopulation of the northern regions that threats of emigration were used as leverage in criminal trials and landlord–tenant negotiations.[12]

Legislators were pressured to hasten the prohibition of this emigration, but before drastic measures could be taken, causes had to be found and remedies tried. In the struggle to understand this phenomenon, those interested in reaching out for solutions looked everywhere for clues and answers. Some questioned customs officials and sheriffs, and even made surveys of particular parishes and farms where emigration was most intense. Others assembled the data and wrote lengthy tracts setting forth causes and guessing

grators" was another group organized in Spitalfields, London. Each member contributed 6 pence a week until the group had enough money to finance every member's trip to America. *Leeds Mercury*, September 23, 1774.

[9] See pp. 94 and 88–90, this volume, for the communities of New Perth, Ryegate, and Barnet.

[10] Thomas Miller to the Earl of Suffolk, April 25, 1774, SP 54/45, PRO.

[11] Miller to Suffolk, April 25, 1774, SP 54/45, PRO; James Sutherland to ?, March 2, 1772, and Sutherland to Alexander McKenzie, July 16, 1772, Sutherland Papers, Dep 313/III/Box 16, National Library of Scotland, Edinburgh; John MacLeod to Mrs. MacLeod, October 9, 1772, MacLeod Papers, Dunvegan Castle, Isle of Skye (access through the National Register of Archives, Scotland); James Grant to Henry Dundas, April 19, 1775, GD 248/244/4/2, Scottish Record Office, Edinburgh (hereafter SRO); Draft of representation of Lords of Trade to the King, November 6, 1773, Papers of William Legge, 2d Earl of Dartmouth, MG 23, A1, Public Archives of Canada, Ottawa, 1: 103, 106.

[12] See, for example, Duane Meyer, *The Highland Scots of North Carolina, 1732–1776* (Chapel Hill, NC, 1961), 62. Also "An Essay on the Late Emigrations from the Highlands of Scotland," MacLeod Papers, p. 29: "I have heard that one whole parish threatened to emigrate, because the patron did not give the presentation to the Minister of their choice."

at cures.[13] Members of Parliament conducted interviews of those knowl-edgeable on the subject.[14] Stories debating the issue filled the newspapers. And in Scotland the worried Lord Justice Clerk collected estimates of num-bers of migrants, which led, finally, to the Privy Council order in 1773 calling for a complete census to be taken of all emigrants leaving the kingdom for any reason.[15]

Much of the momentum of this migration was blamed on economic fac-tors.[16] The most serious complaint heard both in Ireland and Scotland was that of rack-renting: In many places rents were doubled and sometimes tri-pled in the 1760s and 1770s.[17] Tenants complained constantly that they were oppressed by their landlords, not only in having to pay high rents, but also in having to perform unfair or excessive services for their masters.

Farmers were not the only ones who suffered hardships during this period. In the early 1770s a depression in the textile industry in Ireland, Scotland, and England put many weavers and spinners out of work. The depressed linen in-dustry, combined with unusually severe winters, created food shortages, drove up prices, and contributed to higher unemployment. James Campbell, the fac-tor for the estate of the Countess of Sutherland, struggled to find meal for the tenants who were in a "starving Condition." No meal was to be found, Camp-bell complained, "in this corner but at most exorbitant prices . . . [and] the crops so totally failed last year that there is very little to spare."[18]

---

[13] See, for example, *A Candid Enquiry into the Causes of the Late and the Intended Migrations from Scotland in a Letter to J——— R——— Esq; Lanarkshire* (Glasgow, [1771]), 65 pp. This letter was printed because the publisher "had observed that, in some periodical papers, such an *enquiry* was wanted and called for" (preface). Another similar tract written "by a High-lander" was *An Essay on the Late Emigrations from the Highlands of Scotland. Giving an impartial account of the Causes and Rise of that fatal Spirit And Humbly proposing some Methods to stop its present fury: and to prevent its future Return* (1774), 77 pp., MacLeod Papers. He writes this essay "to the Public," because "he thinks it the duty of every highlander to offer his mite on this occasion" (preface).

[14] See *Rivington's New York Gazetteer*, May 12, 1774, for the examination of Dr. Williamson of Philadelphia at the bar of the House of Commons. He reported that 15,000 emigrants from Northern Ireland had arrived in Pennsylvania during the previous two years.

[15] See Bailyn, *Voyagers to the West*, chaps. 2–3.

[16] The causes of emigration from Britain during the eighteenth century have been discussed at length elsewhere and will not be analyzed here. See, for example, Bailyn, *Voyagers to the West*; T. C. Smout, *A History of the Scottish People, 1560–1830* (Glasgow, 1969), chap. XIV; R. J. Dickson, *Ulster Emigration to Colonial America, 1718–1775* (Belfast, 1966), chap. I.

[17] Rack-renting was a constant complaint among emigrants. See, for example, pp. 29, 156, this volume. Dickson, *Ulster Emigration*, 70–77.

[18] James Campbell to Capt. Campbell, Ardmaddy, May 30, 1772, Sutherland Papers, Dep 313/

But economic causes were only part of the story. The exodus was also frequently attributed to encouraging reports from friends and family members who were already in America and to promotional campaigns carried out by American land speculators who wished to populate their lands. The seemingly endless stream of letters, pamphlets, advertisements, and promotional tracts helped to shape the attitude of prospective emigrants, especially those Britons disheartened by economic hardship who were now more receptive to new possibilities. Disaffected people now knew with a certainty derived from letters written by trusted friends that others had left, had lived through the difficult voyage, and were the better for the change. They knew that they did not have to do this alone; they would be able to find help from someone who would guide them through the process of resettlement. This information gave their "discontented spirit[s]" hope, and helped to dislodge them even from "parts, where no oppression could be complained of."[19]

Therefore economic problems only partially explain the motivation of these emigrants in the "provincial" migration; many were *not* destitute. Those who had purely economic motives for emigrating, that is, those individuals who were unemployed and too poor to make any living whatsoever in Britain, were for the most part forced to indent themselves in ways characteristic of the migration from southern England. But approximately 80% of the people from northern England and Scotland did not bind themselves in indentures; they found means somehow to pay for their passage.[20]

This newer, more intense emigration, which started in the early 1760s and continued until 1775, created a crisis. These northern migrants, who were clearly not expendable, were choosing to emigrate, not necessarily for economic reasons alone, but also because of the news they had heard from abroad: They might subsist in Britain, but they could flourish in America. And the British government could do nothing short of flat prohibition to stop this "evil."

The letter writers in this book, for the most part, represent the "provincial" migrants – those who came from Britain's northern provinces. This

III/Box 16. For the collapse in the linen industry in Ireland combined with high prices and scarcity of food, see Dickson, *Ulster Emigration*, 77–80.

[19] William Gilpin, *Observations on Several Parts of Great Britain. . . . 1776*, 3rd ed. (London 1808), 169.

[20] For example, people on the island of Lewis, in the Outer Hebrides, indented because they "were so poor that they could not pay for their passage." They wanted to "Leave the Country in order to procure Bread elsewhere as they could not do it here, so that necessity obliged them to Emigrate." Collectors of Customs, Stornoway, to the Board of Customs, Edinburgh, May 2, 1774, CE 86/2/2, SRO. Bailyn, *Voyagers to the West*, 170–171.

region was where the reports of depopulation were most concentrated, and where the flattering descriptions of America seemed to have the greatest impact.

DISCOVERIES

The information these letters contained was indeed alluring. On the most superficial level, the letters include descriptions of the physical environment and of the various "curiosities" – people, places, and things that seemed unusual or odd to Europeans like Patrick M'Robert who wrote, "There everything is strange."[21] And so it must have seemed to the readers at home who could barely conceive of this exotic world, one very different from their own. The voyage to America was unbelievable in itself. John Wright[22] almost lost his life in a violent storm, and Hester Wylly's friend Mrs. Lewis lost all her belongings and somehow managed to survive nine days in an open boat.[23] But the hazards of three thousand miles of sea travel were no more remarkable than what the settlers saw and touched and marveled at when they arrived.

Few failed to be amazed at the "immense woods," and they groped for ways to describe them to those at home. George Ogilvie wrote from South Carolina to his sister in Aberdeen that he had climbed the tallest building he could find to get an aerial view: "the Eye does not perceive the least inequality nor any kind of opening when it surveys the Boundless forrest . . . the prospect is only bounded by the Horizon."[24] In Nova Scotia, Robinson and Rispin remarked that the "trees here seem to grow out of solid rocks," while writers elsewhere noted their size: "often from 50 to 70 feet high . . . and frequently above 30 feet in circumference." So dense and pungent were the pines in Carolina that "mariners, going upon the coast in spring, have smelt the pines when several leagues at sea."[25] And Janet Schaw, a Scottish

[21] Patrick M'Robert, *A Tour through Part of the North Provinces of America: Being, a Series of Letters Wrote on the Spot, in the Years 1774, & 1775* (1776, offprint Philadelphia, 1935), edited by Carl Bridenbaugh, p. x. This edition is an offprint from the *The Pennsylvania Magazine of History and Biography*, 59(April, 1935).

[22] See letter of John Wright to Jane Wright, New York, May 12, 1774, in Barbara DeWolfe, ed., "Discoveries of America: Letters of British Emigrants to America on the Eve of the Revolution," *Perspectives in American History*, n.s., 3(1987), 34.

[23] See p. 217, this volume.

[24] See, p. 199, this volume.

[25] See p. 57, this volume; [Scotus Americanus], *Informations Concerning the Province of North*

visitor from Edinburgh, was caught one night in North Carolina's dense forest. She found herself "lost in the most impenetrable darkness," hours away from any clearing, and terrified of "monsters" that lurked within those "wilds."[26]

Schaw's feelings of fear and isolation in the Carolina woods were echoed by travelers and immigrants throughout the colonies. Traveling often meant walking or riding 10, 20, perhaps 30 miles between settlements without seeing a house or even a road, making one's way at times by following markings on trees, and finding no lodgings except "in the woods, amongst the howlings of wild beasts, and the crashing of trees."[27]

The isolation that distance and woods created was a rude adjustment for many settlers, especially those in the backcountry where most of the new immigrants were taking up lands. One landowner who lived 30 miles northwest of Augusta, Georgia, found that "society" was "deficient" there, counting only "eight or nine neighbours within twenty miles." A person had to find entertainment in books, or the "amusements of the field," or "by employments of agriculture."[28] Thomas Ridout, who had agreed to settle his brother's Potomac River plantation 140 miles west of Annapolis, Maryland, crossed the "three ridges of mountains" to get there, only to find "one of the most uncultivated and sequestered spots that ever imagination fancied." The plantation was bounded by woods on three sides and by the Potomac River on the other. On the opposite side of the river Ridout could see a 300-foot-high rock face covered with pines, which roared like "the Ocean" when the winds blew "amongst them." He occupied his time with clearing the land and improving the plantation, but had little company, only a "tolerable collection of books, some music, and one pretty rational neighbour."[29]

Carolina, Addressed to Emigrants from the Highlands and Western Isles of Scotland. By an Impartial Hand (Glasgow, 1773), 20, 14. This pamphlet was printed in William K. Boyd, *Some Eighteenth Century Tracts Concerning North Carolina* (Raleigh, NC, 1927), 441, 437.

[26] Evangeline W. Andrews and Charles M. Andrews, eds., *Journal of a Lady of Quality; Being the Narrative of a Journey from Scotland to the West Indies, North Carolina, and Portugal, in the years 1774 to 1776* (New Haven, CT, 1923), 146–147.

[27] M'Robert, *A Tour*, 21, 29; James Whitelaw to William Whitelaw, July 15, 1773, p. 94, this volume. Thomas Taylor, escorting about 50 servants from Savannah to the Georgia backcountry, spent "eight Nights upon the Road," five of which were passed "encamp'd out, part of the Time in Rain, Frost & Snow." See letter of Thomas Taylor, this volume.

[28] Robert S. Davis, Jr., ed., "Letters from St. Paul's Parish," *Richmond County History*, 10(1978), 21, 25. These letters written by "An American" were extracted from *American Husbandry*, 2 vols. (London, 1775).

[29] "Reminiscences of Thomas Ridout," *Maryland Historical Magazine*, 20(1925), 220–221.

All over, in the coastal areas as well as the back parts, the traveler, the settler, and the adventurer encountered, what was for them, new and strange sights. Whitelaw saw Indians in New York who painted their faces with "red and black strokes" and who wore nose jewels and trinkets, but no clothes except "a kind of blanket which they wrap about their shoulders and two pieces of skin which they hang one before and another behind to cover their nakedness."[30] And almost all the observers reported on the abundant variety of usual and unusual flora and fauna. Of the animals, they found large "mousedeer . . . some of them weighing eighty stone," reindeer, "ravenous" bears with heads like those "of a mastiff," beavers, porcupines, tortoises, "fierce" wild cats, otters, minks, sables, martens, tiskers, muskrats, and flying squirrels, "serpents," monstrous hairy wild boars, deer as "numerous as sheep in Scotland," and "hogs running loose through the woods." Fish swam "in great plenty," and birds of vivid color caught the eye.[31]

The produce was likewise remarkable. One could pick "large and lucious fruit" from the trees and had at hand a veritable "kingdom of vegetables" – melons, pumpkins, squashes, gourds, Indian corn, cucumbers, cabbages, turnips, potatoes – and products to cart to market – tobacco, indigo, rice.[32] The list of nature's bounties was as endless as the curious questions about them, and all of them were found "in great plenty," including the miserable "musketoes" – those "devils in Minature" – that buzzed everywhere and bit "the English worst."[33]

America was also strange in its mixtures of goods, currency, customs, manners, architectural styles, and peoples who were not native to its continent. Goods could be bought and sold with pistareens as well as pounds, for "Every Countrys Money goes if peopel know its worth." One could encounter Baptists, Methodists, Anglicans, Roman Catholics, Jews, Anabaptists, Lutherans, Moravians – many "perswations in Religon" existed side by side – as well as people from "many Defrent Countreys."[34]

---

[30] James Whitelaw to William Whitelaw, July 15, 1773, this volume.

[31] See p. 69, this volume. *Informations Concerning . . . North Carolina*, 16; See John Campbell to William Sinclair, July 26, 1772, this volume; G. Melvin Herndon, "A Young Scotsman's Visit to South Carolina, 1770–1772," *South Carolina Historical Magazine*, 85(1984), 192.

[32] *Informations Concerning . . . North Carolina*, 21, 14. See p. 97, and p. 113, this volume; Davis, ed., "Letters from St. Paul's Parish," 25–26.

[33] George Ogilvie to Margaret Ogilvie, November 22, 1774, this volume; and Luke Harrison to William Harrison, June 30, 1774, this volume.

[34] James Metcalf to Ann Gill, August 1772, this volume; "Journal of Colonel Alexander Harvey of Scotland and Barnet, Vermont," *Proceedings of the Vermont Historical Society for the years 1921, 1922 and 1923* (Montpelier, VT, 1924), 238.

These endless varieties of "importations" and nonnative implants seemed all the more strange in their juxtapositions with elements of the native environment, each transforming the other and creating a new, constantly changing synthesis of culture. Robinson and Rispin, while traveling through the barren wilderness of Nova Scotia, stopped at an isolated lodging where they were surprised to find "chocolate, coffee, and tea, in china, with silver spoons, and every thing very elegant."[35] And Janet Schaw, who viewed the handsome Carolina houses of the well-to-do and attended their dress balls, was amazed "to find that every instrument of husbandry was unknown" there – except the hoe, which is used both to "till and plant the corn."[36]

One's encounters must have seemed bizarre at times, as Alexander Harvey,[37] a visitor from Scotland, might have thought one night when supping with an "indian King" in Perth Amboy. Since the Indian could not speak English, he communicated through an interpreter who informed Harvey that the "King" was "Going throw [through] the provinces in ourder to Establish peace withe the Colinies."[38] How strange it must have seemed to Harvey to have dined with an Indian king, who wore "a Star on his Breast" and "Large Rufles Round his wristbands." These experiences were odd, not because the newcomers were traveling in a culture different from their own, but because they were traveling in many different cultures mixed together and superimposed on the remnants of an older, native culture that was in, but not of, that newer world of European transplants.

For almost two centuries Europeans had been fascinated by this remote exoticism. They wanted to see and feel this strangeness, and begged for "specimens" to examine – plants and produce of all kinds, ores and minerals, Indian souvenirs, and other rareties. Some of the more well-off of these curiosity seekers kept special cabinets in which they displayed their specimens from all over the world. The most renowned of these collections was that of Sir Hans Sloane, a British physician, who traveled widely looking for rare and unusual objects. So well-known was his "museum," which housed many cabinets in at least nine rooms, that it was an attraction for visitors from abroad, like Benjamin Franklin, who sold Sloane an asbestos purse from America, and Pehr Kalm, a student of Linnaeus. Sloane's col-

---

[35] See p. 57, this volume.
[36] Andrews and Andrews, eds., *Journal of a Lady of Quality*, 163.
[37] Alexander Harvey was an agent for the Perth and Sterling Company of Farmers who toured America in 1774 looking for lands on which to settle prospective emigrants. "Journal of Colonel Alexander Harvey . . . ," 201.
[38] "Journal of Colonel Alexander Harvey . . . ," 238–239.

lection contained artificial as well as natural curiosities: plants and animals, gems and stones, insects, shells, minerals, art work, and coins. Four hundred different kinds of agate filled one entire cabinet. His tens of thousands of objects included an Egyptian mummy, a stuffed camel, a black stone from Connecticut, the head of a two-horned rhinoceros, a Queen's hat from Tunquin, a Sicilian sea-urchin fossil, and the 14-foot horns from an Indian buffalo. But collections such as Sloane's were not primarily for show; they were used for research, study, and teaching. And some of them, including Sloane's, eventually became "the core of what are at present considered to be the great ethnographical museums of Great Britain and Western Europe."[39]

Sloane's "museum" was exceptional, but many people collected on a small scale and asked their friends going to America to send them curiosities. No one knows whether the bones Thomas Feilde sent to his botanist friend in London ever ended up on display, or how Hester Wylly's green oranges were received by Mrs. Gaylord, but they represented ways that Europeans could share in the discoveries of America without having to go there.[40] What was America like? Give us "an account," wrote William Harrison from Yorkshire to his cousin in Nova Scotia, "of all the Curosities that you have seen." And David Duff promised his benefactor, "If you have any desire to see any of the curiosities of whatever kind which this part of America can produce, I shall do all that lies in my power to have them transported to you."[41] At times the competition for specimens was so fierce that some of the items of curiosity were hard to find. Andrew Porteus, a trader at Michilimackinac, wrote in his journal in 1767 that he found it hard to get Indian artifacts because many people had been there looking for them.[42]

These specimens, then, were taken out of their contexts and sent to curiosity seekers who collected and enshrined these treasures from America. But though the "wild" stories made good reading and the "unusual" objects were interesting to look at, they did not reveal much about what America

[39] G. R. de Beer, *Sir Hans Sloane and the British Museum* (1953, reprint New York, 1975), 111–113, 116–117, 120–123, 130, 133. George R. Hamell, "One Culture's 'Truck' is Another Culture's Treasure: Cabinets of Curiosities and Northeastern Native American Ethnological Specimens of the 16th through 18th Centuries" (unpublished paper delivered at the Conference on Historical Archaeology, September 24–25, 1982), 2, 3. I would like to thank George Hamell for permission to cite this article.

[40] See letters in this volume: Thomas Feilde to Dr. Mackenzie, February 16, 1771; and Hester Wylly to Helen Lawrence, December 14, 1768.

[41] William Harrison to Luke Harrison, March 25, 1775, p. 51, n. 39; David Duff to James Grant, 1772, this volume.

[42] Hamell, "One Culture's 'Truck'," 10–11.

was like, nor did they, for the most part, lure the European thither. Occasionally an eager adventurer was curious enough to want to see America in person, and a fair number of people were attracted by profits to be made in meeting the demand for American oddities, but most emigrants who wanted to settle in America permanently were drawn there for other, more compelling, reasons.

*   *   *   *   *

One of the most alluring messages prospective emigrants received from their contacts across the Atlantic was that the poor of Britain would be able to better their lives and the lives of their children. The idea that America was a good place for the poor dated back to the beginning of the seventeenth century. In *A True Discourse of the Present State of Virginia*, written in 1615, Ralph Hamor gave encouragement to "painefull people" who lived in Britain in "extreame poverty." He urged them to come to Virginia where they "shal soon find the difference between their own and that Country." In Virginia the poor adventurer with his family would have a house in which he could live free of rent, in addition to 12 English acres for his own use. He would be provided with a 12-month supply of provisions from the store, as well as "necessary tooles of all sorts," poultry, swine, and perhaps a "goate or two" or a cow. Hamor was sure that if these poor people came they would "never returne" to Britain.[43] Forty years later, in 1656, John Hammond extolled the virtues of Maryland in order to attract the English poor. He was appalled at the "dull stupidity" of people "who rather then they will remove themselves, live here a base, slavish, penurious life." He addressed the destitute: people so poor they would either end up in jail, or have to "itch out their wearisom lives in reliance of other mens charities," or "betake themselve to almost perpetuall and restlesse toyle . . . [making] hard shift to subsist from hand to mouth, untill age or sicknesse takes them off from labour and directs them the way to beggerie." He pitied them their "degenerate and base" ways of living, remarking that their condition was "far below the meanest servant in Virginia."[44]

These two early seventeenth-century authors exaggerated the benefits of living in Maryland and Virginia, perhaps in order to attract useful hands to

[43] Ralph Hamor, *A True Discourse of the Present State of Virginia* (1615, reprint, Richmond, VA, 1957), 19–20.

[44] John Hammond, "Leah and Rachel, or, the Two Fruitfull Sisters Virginia and Mary-Land," in Clayton Colman Hall, ed., *Narratives of Early Maryland: 1633–1684* (New York, 1910), 296–297.

the labor-short Chesapeake. They neglected to mention the drawbacks, like the extraordinarily high mortality rate, particularly for new arrivals. But if people did survive, they found opportunities in the early decades of the 1600s that enabled them to prosper. By the middle of the century, the Chesapeake was deemed a "good poor man's country" for those who had started out as impoverished servants or as freemen with little or no capital. These poor and middling planters were able to get some land and/or property, maybe in cattle, and start building a farm. They also found it fairly easy to obtain official positions in their colony's government. However, toward the end of the century, as the tobacco market declined, opportunities decreased. Lands in well-settled areas began to fill up and newly freed servants were forced to migrate to the frontier areas or to areas of poorer soil, in order to find lands to patent.[45] Nevertheless, the *belief* that America was the best place for a "poor man" without capital persisted throughout the colonial period, in spite of growing evidence that opportunities had smartly diminished by 1700. Robert Beverley's declaration in 1705 that Virginia was "the best poor man's country in the world" was commonplace by the end of the eighteenth century, not just in Virginia, but in all the colonies.[46] It was used repeatedly in letters,[47] but appeared most often in the printed emigration literature.[48] The oft-repeated message – "land is cheap, provision plenty, and labour well paid for"[49] – was always used in comparing the quality of life in America to that in Europe: The ease of living and bountiful produce had reduced poverty,

[45] Russell R. Menard, "British Migration to the Chesapeake Colonies in the Seventeenth Century," in Lois Green Carr, Philip D. Morgan, and Jean B. Russo, eds., *Colonial Chesapeake Society* (Chapel Hill, NC, 1988), 111; Russell R. Menard, P. M. G. Harris, and Lois Green Carr, "Opportunity and Inequality: The Distribution of Wealth on the Lower Western Shore of Maryland, 1638–1705," *Maryland Historical Magazine*, 69(1974), 182; Lorena S. Walsh, "Servitude and Opportunity in Charles County, Maryland, 1658–1705," in Aubrey C. Land, Lois Green Carr, and Edward C. Papenfuse, eds., *Law, Society, and Politics in Early Maryland* (Baltimore, 1977), 126–127; and Lois Green Carr, Russell R. Menard, and Lorena S. Walsh, *Robert Cole's World: Agriculture and Society in Early Maryland* (Chapel Hill, NC, 1991), 12–17.

[46] Robert Beverley, *The History and Present State of Virginia* (London, 1705; reprint ed. by Louis B. Wright, Chapel Hill, NC, 1947), 275.

[47] See letters in this volume, for example, Baikia Harvey to Thomas Baikie, December 30, 1775; Alexander McAllister to Angus McCuaig, November 29, 1770; and Alexander Cumine to Alexander Ogilvie, June 17, 1763.

[48] See, for example, *Informations Concerning . . . North Carolina*, 29; Thomson, *News From America*, p. 115, this volume; M'Robert, *A Tour*, ix; *A Candid Enquiry . . .*, 39; [William Smith], *Information to Emigrants* (Glasgow, [1773]), 7.

[49] *A Present for an Emigrant* (Edinburgh, 1774), 39–40.

so that in America the poor were not the same as the poor in Britain. "The people who are reckond poor here are not in the condition they are wt [with] you difficulted to get a Subsistance; but eat and drink well who tho they have not plantations and Negroes yet have houses and small pieces of Land where they bring up Horses & Cattle & Fowls . . . by which means they live very happily . . . whereas the poor att home very oft cann't get where with to Cloath & keep themselves alive."[50] Those "of small substance if upon a precarious footing at home" could "do well" for themselves in America.[51]

Various elaborations usually included a listing of prices (especially the value and quality of land), provisions, wages, and opportunities for different kinds of work. Lands in well-settled areas were expensive, Campbell reported, selling for 40s to £3 sterling an acre in Maryland. But cheaper lands could be taken up in the frontier areas, like backcountry New York where land was selling for 6s sterling per acre, and if one were willing to journey to the Ohio region, one could buy 2000 acres for £200 to £300. Immigrants short on capital could lease land at low prices.[52]

The letter writers sometimes gave breakdowns of costs and profits of leasing and buying lands. For example, John Campbell gave details of a hypothetical "case history" of a typical farmer with a wife and children. Such a farmer could lease a 150 to 200-acre farm (with 50 acres cleared) in Maryland for £10 currency; this would enable him to make 5000 weight tobacco a year, not including rent, with no help other than the labor of his own family, and turn a profit of £50 currency. He would not need to spend any money on produce, as he could raise what he needed himself.[53] Someone else pointed out that those who could afford to buy land could live like "lairds": An investment of £500 sterling in North Carolina could render a farmer "equall to any Laird of £500 P Annum in any part of great Brittain."[54]

Wages and opportunities for work were also good. All sorts of tradesmen, especially "mill-wrights, coopers, wheel-wrights, house and ship-carpenters, blacksmiths," would "have the greatest encouragement" in North Carolina,

[50] See letter from Alexander Cumine to Alexander Ogilvie, June 17, 1763, this volume.
[51] *Informations Concerning . . . North Carolina*, 31.
[52] See letter from John Campbell to William Sinclair, July 26, 1772, p. 157, this volume; "To All Farmers and Tradesmen, Who want good Settlements for themselves and Families" 1772, Broadside, SM# Am 1772, Accession #960.F.19, Americana Collection, Library Company of Philadelphia. Many of the Yorkshire settlers to Nova Scotia leased rather than bought lands. See, for example, the letters of Luke Harrison and James Metcalf, this volume.
[53] See p. 155–156, this volume.
[54] See letter from Alexander Campbell of Balole to Lachlan Mackinnon, 1772, this volume. See also Thomson, *News from America*, p. 115, this volume.

where masons and wrights took home 5s a day, and ship carpenters got 13s.[55] In Maryland, "every branch of Manufactures" met "with good encouragement," while in New York City tradesmen and laborers who were "good hands" commanded high wages. But even bad hands could find work in the "back settlements" where they could find "plenty of room and employ."[56] Schoolteachers were in demand in all the colonies. The schoolteacher David Duff hoped to clear £40–£50 sterling a year in Maryland, which he "reckoned very handsome," and Hugh Simm's first teaching job in New Jersey brought him a salary of £50–£55 currency.[57]

These recitations of opportunities were tantalizing to those left behind. William Harrison wanted information, not just on "all the Curosities that you have seen," but also on "the Produce of the Country and what Sort of a Winter You have had and if their is any Prospect of Making a Good Settlement."[58] The answers to such questions – about prices and produce and good settlements – were often attractive even beyond expectation, as one Pennsylvanian discovered: "It is Much better than I expected it to be in every way I assure you."[59]

But the heart of the message – the animating force – was something else: America was not just a good poor man's country, where one could enjoy the abundance of America's bounty; it was also a land of liberty, where one could be independent. Not only did higher wages and cheaper living in America provide opportunities for the poor to become financially independent, but farmers were not bound to the land in semifeudal obligation as they were in many parts of Britain. In the colonies, British farmers were told, they could own their own land and reap its profits, without having to pay heavy rents and perform services for landlords, and without having to worry about their rents or taxes increasing.[60] The attraction was not only that one found

---

[55] *Informations Concerning . . . North Carolina*, 30.

[56] See letter of John Campbell to William Sinclair, p. 157, this volume; *Informations Concerning . . . North Carolina*, 30; M'Robert, *A Tour*, 9.

[57] David Duff to James Grant, 1772, this volume; Hugh Simm to Andrew Simm, June 8, 1769, this volume.

[58] William Harrison to Luke Harrison, March 25, 1775, p. 51, n. 39, this volume.

[59] Job Johnson to Messrs John, Robert, & James Johnson, November 27, 1767, in Alun C. Davies, " 'As Good a Country as any Man Needs to Dwell in': Letters from a Scotch-Irish Immigrant in Pennsylvania, 1766, 1767, and 1784," *Pennsylvania History*, 50(1983), 319.

[60] During the second half of the eighteenth century, many landlords forced their tenants to submit to increased rents in order to pay for improvements on their estates and fund their extravagant lifestyles. For these and other grievances of tenants against their landlords during this period, see Bailyn, *Voyagers to the West*, 43–49.

in America abundant lands or cheap lands or fertile lands, but also that one might own land and thereby gain control over one's life and destiny and ensure the future independence of one's family.

The meaning of liberty when used in the context of emigration is sometimes confusing. Many of the published sources about emigration used the term "liberty" in the way that the American rebels used it – in reference to no taxation without representation, religious and civil liberties, and America as an asylum from British despotism. In fact, Thomas Miller was afraid that "the minds of these unhappy people may be corrupted with American principles, before they leave this Countrey."[61] But few of the British radicals, who heartily embraced the ideals of the American rebels and talked about going to America, actually emigrated.[62] The people migrating in large numbers from northern Britain – those Miller was so worried about – were attracted by the ideals of liberty and independence, but they did not think about them in such abstract terms. It was not freedom from the tyranny of Parliament or the Crown that concerned them, but freedom from the tyranny of their landlords, freedom to own land, and freedom to be their own masters. For them, America represented "some happier land where freedom reigns, and where, unmolested by Egyptian task-masters, they may reap the produce of their own labour and industry."[63]

With this hope of liberty, then, the victims of economic oppression in Britain crowded the ships to get to the "best poor man's country in the world," where they had been promised by kin already there that they could have a better, and more independent, life. However, in looking closely at the perceptions of these new Americans, one discovers that hidden behind the enthusiastic appeals and rosy accounts, the high wages and cheap lands, was the message that "poor" did not mean destitute or beggarly – it meant *poor with some assets*. Assets in capital were preferable to other kinds of assets, but occupational skills and personal contacts were also considered valuable. Therefore one often finds the use of the term "best poor man's country" qualified or even, in some cases, defined. For example, William Smith, a member of the New York Council, was careful to explain what poor meant in his 1773 promotional pamphlet *Information to Emigrants*: "The European Emigrants in America, have heretofore too generally been very poor persons, who being utterly destitute, were exposed to insuperable difficulties; for tho'

---

[61] Thomas Miller to the Earl of Suffolk, August 14, 1775, SP 54/46, PRO.

[62] Arthur Sheps, "Ideological Immigrants in Revolutionary America," in Paul Fritz and David Williams, eds., *City and Society in the Eighteenth Century* (Toronto, 1973), 231.

[63] *Informations Concerning . . . North Carolina*, 11.

this is allowed to be the best poor man's country in the world, yet it has very little advantage of others to such as are so necessitous as to depend upon mere charity. 'Tis to farmers of estates from £. 100 to £. 300, that this is a situation superior to other countries: These are able to purchase much for a little, but none can expect to have the lands given to them for nothing."[64] Others made the same observation. America was "the best country in the world for people of small fortunes," noted Patrick M'Robert.[65] And John Campbell took for granted that "emigrants" meant "people possessed of some property at home, but rather discontented with their Situation, who would wish to convert what little they have into some of the fruitful acres of the West." His calculations on the ease of living in America were therefore based on people of "slender fortune."[66]

The observations of Smith, M'Robert, and Campbell were similar to those of other colonists and travelers. They saw America as a diminishing area: The lands in the settled parts, they knew, had been taken up, and re-sales were often quite expensive. Cheaper lands could be found in the back parts or frontier areas, especially as far west as Ohio, where land speculation was in full swing by the 1770s. George Haworth, an immigrant weaver who earned about £19 a year in 1700, was able to purchase 450 acres in Buckenham, Bucks County, some 20 miles from Philadelphia.[67] Seventy years later, however, a visitor was astonished when he inquired about the cost of property for sale in the neighborhood of Philadelphia and found that "every Object . . . was full as dear as any in the Vicinity of London."[68] This may have been why Alexander Thomson had to go 150 miles west of Philadelphia in 1772 in order to find a 430-acre farm he could afford at £300 sterling.[69]

Large tracts were almost impossible to find near settled areas. When James Whitelaw and David Allen were looking for a tract of about 16,000 to 20,000 acres on which to settle the shareholders of their emigration association, Alexander Thomson informed them that they would not be able to find any tract that large in the "middle provinces." "[P]lenty of single

[64] [Smith], *Information to Emigrants*, 7.

[65] M'Robert, *A Tour*, ix.

[66] See John Campbell to William Sinclair, pp. 154, 155, this volume.

[67] "Early Letters from Pennsylvania, 1699–1722," *Pennsylvania Magazine of History and Biography*, 37(1913), 330, 332, 334.

[68] Patrick Brett, "America 1770–1771 from the letters of a middle-class Englishman to his son . . . ," *British History Illustrated*, 6(1979), 11.

[69] See Thomson, *News from America*, pp. 112, 113, this volume.

plantations here and there" could be purchased, but they would have to go farther west, perhaps as far as the Ohio, in order to find such a large tract.[70] Whitelaw and Allen ended up buying 10,000 acres in the township of Ryegate, New York.[71] This township was "very far back being more than 300 miles from New york and tho it lies along the banks of Connecticut river it is 200 miles above Hartford which is the highest that sloops come up that river[.] the nearest seaport to it is portsmouth which lies about 100 miles east from it."[72] So at 16 pence an acre, on the far fringes of European settlement at least 100 miles from the nearest seaport and coastal market, the agents for the Inchinnan Company finally found a tract large enough to settle all of their members.

Reports from other colonies were similar. Alexander McAllister warned a friend in Scotland that the best lands in his part of North Carolina had been "taken up many years ago."[73] This was also true of Virginia, Helen Rose wrote in 1767: "All the Good lands within the bounds of this Colony are allready taken up" and, as a result, good riverfront property was expensive – £2.8 sterling an acre. She too recommended settlement on the Ohio, but "many thousand men woud be required to mack [make] good sittlement" there. Five years later, in 1772, she reported that settlement had pushed beyond the Allegheny Mountains to the Green Briar area.[74]

Thus immigrant farmers needed capital to buy or lease lands, even the cheaper lands in the backcountry. But even if settlers were able to lease lands for low rent in the backcountry areas, they would still need money for tools, livestock, household items, and transportation to distant markets in order to set up self-sufficient plantations. William Manson brought his own tools, staples, European goods, tradesmen, and laborers to his plantation in the newly ceded lands in upcountry Georgia, 180 miles from Savannah, so that

---

[70] Thomson, *News from America*, p. 117, this volume; see also, "Journal of General James Whitelaw . . . ," *Proceedings of the Vermont Historical Society* (1905–1906), 137.

[71] Now Vermont.

[72] See James Whitelaw to William Whitelaw, July 15, 1773, this volume.

[73] Alexander McAllister to Angus McCuaig, November 29, 1770, this volume.

[74] Helen Rose to Jeanie Grant (1766?), and Helen Rose to Archibald Grant, May 26, 1772, GD 345/ 1171/2/70 & 71x, SRO. John Campbell remarked that lands near trade and navigation in Maryland were "well peopled" and therefore expensive, selling for as much as £3 sterling per acre. But he notes that even good lands 80 to 90 miles inland sell for that amount. See John Campbell to William Sinclair, this volume. See also Brett, "America 1770–1771 . . . ,": "There is no doubt but that the back Part of Virginia, of Georgia, or the Carolinas, near some navigable River, are the most promising Places for new Settlers to make an Advantage of their Money" (p. 11).

he could establish a bartering system with other settlers nearby, and thereby make the remote area more or less self-sustaining.[75]

The colonists' message, then, was the more money the better, but at the very least, one should have enough money to pay for passage. Then, if one had contacts or much-needed skills, one could eventually do fairly well. David Duff, Hugh Simm, and Alexander Cumine all had skills or personal contacts to help them find work. Simm, whose starting salary as a teacher was £50–£55 currency, found a job for £120 a few years later. But even with his skills it took time and several moves for him to get well settled. So when he wrote to his brother in Paisley, who was thinking about moving to America with his family, Simm wanted to be sure that his brother was "Skilled in working any kind of cuntry work Such as table Cloaths hand Cloathes and the like and Can bring £50 with you ashoare." He also advised him to bring not just one, but *two* looms, and to get more training in the skill of dying textiles, "especially what they Call the Cold fat this will be of Considerable advantage."[76]

Those with no skills or contacts were more likely to face severe trials. Baikia Harvey, the only writer in this collection who had not paid the money for his passage, deeply regretted that he had not come free. He pleaded with his godfather to send him "all the Money" he could so that he could buy his time and apprentice himself "to some Tradesman to Learn his calling," and he further warned that no one should come to America unless "they are able to pay their passage thir Selves and then they may come as soon as they like this is a good poor mans Country *when a man once getts into a way of Liveing*."[77]

But a "way of Liveing" was sometimes hard to get "into," as William Roberts found out at the end of his three-year term of indentured servitude. In 1761, two years after his release, he was poor, landless, wore tattered clothes, and took pick-up jobs in order to survive. Six years later he was still poor and did not have enough money to rent a plot of land and set up a household. He wore his brothers' second-hand clothing. At this time, in 1767, he estimated that he would need £28 sterling to establish himself on a small farm. The rent was only £10 currency a year, but he would need money in order to buy livestock and provisions. However, he was not able to earn or raise the money, so the following year he took a job as an overseer of 20 slaves. He was finally able to rent a plantation with someone else, but then

---

[75] See Bailyn, *Voyagers to the West*, 558–567.
[76] See Hugh Simm to Andrew Simm, September 27, 1774, this volume.
[77] Baikia Harvey to Thomas Baikie, December 30, 1775, this volume. Italics added.

sank into debt.[78] All he asked his mother and uncle for in 1769 was about £20 sterling and some bedding, and then he would be able to "live veary well." After ten years, Roberts's circumstances were no better than they had been after his release from servitude. He, like Harvey, wished that he had learned a trade, for "Tradesmen hear [here] lives like Gentlemen."[79]

Therefore many American colonists who knew these realities about the costs of getting settled and the perils of trying to make one's way without assets wrote with urgency to their relations, begging them to emigrate before they got too poor to come. As Alexander Thomson warned, "If tradesmen, or labourers, or farmers design to come over at all, they ought by all means to come immediately, before they be too old or turn so poor, that they will have no money to bring with them, nor even to pay their freight."[80] And McAllister, happy to "See So many f[l]ying" from oppression, was nevertheless angry at those who waited too long to leave: ". . . all I bleam the pople for is that they do not com to this Country be fore they geet So poor."[81] Not only would leaving Britain without any money be difficult, but if they waited too long, they would also have to spend more money for good quality lands which were being settled rapidly.

Thus informed, many in reduced but not desperate circumstances took heed and converted their stock and worldly goods into capital. Some even left without paying their debts, because they were afraid that they would not have enough money to start anew in America. James Campbell, a factor to the Countess of Sutherland, remarked that "hither to the american emigrators have honestly settled [with] me before they set out but I find now that they have no such intentions for this reason if they were to pay all they owe they would have nothing remaining to carry them of[f] the Country & off they are determined to be." The result of the money-hoarding was that "not a farthing of money" could be found "in the Country at present the emigrants

---

[78] In a recent study of Augusta County, Virginia, Turk McCleskey discovered that out of 216 adult men who had been indentured servants before 1770, only 16 were able to get their own land there, and not one freed servant was able to get land in Augusta County after 1761. Turk McCleskey, "Rich Land, Poor Prospects: Real Estate and the Formation of a Social Elite in Augusta County, Virginia, 1738–1770," *Virginia Magazine of History and Biography*, 98(1990), 452–453.

[79] James P. P. Horn, "The Letters of William Roberts of All Hollows Parish, Anne Arundel County, Maryland, 1756–1769," *Maryland Historical Magazine*, 74(1979), 117–132, quotes at p. 129 and p. 128.

[80] Thomson, *News from America*, p. 120, this volume.

[81] See p. 176, n. 23, this volume; Alexander McAllister to James McAllister, December 1771–January 1772, this volume.

have drained it of what littled remained in the peoples hands."[82] Similar
alarming reports were coming from other places as well. A writer from Wigton was worried that the "country will suffer not only from the loss of its
inhabitants but also from the loss of its wealth."[83]

Those who had no stock to convert into capital or who did not have
enough capital to get comfortably settled in America tried other ways to
compensate. Some borrowed money or joined an emigration association. At
least four emigration societies were formed in the 1770s in Scotland alone.[84]
Shareholders of these joint stock companies could later receive allotments of
land in America based on the number of shares owned. This enabled poorer
emigrants to settle on small parcels of their own land while receiving help
from fellow company members.

Although "the material standard of living enjoyed by the typical white
family unit in the thirteen mainland English colonies was almost certainly
the highest in the world by the 1770s,"[85] the experiences of settlers helped to
continually redefine the meaning of that persistent but ever-changing standard for future migrants. America was a good poor man's country, but by
the 1770s, this was true only if the poor had assets, preferably in capital. A
few contemporaries, like Father Joseph Mosley, had begun to think that
America had outlived its reputation. In 1772 the Jesuit missionary wrote his
sister that America "has been a fine poor man's country; but now it is well
peopled; the lands are all secured; & the harvest for such is now all over.
The lands are mostly worked by the landlords' negroes; and, of consequence,
white servants, after their term of bondage is out, are stroling about the
country without bread."[86]

Therefore, even though the letters contained the encouragement that the
disheartened Britons needed to hear – that America had a healthy climate,
abundant produce, fertile lands, high wages, good prices, and cheap lands
for sale – many also contained a warning, sometimes subtle or silently bracketed between promises of abundance, but nevertheless urgent: Come before
it's too late; come before you get too poor.

---

[82] James Campbell to Alexander Mckenzie, August 10, 1772; and same to same, August 1, 1772,
Sutherland Papers, Dep 313/III/Box 16.
[83] Quoted from "Extract of a letter from Wigton, in Galloway," with a dateline of London,
April 7, *South Carolina Gazette & Country Journal*, June 7, 1774.
[84] See p. 4, n. 8, this volume.
[85] Edwin J. Perkins, *The Economy of Colonial America* (New York, 1980), 145.
[86] Thomas Hughes, *History of the Society of Jesus in North America* (London and New York,
1908), 1: 342.

NETWORKS

In addition to the "discoveries" and "curiosities" written about in these letters, the writings as a whole reveal much about the emigration process and its context. The letters expose personal connections that are laced together to form networks through which these discoveries about America circulated. Not only did the contents of the letters influence the decisions of those back home, but the networks themselves also had a decisive impact on the character and intensity of this migration.

The more formal, well-organized networks have been well documented. Among these are the indentured servant and convict trade, centered mainly in London, Bristol, and Northern Ireland, but active all over the British Isles; the slave trade; merchant and business firms, for which young men were sent to the colonies as factors, storekeepers, and apprentices; and church organizations that sent men and women to the colonies as clerics and missionaries. Some of the letter writers in this book belonged to one of these formally established networks: John Campbell was a factor for a Scottish tobacco firm; Thomas Taylor and Baikia Harvey belonged to two separate but related indentured servant enterprises; and Thomas Feilde was licensed for America by the Anglican Church.[87]

But most of the letters printed here were written by emigrants who belonged to one of the countless informal kinship and friendship networks that spanned the Atlantic. These were often started by one family or a closely knit group of emigrants who, after settling in America, wrote back home and encouraged others to follow. Some were quite small: Hester Wylly, for example, came to America to join her brothers.[88] Others were huge and kept expanding and forming subnetworks, like the Glasgow–Paisley/middle colonies network in which Hugh Simm, Alexander Thomson, and James Whitelaw shared a number of connections that centered around Simm's mentor, John Witherspoon, and the latter's contacts in the Associate Presbyterian (or Seceder) Church.[89] Within these three sets of letters, a pattern

[87] See letters of John Campbell, Thomas Taylor, Baikia Harvey, and Thomas Feilde, this volume.

[88] See letter of Hester Wylly, this volume.

[89] Three of these large networks are represented in this book: Yorkshire/Nova Scotia; the Glasgow–Paisley/middle colonies; and Hebrides/Sutherland/North Carolina. John Witherspoon, a Scottish divine, was the minister of the Laigh Kirk in Paisley, Scotland, at the time he was offered the Presidency of the College of New Jersey (later Princeton University). He accepted the post and arrived in America in 1768, accompanied by his family and Hugh

emerges, and common elements appear: Whitelaw stopped at Thomson's plantation on his way south after first having received directions from Witherspoon. With supplementary documentation, this network can be traced to its fullest extent, at least as far north as Nova Scotia – where Witherspoon was involved in settling Pictou with Scots – then south to Carolina, and east, across the ocean, to lowland Scotland. And, too, many of these people belonged to subnetworks within this larger framework: Thomas Clark, the minister who settled New Perth (now Salem) New York, was an important contact for Witherspoon and Whitelaw, but he was also a crucial link in his own Irish emigrant community.[90]

These informal connections, through which information about America was circulated by word-of-mouth and by letter, were so powerful in generating emigration that they were responsible for the majority of free British migration to America during this period.[91] Their influence was, to a large extent, the result of the type of public information available to prospective emigrants and its reliability.

Public information about emigration was widespread and often confusing. Newspapers were the primary means of disseminating reports on the pros and cons of migrating to America. These reports ranged in length from one or two sentences to several pages, and took many forms. Some were extracts of emigrant letters, printed in the hope that firsthand information would be more persuasive in encouraging or discouraging emigration. Some were advertisements for different kinds of artisans, or for people with capital who could be tempted to buy or lease lands in America. Some were strictly informational – for example, those informing the public that an emigration society had been formed, or that a group of Highlanders had left for America. The longest accounts were essays on various aspects of emigration: the reasons for leaving and the benefits of the change, the loss to the kingdom of capital and useful people, the exaggerated descriptions of America and the deluded notions that people had about it, and the attention that gov-

---

Simm. See p. 123, n. 67, this volume, and see letters of Hugh Simm, Alexander Thomson, and James Whitelaw, this volume.

[90] For Thomas Clark, see p. 94, n. 17, this volume.

[91] Many contemporary observers remarked on the impact that these encouraging letters from America had on emigration. See, for example, Customs Officers at Wigtown to the Board of Treasury, January 5, 1774, T1/500, PRO; *Lloyd's Evening Post*, under "London" December 6–8, 1773, and under "York" March 18–March 21, 1774; "Unto the Honourable the Vice Admiral of Zetland," James Hogg Papers, M-341, Southern Historical Collection, University of North Carolina, Chapel Hill; and Archibald Campbell to Thomas Miller, March 3, 1774, SP 54/45, PRO.

ernment was or was not giving to this matter. In addition to the newspaper reports, handbills and pamphlets were circulated by private publicists and agents acting on behalf of merchants, who were hoping to make a profit on a shipload of paying emigrants or indentured servants, or by landholders wishing to people their lands in America.[92]

In sifting through this information, people interested in emigrating had to be wary; the truth about the emigrant experience was not easy to find. For example, antiemigration factions like Highland landlords, who did not want to lose their tenants, printed false information about America in order to discourage mass emigration.[93] And some promoters of emigration, especially those eager to make profits from taking shiploads of people overseas, also found it in their best interest to distort the truth by exaggerating the bounties America provided. "[W]hile one represented the case of the emigrants as a state of perfect felicity, as if they had entered into elysium upon their setting foot on the American shore; another described it to be the most deplorable, as if when they crossed the Atlantic, they had plunged themselves into labyrinths of endless misery."[94]

In order to correct the biases in the printed literature, some of those who had emigrated or who had toured parts of America agreed to have their observations published in pamphlet form. Patrick M'Robert, who toured the northern colonies in 1774 and 1775 and claimed to have "an inviolable regard to truth," wanted to correct the "misrepresentations and contradictory accounts."[95] John Robinson and Thomas Rispin promised a "faithful description" of Nova Scotia to those who were still interested in emigrating in spite of the "late unfavourable accounts."[96] In fact, so strong was the demand for these "truthful" accounts that when Alexander Thomson's pamphlet *News from America* was published in Glasgow in 1774, "several thousand copies"

---

[92] See, for example, the *London Chronicle*, September 30–October 3, 1775, p. 7.

[93] Hector McAllister wrote from the Scottish island of Arran to his brother Alexander in America that "the lairds here are much affraid to have their lands waste & give Strange Characters of all that Country." And Alexander's cousin John Boyd wrote from Kintyre that since he had not received his letter, he suspected that if Alexander had given "a good Account of the Countrey," the letter may have come "to some of the Lairds hands in this Countrey and No doubt they would keep from me knowing well I am a great Friend to adventurers," as they do "all they can do to keep the poor people back from Going." Hector McAllister to Alexander McAllister, June 26, 1754; and John Boyd to Alexander McAllister, September 29, 1774. Papers of Colonel Alexander McAllister, North Carolina Department of Archives and History, Raleigh (hereafter McAllister Papers).

[94] M'Robert, *A Tour*, ix.

[95] M'Robert, *A Tour*, ix.

[96] See p. 54, this volume.

were sold in one week.[97] But, despite these testimonies of truth, people often remained skeptical of any published account no matter who the author was. Some even mistrusted the pamphlet written by Thomson, who was a former countryman and friend to many in the Paisley community: "Some people is Mightily lifted up with it and others laughing at it."[98]

Therefore, the only way people interested in emigrating believed they could get accurate information was to ask those they knew and trusted who had already settled in America. Earnest pleas for honest assessments appear frequently in letters to emigrants. Sarah Bentley wrote to friends in Nova Scotia that she wanted "the truth and nothing but the truth";[99] William Whitelaw had heard "many various accounts" and wanted his son James to be honest in his account of America – was it "a Canaan or a barren wilderness"?;[100] and Hector McAllister asked his brother in North Carolina to tell everyone to "write home the best encouragement you can with truth" to counteract the false reports spread around by the Scottish landlords.[101] So great was the hunger for accurate information that people in these networks – friends, kin, acquaintances, business associates, ship captains – who had firsthand knowledge of America or who had received letters from America, were sought out and questioned, and the information was repeated and talked about in detail.

In general, the networks had two nuclei – one in Britain and the other in America – tied together, of course, by people who knew each other. The British side of the network originated with a group of people in a small geographical area – a valley or glen, a single parish or county, or a cluster of several islands – some of whom migrated to a township or county or valley in America, where they established a new settlement. As their encouraging letters drew more and more former neighbors across the Atlantic, the networks on both sides expanded beyond their original geographical areas. The peopling of these American enclaves took different forms, but some elements

---

[97] Extract of a letter from Edinburgh, May 28, 1774, in *Lloyd's Evening Post*, June 3–6, 1774. This news item refers to this pamphlet as *Good News From America*. The actual title was *News from America* (in this volume). Thomson had asked his friend in Glasgow to send his letters to the press in order to make a public refutation of false rumors that had been circulating in Scotland regarding his unhappy condition in America.

[98] William Whitelaw to James Whitelaw, March 25, 1774, James Whitelaw Papers, MS 29, Vermont Historical Society, Montpelier, VT (hereafter Whitelaw Papers).

[99] Sarah Bentley to William and Ann Truman, February 9, 1776, Webster Chignecto Collection, 7001/313, Mt. Allison University Archives, Sackville, New Brunswick.

[100] William Whitelaw to James Whitelaw, June 14, 1773, Whitelaw Papers.

[101] Hector McAllister to Alexander McAllister, June 26, 1754, McAllister Papers.

were common to all networks: News was passed back and forth informally by letter and word-of-mouth; the flow of emigration was primarily one way; and certain people were more prominant than others in stimulating this flow. Those who knew the most about America became the natural facilitators. Some may have visited there, but most had probably received their information from their American correspondents. These "friends of adventurers" were not just sources of information; many took a more active role by arranging group or family emigration. They knew where to charter ships. They collected money, made lists, organized food supplies, and wrote letters of reference. When necessary, they called meetings by posting notices at church doors, summoning all those interested in emigration to meet and collectively discuss how to move themselves and their families to America. As leaders to whom all others looked for information and safe guidance, they were a vital part of the mechanism, making emigration possible for many poor tenants who otherwise would have had little knowledge about how to make so radical a change. A closer look at how one of these networks operated in Britain and America will reveal something of the power that these letters, personal contacts, and facilitators had in generating emigration.

One such network extended from Cumberland County, North Carolina, across the Atlantic to the inner Hebridean isles and parts of Argyleshire, north to Skye in Invernesshire, and then up to the northern counties of Sutherland and Caithness. After the first load of 350 Scots from the inner Hebrides landed in North Carolina in 1739, information was sent back and forth across the Atlantic as more and more Scots settled near their former neighbors in the upper Cape Fear region of the Carolina backcountry. As the followers, who trickled in slowly during the 1740s and 1750s, claimed lands and settled in, they wrote to those left behind, enticing them with promises of cheap land and general abundance.

Information about this network can be found in several sources, but most of it comes from the McAllister family papers deposited at the State Archives in Raleigh, North Carolina.[102] More than 50 letters written by Alexander McAllister, who was a member of the 1739 group, and his friends and relatives in Scotland have survived. Among Alexander's eight correspondents in Scotland were his brother, sister-in-law, and several cousins, as well as a few acquaintances, all of whom lived on the islands of Arran and Islay, or the peninsula of Kintyre in the inner Hebrides. From them, information passed along land and sea lanes to their friends and acquaintances, at least as far north as the isle of Skye and east to Greenock.

---

[102] See p. 170, this volume.

The bulk of Alexander's correspondence was to and from his brother Hector, who lived on the island of Arran in Buteshire. Hector had accompanied his family to Carolina in 1739, but returned to Scotland shortly thereafter, and never went back to America. However, as a result of his brief visit and continued communication with his family there, he acquired a great deal of knowledge about this part of America, and was widely regarded in his neighborhood as somewhat of an authority on Carolina. Hector passed along his news from abroad to many of the McAllisters still living in Scotland, as well as to friends in Jura, Islay, Kintyre, and Greenock. Transportation between islands by packet and express boats enabled Hector and his friends to visit each other without too much difficulty, to share information, and to give those going to Carolina letters or family news.

One person who went to Hector for advice about emigrating to Carolina was his kinsman Angus McAllister, who lived in Tarbert, Kintyre. Angus and his son had sailed the short distance to Arran to consult Hector and to get a letter of recommendation before setting out for Carolina to "try their fortune." Hector agreed to write his brother Alexander on their behalf, asking him to do everything in his "power to recomend [Angus] to business either by Sea or land as he will Judge it most his Intrest or as you yourself may think most for his advantage." He went on to describe Angus' abilities and the talents of his 13-year-old son.[103] Such personal recommendations were common, and Alexander McAllister received many of them. They were extremely important as a form of introduction for emigrants who did not know anyone in America.

Hector's role as "friend to adventurers" was not just to give personal advice to friends or to write letters of recommendation. His reputation was so widespread that when he decided to plan his own emigration to Carolina in 1769, hundreds of people on Arran and the neighboring islands wanted to go with him and begged him to "procure them undoubted intelligence" about where they could settle. He then wrote to the governor of North Carolina, as well as to his brother, in order to find out where good lands could be purchased for all of these people. He would charter a ship as soon as he knew the place where the governor wanted them to land. He estimated that plans would take at least a year, because the people had to dispose of their stock of cattle and other goods.[104]

Hector, though a prominent figure in this network, was only one person through whom information about America was circulated. Alexander had at

---

[103] Hector McAllister to Alexander McAllister, May 31, 1774, McAllister Papers.
[104] Hector McAllister to Alexander McAllister, March 15, 1769, McAllister Papers.

least seven other correspondents, all of whom had similar contacts. Some,
like Hector, wrote letters of recommendation and actively assisted emigrants
in planning their departure. Others just exchanged news and gossip. When-
ever a ship from Carolina arrived at one of the island stops, residents were
eager to see if any letters had come from their friends or relatives, and often
made special plans to arrange meetings with Carolina visitors so that they
could get the latest news from abroad.

One frequent visitor, who was known to just about everyone, was one of
the most important facilitators in this network: Alexander Campbell of Balole, a native of the isle of Islay.[105] As a shipmaster and trader, whose business
had taken him to Jamaica for 12 years, Balole was a frequent trans-Atlantic
traveler. He knew many people on both sides of the ocean. Alexander and
Hector McAllister were close friends, as were many other Carolinians and
their relations, including members of his own family who had gone to North
Carolina in 1739 with the original settlers. An avid supporter of emigration,
Balole did all he could to help people get to Carolina, taking emigrants,
letters, and news with him whenever he went. These contacts and frequent
trips gave him a widespread reputation as an excellent source of information
about emigration.

One tacksman[106] from the Isle of Skye, Lachlan Mackinnon of Corrychatachan, had heard about Balole, and wrote him asking for information
about Carolina, as he was planning to give up his tack and leave Skye. He
and his family were among many who wanted to leave that island, because
their landlord, Alexander MacDonald of Sleat, was doubling and trebling
their rents. In 1771 some of MacDonald's tenants designed an emigration
plan that became known to some as the "Carolina Scheme." They wanted
to sell shares of stock to prospective emigrants in order to raise capital for
the purchase of a tract of 100,000 acres in Carolina for the settlement of all
shareholders. Each would receive land in proportion to the amount of shares
owned. In order to find out as much as they could about Carolina and how
to prepare for their departure, they solicited advice from people, like Balole,
who were knowledgeable on the subject. When Balole replied to Corrychatachan, he wrote a brief but enticing letter: Cross Creek, where the High-

---

[105] See Alexander Campbell of Balole letter, this volume; McAllister letters, this volume; and
Donald Campbell to Colin Shaw, August 23, 1770, and Duncan Shaw to Colin Shaw,
September 23, 1773, Colin Shaw Papers, North Carolina Department of Archives and His-
tory, Raleigh.

[106] A tacksman was a tenant who leased a farm or "tack," often the head tenant, who collected
rents from his subtenants.

landers were settled, was a "thriving place" where "each has a plantation of
his own on the river Side & live as happy as princes, they have liberty &
property & no Excise, no dread of their being turned out of their lands by
Tyrants." This encouraging letter, written by a man who knew Carolina well,
was copied and passed around to all who were interested.[107]

Balole's influence in generating emigration from Skye cannot be mea-
sured, but many people emigrated from that island in the early 1770s because
they were tempted by letters and information from abroad. As one observer
of Skye remarked, "the flattering accounts receivd from America has rais'd
a spirit of emigration, which if not soon suppress'd may have dreadfull consequences." When a large group of people left Skye in 1771, Hector McAllister wrote his brother Alexander that he heard "their are some hundred
families going this year from the Island of Skye." In fact, the migration from
Skye became notorious in itself; estimates for the early 1770s went as high
as 2,000.[108]

The emigration from Skye and the "Carolina Scheme" drew so much
attention that they attracted the interest of other emigration organizers as
far north as the county of Sutherland, where George Mackay of Mudal lived.
He was in the process of making arrangements to ship about 200 people
from Sutherland to North Carolina, and he wanted details on how the Skye
tenants had organized themselves. Mackay had been told that he could not
buy land in North Carolina, that all the property was owned by "other trading people," a few noblemen, Army officers, and merchants. He therefore
made the trip to Skye, "desirous to be informed minutely in this affair."
While there, in March 1772, he wrote to a gentleman who might know
whether or not these rumors were true, and who, he was told, might be able
to explain more about the "Carolina Scheme."[109] The reply was reassuring:
Mackay had been misinformed – "a twentieth part of that province is yet
no Mans property but the Kings"; furthermore, Carolina was a good place
to live: The climate was healthy, wages were high, and the ground fertile.
An enclosed copy of the letter from Campbell of Balole to Corrychatachan

[107] See Campbell of Balole's letter to Corrychatachan, this volume.
[108] John MacLeod to Mrs. MacLeod, October 9, 1772, MacLeod Papers; Hector McAllister
to Alexander McAllister, September 12, 1771, McAllister Papers; Robert Forbes, *The Lyon
in Mourning . . .* , Henry Paton, ed., 3 vols. (Edinburgh, 1895–1896), 3: 259.
[109] George Mackay of Mudal was a tacksman on the Sutherland estate in Strathnaver, northern
Scotland. Alexander Murdoch, "A Scottish Document concerning Emigration to North
Carolina in 1772," *North Carolina Historical Review*, 67(1990), 445, 447; R. J. Adam, ed.,
John Home's Survey of Assynt (Edinburgh, 1960), xxiv, n. 75, and xxv, n. 78.

gave fuller details.[110] This news must have reinforced Mackay's resolve to take a shipload of people from Strathnaver to Carolina, because early in the summer of 1772 he went to Edinburgh to charter a ship. News of this quickly spread to the general commissioner of the Sutherland Estates, who, fearful of losing his tenants, accused Mackay of being a "ringleader" intent on imitating the Isle of Skye people.[111] But Mackay ignored Sutherland's attempts to thwart his plans. When the passage money had been collected and the ship was ready for the voyage, the *Adventure* arrived at Loch Eriboll, took on its full complement of adventurers, and set sail for Carolina on August 19, 1772.[112]

When the Strathnaver people arrived in Carolina, they "sent back such favourable accounts . . . setting forth the richness of the Country, the Cheapness of living and the certain prospect of bettering their fortunes &c &c" that they advised "all their friends to follow them."[113] This, then, was the beginning of a new trans-Atlantic network – of Carolina-Sutherland people. The letters sent from Carolina intensified interest in emigration to such an extent that during the next few years several emigrant ships left the northern coast of Scotland with people from the counties of Sutherland and Caithness.[114]

Thus, from the small inner Hebridean islands, to the isle of Skye, then north to the county of Sutherland on the northernmost coastal fringe of mainland Scotland, news about living in America found eager listeners, who in turn established their own small networks in which emigrants and prospective emigrants could share knowledge and provide assistance. Equipped with all the information they could gather, people who were determined to leave converted their stock into capital, obtained letters of reference and directions about where to go, made sailing arrangements, said goodbye to friends and relatives, and left. The risk was enormous. They left leaseholds that their families had held for generations, gave up possessions they could not carry, took one final look at the countryside they knew so well, and sailed in a small wooden ship across 3000 miles of open sea to an unfamiliar

[110] Letter to George Mackay and enclosure, in Murdoch, "Scottish Document," 447–448. See Campbell of Balole letter, this volume.

[111] James Sutherland to Alexander Mackenzie, February 17, 1772, Sutherland Papers, Dep 313/III/Box 16.

[112] *Scots Magazine*, 34(September, 1772), 515.

[113] "Unto the Honourable The Vice Admiral of Zetland," n.d., pp. 2–3, James Hogg Papers.

[114] James Campbell to Alexander McKenzie, February 22, 1773, Sutherland Papers, Dep 313/III/Box 16; May 30, 1774–June 3, 1774, T47/12, PRO.

place. But most at least had a safety net: They were not going alone, and they knew, or knew of, American friends who could help them get settled.

One family that had taken this bold step were the Campbells from the Isle of Skye. When young Dugald Campbell and his family left their home on Skye sometime in late 1771 or early 1772, they carried a letter of recommendation written by their friend, Alexander McAllister's cousin John Boyd.[115] They were probably leaving with many other Skye people, who were going to America to "try their fortunes," most of them unable or unwilling to pay the exorbitant rents at home.

When the ship carrying the Campbells arrived in Carolina, probably at Wilmington, Dugald and his family had to transfer to a smaller boat – a long-boat or lighter – to carry them about 100 miles up the Cape Fear River to Cross Creek, a center of Highland settlement, where Alexander McAllister lived. The slow trip added another week to their voyage.[116]

Alexander was not expecting them, but he welcomed them, as he had many others, and was glad to see that more people had broken free of the tyranny of their landlords. He opened his cousin's letter, and after reading Boyd's unnecessary apology for always being "very troublesome" with "Epistles of recomendation in favours of people whose Interest I have so much at heart," he learned that Dugald was a young gentleman and a "good Classicale scholar" who "writes a Good hand and understands figures." Dugald's father was a surgeon and needed no recommendation to help him find work, as his qualifications would be enough. But the one-page letter served a greater purpose – that of introducing the Campbells to the McAllisters, who no doubt entertained them and shared conversation about friends and relations back home. And, more important, it introduced the Campbells to McAllister's world – not only to the people he knew, but also to his extensive knowledge of lands for sale, job opportunities, crops, prices, distances, and all the necessary information they would need to get the "proper Settlements" that Boyd had wished for them.

Alexander lived in the small community of Cross Creek, near Campbelton, a mile and a quarter away. Together these two places made up the trading hub of backcountry North Carolina. Main roads that cut inland across North Carolina met at Cross Creek, which became the market for the Upper Cape Fear River. One observer noted that in the early 1770s, as many as 40 or 50 large wagons carrying produce from the Carolina backcountry could be seen in Cross Creek on any given day. Though the town

115 John Boyd to Alexander McAllister, November 15, 1771, McAllister Papers.
116 Meyer, *Highland Scots*, 77, 75.

was relatively small, it had three gristmills, a place for slaughtering cattle and hogs, tradesmen of various kinds, merchant houses, and branch stores of Wilmington merchants whose agents in Cross Creek carried on a lively trade with the backcountry settlers.[117]

Surrounding this market center was the local population, which spread out in all directions. It was far from being a transplanted Highland community, for at least half the people were from other places: England, Wales, Germany, France, and the lowlands of Scotland. Most of these residents raised livestock and farmed their lands along the river or creeks, but a few were tradesmen and merchants in and around Cross Creek and Campbelton. Some, too poor to pay the land-grant fees and buy tools, either worked as tenants or as indentured servants.[118]

Alexander was himself a planter of considerable means and a prominent figure in the Cape Fear community, where he had lived since 1740. By 1787 he had accumulated 2599 acres of land and owned 40 slaves. So as a planter he was well-acquainted with crops, soil, prices of livestock and produce, clearing land, building shelters, tending animals, and transporting goods to market. As a mill owner, he knew about grinding corn and milling wheat. And as an employer of tradesmen, he knew which kinds of services were available nearby and which were desperately needed – the latter including weavers, blacksmiths, shoemakers, and carpenters. He spoke from experience. Poor people will have difficulty settling in, he wrote, and it will take one or two years to get "comodiously Settled," but when they do get settled, it will be for life, and they will be able to grow a great variety of crops. Indian corn was the "cheaf griane" for "man & Beast," but they would also be able to grow wheat, barley, rye, oats, potatoes, tobacco, and "every other thing" and make tar and indigo.[119]

In addition to being a planter, McAllister took on other responsibilities in the colony. He was an elder in the Presbyterian Church, a representative to the North Carolina House of Assembly, member of the Committee of Safety for Wilmington district, lieutenant colonel in the Cumberland County militia, and later a state senator. All of these responsibilities put him in touch with a wide variety of people scattered throughout the colony.

Alexander's most important connections in the colony were his relatives and friends, of whom he had many. The three sisters who had come with

[117] Meyer, *Highland Scots*, 79, 110; *Informations Concerning . . . North Carolina*, 29.

[118] Meyer, *Highland Scots*, 116, 103, 107. Tenants rented plots from those with large holdings and paid a rent of one-third of the crops produced and one-third of the livestock.

[119] See letter from Alexander McAllister to John Boyd, c. April 1772, this volume.

him from Scotland lived near him.[120] One of them, Mary, had married Hector McNeill, an attorney and sheriff. They lived nearby on their own property above Cross Creek, near the bluffs overlooking Cape Fear River. Like his brother-in-law, McNeill served as a church elder and as a representative to the North Carolina House of Assembly in 1761 and 1762.[121] Another of Alexander's sisters, Isabella, married Farquhard Campbell, who by the early 1760s was a wealthy landowner and church elder. His properties, scattered throughout Cumberland County, included lands that joined Alexander's "on the lower Side." He also served as a representative to the Assembly and as a delegate to revolutionary conventions. Alexander's unmarried sister, Grisella, lived with them.[122]

These were Alexander's closest kin, but he had other relatives scattered throughout the colony and elsewhere in America with whom he was constantly sharing news. His cousin Hector McAllister, married to his niece Isabella Campbell, lived in Wilmington and was the commander of a ship. His cousin Jean McNeill also lived in Wilmington.[123] Alexander Colvin and Margaret Robinson, parents of his second wife, Jane, lived 60 miles below him on Black River, a branch of the Cape Fear.[124] Through his in-laws, Alexander was able to get news about the settlers from the island of Arran, clustered along Black River. His cousin Peter Stewart and his brother-in-law had gone to the island of St. John, and a McAllister lived on Antigua. Alexander even had a relative in Virginia – young Archibald McAllister from Greenock, who was working on the James River as an apprentice storekeeper.[125]

Aside from relatives, Alexander had also gotten to know many others through his various roles as neighbor, Presbyterian elder, farmer, mill-owner,

---

[120] One sister, Ann, stayed in Scotland.

[121] A. I. B. Stewart, "The North Carolina Settlement of 1739," *The Scottish Genealogist*, 32(1985), 11; Meyer, *Highland Scots*, 105, 129; William L. Saunders, ed., *The Colonial Records of North Carolina*, 10 vols. (Raleigh, NC, 1886–1890), 5: 1195, 1197.

[122] Meyer, *Highland Scots*, 115, 129; Hector McAllister to Alexander McAllister, August 22, 1775, McAllister Papers; and Alexander McAllister to Angus McCuaig, November 29, 1770, this volume.

[123] Hector McAllister to Alexander McAllister, September 12, 1771, McAllister Papers; and Alexander McAllister to Hector McAllister, November 29, 1770, this volume.

[124] D. S. McAllister, *Genealogical Record of the Descendants of Col. Alexander McAllister of Cumberland County, North Carolina . . .* (Richmond, VA, 1900), 149.

[125] Hector McAllister to Alexander McAllister, August 22, 1775, McAllister Papers; Alexander McAllister to John Boyd, April 1772, and Alexander McAllister to Alexander McAllister of Cour, late 1771–early 1772, this volume; Hector McAllister to Alexander McAllister, September 12, 1771, McAllister Papers.

politician, military officer, and friend. The minister at his church, Rev. James Campbell, was a fellow countryman from Kintyre, who had arrived at Cape Fear in 1757 via Philadelphia, where he had lived since about 1730. As the only Presbyterian minister in that area in the 1760s, he traveled regularly to two other meetings, one at Alexander Clark's on Barbeque Creek, the other at a Mr. McKay's. At the Barbeque Church, Campbell ministered to some of the settlers from the Hebridean island of Jura. Campbell also had connections with Presbyterians in South Carolina.[126] So through James Campbell, Alexander was able to tap into a much wider Presbyterian network than that of his own church by the Bluff.

As a delegate to the general assembly, Alexander was in touch with prominent people throughout the colony. One colleague on the assembly was Thomas Rutherford, who lived south of Cross Creek. Rutherford had been Deputy Secretary of the Province and Clerk to the Council in 1763, a surveyor of the boundary between North and South Carolina in 1772, clerk of the court in Cumberland County in 1772, and delegate to the provincial congresses from 1774 to 1776.[127] His brother was John Rutherford, a wealthy merchant-planter and receiver-general of quit rents for the colony, who sat on the governor's Council, and was a frequent traveler out of the colony to places such as England, South Carolina, Georgia, and the Carolina backcountry. John Rutherford owned a plantation of 1920 acres outside Wilmington on the northeast branch of the Cape Fear as well as other properties in the colony, including land in Wilmington, and a tar house on Eagles Island – probably the destination of the tar his brother Thomas produced from the plentiful longleaf pine.[128] Alexander may have been connected to the Rutherfords by marriage as well; one of his cousins was a Mrs. Rutherford, who was "Well marry'd."[129]

Others of Alexander's acquaintance were Chief Judge John Smith, who lived next door, the surveyor John Dickson, the sheriff in Campbelton where the county court was located, tradesmen like his cousin Hector McNeill who made saddles, and business associates, not just in Cross Creek and Campbelton, but in other parts of the colony as well. Edward Holland

[126] Saunders, ed., *Colonial Records of North Carolina*, 5: 1196–1197.

[127] John H. Wheeler, *Historical Sketches of North Carolina, From 1584 to 1851* . . . , 2 vols. in 1 (Philadelphia, 1851), 2: 125; Meyer, *Highland Scots*, 106; William S. Powell, ed., *The Correspondence of William Tryon*, 2 vols. (Raleigh, NC, 1980–1981) 1: 108n.

[128] Andrews and Andrews, eds., *Journal of a Lady of Quality*, 291–296; Meyer, *Highland Scots*, 106.

[129] Hector McAllister to Alexander McAllister, May 31, 1774, McAllister Papers.

lived in the Buffalo settlement north of Cross Creek, and Mr. Wilkinson was a merchant in Wilmington who sent Alexander "Negros, Cloth, Blankets, and Keg of Rum."[130]

These friends, relations, and business connections were of course only a small number of the people who populated Alexander's world. But the sample tells us that he knew a wide range of people – from struggling tenants to members of the Governor's Council – who lived in various parts of North Carolina, in nearby colonies, and on the Caribbean islands. He certainly knew enough to be enormously helpful to newcomers: He could assist them in hunting for jobs, or provide information to help them buy or lease lands or build their farms, or introduce them to someone who could answer questions he could not. And he certainly knew enough to be able to give an accurate assessment of what Carolina offered.

Alexander was in a position to help new settlers, and he did his best. He wasted no time informing his cousin John Boyd that "your frind Dougal Campbel is with a merchant at Campbelton I belive the lade will do very well," and his father had already bought a plantation with good houses and cleared land.[131] In other letters he sent back more news of people's successes – cousin Hector McNeill was making saddles, and John McCallum was an overseer for his (Alexander's) father-in-law.[132] Of one group of the "poorest Sort" who arrived in 1770 or early 1771, he wrote, "ther is not one of them that I know but is in a way of doing well they mad[e] all plenty of Corn for them Selves & famile and seemes to be very well Satisfied . . . the most of them is now leards [i.e., lairds] for I beleve too pearts of them have gote land of ther one [own]."[133]

The dissemination, throughout just one network, of what the potential emigrants considered to be reliable information had its effect. The trickle of people who had departed from the Hebrides in the 1740s and 1750s and from Skye in the 1750s grew to an "immense number" in the 1760s and 1770s.[134]

---

[130] Hector McAllister to Alexander McAllister, June 26, 1754, and Jo. Dickinson, Surveyor, September 29, 1771, McAllister Papers; Alexander McAllister to Angus McCuaig, November 29, 1770, this volume; Alexander McAllister to Hector McAllister, n.d. (c. 1766–1768), Ed. Holland to Alexander McAllister, February 15, 1769, and Mr. Wilkinson to Alexander McAllister, November 29, 1766, McAllister Papers.

[131] Alexander McAllister to John Boyd, April 1772, this volume; Alexander McAllister to Hector McAllister, n.d. (c. 1766–1768), McAllister Papers.

[132] Alexander McAllister to Alexander McAllister of Cour, n.d. (c. late 1771–early 1772), this volume.

[133] Alexander McAllister to James McAllister, December 1771–January 1772, this volume.

[134] Alexander McAllister to Alexander McAllister of Cour, n.d. (c. late 1770–early 1771), Mc-

In the three years prior to April 1772, reports from North Carolina stated that 1600 men, women, and children had landed there from the Hebridean islands of Arran, Jura, Islay, and Gigha alone. In 1772–1773, 1500 people from Sutherland emigrated, most bound for North Carolina.[135] And, as noted earlier, as many as 2000 may have left Skye in the early 1770s. These people, well over 5000 in all, were all drawn from the Hebrides/Sutherland–Caithness network of kinship and friendship ties.

* * * * *

The letters that follow provide numerous illustrations of the matters discussed in this introduction, but they also reveal a wide variety of other issues as well – for example, the impact of the changing political climate on these new Americans, and the quality and variations of written literacy. Taken singly, they show how individuals understood and defined the meaning and measure of emigration to America in the decade before the Revolution. They are full of fascination, fear, wonder, doubt, curiosity, courage, and astute observation. But these are more than stories of individuals. As a whole, they can be compared for similarities and differences, because the selection is limited to one particular group in time – British migrants before the Revolution. Also, the collection exposes patterns and networks – some small, some huge – that sustained and nourished these individuals. Hundreds of such networks and subnetworks and extensions of networks existed, as this collection makes apparent through the combination of groups of letters. They provide collective clues to the complex process of trans-Atlantic migration, of people linked together in webs of connections that intersect and blend, while continually forming newer, larger networks or feeding into older, more established ones.

Allister Papers: "as to Settleing our Colony I beleive this part of it will Soon be a new Scotland for within these three or four years there is an imense Number Come in to this place." When Hector tried to find people to go to Carolina in 1754, he could get only about 20–30 families. In 1769, he had hundreds of people who were interested in going with him. Hector McAllister to Alexander McAllister, June 26, 1754, and same to same, March 15, 1769, McAllister Papers.

[135] Saunders, ed., *Colonial Records of North Carolina*, 8: 526; Meyer, *Highland Scots*, 55.

NOVA SCOTIA

Narrative of Charles Dixon, Cumberland County, Nova Scotia, September 21, 1773[1]

CHARLES Dixon and his family came to Nova Scotia with the first wave of Yorkshire migrants to the maritime provinces. They left Liverpool on the *Duke of York* in March 1772 with 56 others, most of whom had been recruited by agents of Nova Scotia's lieutenant governor, Michael Francklin. Francklin, an Englishman by birth, came to Nova Scotia in 1752 where, as a successful merchant and politician, he was able to speculate heavily in the Nova Scotia land grab of the 1760s. Desperate to settle these lands with enterprising farmers, he visited Yorkshire in the early 1770s, where he was able to tap into a restless pool of potential emigrants. These people for the most part were victims of the late eighteenth-century economic and agricultural improvements that had led to high rents and evictions. But other forces were working as well to uproot the farmers. Many had converted to Methodism, which was prevalent in Yorkshire in the mid-to-late eighteenth century, and were eager to find a place where they could practice their religion without fear of abuse and derision. Nova Scotia beckoned with promises of cheap lands and freedom of religious worship.[2]

---

[1] *Source*: Dixon Family Papers, MC 251, MS 1D, Charles Dixon Memoirs, Provincial Archives of New Brunswick, Fredericton, New Brunswick. *Courtesy*: Provincial Archives of New Brunswick. The letter has been printed but contains transcription errors: See James D. Dixon, *History of Charles Dixon . . .* (Sackville, N.B., 1891), 1–5.

[2] Bernard Bailyn, *Voyagers to the West: A Passage in the Peopling of America on the Eve of the Revolution* (New York, 1986), 373–374, 378; James Dean Snowden, "Footprints in the Marsh Mud: Politics and Land Settlement in the Township of Sackville, 1760–1800" (M.A. thesis, University of New Brunswick, 1974), 73–74.

By 1772 the Bay of Fundy area had been fairly well populated by Acadians and New Englanders, but many of them were later removed from their land by the British government or else they had left voluntarily for economic reasons. As a result, the Yorkshire emigrants were able to find inexpensive lands to buy or lease that had been previously cleared and cultivated. Their successes in finding these choice lands encouraged others to follow them across the Atlantic. No fewer than nine vessels from northern England, carrying about 1000 people, followed the *Duke of York* to Nova Scotia before the outbreak of the Revolution.[3]

In his memoir, Charles Dixon provides us with much biographical information about himself. He also gives a rare look at the internal and external forces behind his decision to emigrate. Step by step, he traces the evolution of this transformation, which actually started, not in 1772, but in 1759, when he converted to Methodism. Of his wife Susanna's opinion, we know little from this memoir, other than that he consulted her and she evidently agreed to go, even though she was pregnant with her fifth child. It could not have been an easy decision for either of them, and Charles' hesitancy to leave reflects that. They were well established in Hutton Rudby and fairly well-off financially, and they were not young: Charles was 42 and Susanna 34. They left friends and relatives in England, most of whom they would probably never see again. Only Susanna's sister, Isabella, and her husband, John Trenholm, joined the Dixons in Nova Scotia.

Nevertheless, the Dixons took the risk. They sustained hope throughout the long, difficult, and sickly voyage, and through their initial disappointment after landing at Cumberland, that place of "gloomy aspect." But after their early struggles, they settled down on their 2500-acre farm in Sackville and raised eight children. In addition to being one of the largest landowners in the township, Charles Dixon started a small retail business, held several county offices, was Judge of Common Pleas, representative to the legislature for the province of New Brunswick, and collector of customs. He died in 1817, two years after writing a short memoir saying

---

[3] See pp. 65–66, this volume, for a description of the area where the Yorkshire emigrants settled. Graeme Wynn, "Late Eighteenth-Century Agriculture on the Bay of Fundy Marshlands," *Acadiensis*, 8(1979), 80–89; T47/9-12, Public Record Office, London (hereafter PRO). See also John B. Brebner, *The Neutral Yankees of Nova Scotia* (New York, 1937), 119.

that his descendants numbered 130. Susanna lived another nine years, dying in 1826.[4]

I Chas Dixon was Born in March 8th old Stile 1730 at Kirleavington near Yarm in the East Riding of Yorkshire[5] in old England was brought up to a Bricklayor by trade with my father till I was about 19 followd that calling till about ye 29th year of my Age after that Engaged in a paper Manufactory at Hutton Rudby[6] and followed it for the space of about 12 years with Success during that period at 31 I married Susanna Cottes[7] by whom I have had one [son] & four Daughters[8] During the Cours of my life I was brought up a Protestant or a member of the Church of England after I was sencible of [a fitter?] state of rewards & Punishments I indeavourd to demean my self as one on his Christtian Rase to live Soberly Righteously & Godly in this present Evill world thinking or at least had no doubt but I sho'd obtaine heaven at last but being one time at Robin Hoods bay near Whitby I went to hear Thos Secomb,[9] a Methodist preacher so Calld by way of derishion but his Preaching was such as I neavour heard before for his word was with power it made me cry out in ye bitterness of my Soul what must I do to be savd I found that I was co[n]demd by the [Laws?] of God for it says whoever offends one point is Guilty of all, and all my pretences to being A Member of the Church fell to the ground, I was Condemd by her articules, her Homilies, I had broke my Batismall Covenant, so I was in fact a Babtised Heathen with a Christian Name, I was made to posess Months of Vainity & bear ye Reproach of my Youth, for about 12 Months I went mourning all my Days under a Sence of Guilt, and born'd down with a spiritt of bondage,

4 Dixon, *History of Charles Dixon*, 7, 8, 11, 12, 5, 16.

5 Kirk Levington was actually in the North Riding about two miles south of Yarm and the Tees River, which is the northern boundary of Yorkshire.

6 Hutton Rudby, on the Leven River, was six miles south of Yarm.

7 Susanna Coates (1738–1826).

8 These were Mary, Charles, Susanna, Elizabeth, and Ruth. Ruth was born on September 16, 1772, four months after the Dixons' arrival. Charles and Susanna had three more children: Martha, Edward, and William. Dixon, *History of Charles Dixon*, 16.

9 Thomas Seccombe was an itinerant Methodist preacher, primarily in Ireland, where he was assigned in 1755 until his death in 1759. It must have been during one of his visits to England when Dixon heard him. C. H. Crookshank, *History of Methodism in Ireland* (Belfast and London, 1885), 1: 104, 139.

not being able to fight, nor willing to fly, but seeking for and asking of God that Spiritt were with he made his Children free, that I might Rejoice with his Chosen, & give thanks with his Inheritance, after thus seeking and striving upon my knees, the Lord Proclaim'd his Name Mercifull & Gratious to forgive my Iniquities, heald all my diseases and set my Soul at Liberty, it was on Wednesday ye 21st of Sept 1759 I then was a Member of the Methodist Society at Hutton[10] & continued till the Year 1772 being the 42d year of my age being wearied with Publick Buiseness, and I saw the troubles that was befalling my native Country opreshions of every Kind abounded, and it was very dificult to Earn bread & keep a Consience void of offence, & tho I was involv'd in Buiseness without ye least appearence of being freed there from, till Providence so order'd it, the Honourable Leautenant Governor Franklin of the Province of Nova Scotia ye year 1772 Made som proposalls for Settlers, an aquaintance of Mine being his agent,[11] whith whom I had som Intercourse, and when ye advertisments came out I frequenly recomended them, to others not seeing a way for me to Embrase them my self, till about 2 Months before ye Embarkation (at Liverpool, on board the Ship calld the Duke of York Capt. Benn[,] Master) a Gentelman calld at my House whom I had neaver seen before and ask'd me som Questons about my affares Buisness &c and told me he had been Inform'd I was Inclin'd to Embrace Governor Franklins Proposalls if so he wo'd undertake my afares my Stock in trade Lease Other bills &c that I might not be retarded I was brought to think of it more seriously and gave him for Answer I wo'd weigh it more narowly and give him a deliberate answer in a little time after many thoughts and Consultations with my Wife & frinds I came to a Resolution to leave all my frinds and Intrests I was Invested with, and go to Nova Scotia the time Comcnc'd that wc was order'd to be at Liverpool being ye 18th of Feb we arrivd at Liverpooll on ye 27th & Saild ye 16th of March 1772 on board ye Duke of York[12] with 62 Souls Men Women & Children bound for Nova Scotia as Settlers, in my fambly was Containd my self & my Wife &

---

[10] Hutton Rudby.

[11] Francklin appointed agents for different areas, e.g., the towns of Rillington, Skelton, Thirsk, Hovingham, Sowerby, and Whitby. Snowden, "Footprints in the Marsh Mud," 74.

[12] The advertisement for the sailing of the *Duke of York* for Halifax, Annapolis Royal, and Fort Cumberland, Nova Scotia, appeared throughout February and early March. It instructed people to apply for passage to James Shanks, who had "Lands to give to such as chuse to become Settlers in said province." Shanks was a merchant in Liverpool with whom Francklin had left his terms of settlement. (*The General Advertiser*, Liverpool, February 7, 1772.) The ad was repeated weekly until the second week of March. (*The York Courant*, May 19, 1772, p. 4, col. 1.)

4 Childer viz Mary, Charles, Susanna & Elizebeth Dixon,[13] we had a Rouf
pasage none of us being at sea before was Much Sick after 6 weeks & 4 days
we arrived at Halifax ye Capitall of the Province and was receivd with much
Joy by ye Gentelmen in Generall, but much discourged by others and the
accounts we had of Cumberland ye place intended for our [reception?] was
Enough to make [ye?] Stoutest heart give [place?], I had all this time an
Eye to that providence that calld & made things plain before me hitherto,
& frequently told My Wife all things wod work togeather for good not to
be cast down for I was Sure we Sho'd meet with good Sucess at our Jorneys
End, for we had a many Difficulties in our Jorney and Endeavourd to per-
swade others he that had Inclind us to com hither wo'd surly not leave us
if we was not a Wanting to our Selves thro many discourgements we arrive'd
before Fort Cumberland and things at first Glance wore a gloomy aspect
their was almost none of the Inhabitants about Cumberland but wanted to
sell their Land & go hence, I thought their must be a Cause for this disorder
it being so universall, we Landed on May 21st and the spring being very late
we was not so able to Judge of things, went into the Barracks with our
famblys till we could find a Resting place, as Soon as I was Satisfied in my
own Mind and perceived ye Cause of the Disorder that so much abounded
(viz Indolence, and want of Knowledg) I frequently walkd about ye Country
& at Sackville Bot. a tract of Land of Daniel Hawkins of 2500 Acres[14] for
260 £[15] which I remov'd to June 8th most of the rest of the Settlers & had
Bot. & Settled Elswhere one thing in ye Inhabitance was very Comendable
ye not forsakeing but Asembling them selfs togeather to worship,[16] tho Un-
happily devided in parties & ready to say to each other Stand off I am [   ]
Holier then thou that partie & Unchristian spiritt Prevaild much [   ] so
that ye Divishions amongst them had in great Measure eaten up all their
[   ] Christianity & their attachment to Calvinism had [   ] them of

[13] Their ages were 7, 6, 4, and 1. Dixon, *History of Charles Dixon*, 16.
[14] Daniel Hawkins, a trader, was one of 50 New England grantees who left Sackville, Cumberland (now New Brunswick) between 1770–1774. (Snowden, "Footprints in the Marsh
Mud," 64.) The deed was dated September 8, 1773, and was registered on November 16,
1773. (For the deed, see "Appointments, Agreements & Legal Documents, 1773–1827," MC
251, 8.9.773, Dixon Family Papers.) Dixon bought the land fully stocked with 13 cows, 6
oxen, 34 young cattle, 7 horses, 36 sheep, 13 hogs, and 2 goats. In addition, the property
contained 2 houses, 2 barns and cow houses. (General Accounts, 1774–1818, Dixon Family
Papers.) Dixon leased half his land for £30.8 a year. See p. 66, this volume.
[15] Nova Scotia currency. See General Accounts, 1774–1818, Dixon Family Papers. The exchange
rate was £111.11 currency to £100 sterling.
[16] See p. 46, this volume.

that Universality so Conspickious in a Christian Spiritt & so agreeable to Gods Attributes; who wo'd that none sho'd perish but that all men sho'd be saved It's much to be Lamented when Men are thus Contracted & have Imbibed a parte Spiritt, so we may justly name them & their Reliegeon as Phineas Wife did her Child Sam 1st & 4 Chap,[17] his name is Ichabod for ye Glory of the Lord is departed from them, but to leave persons & things let us admire that Providence who has preserv'd & brought us from our fathers house, who has preserv'd us through many Seen & Unseen [dangers?] and given us a Lott in a Strange Land, and an Earthly Inherittance that we neavour Expected, nor diserv'd   oh that it may Excite us to Gratitude & thanksgiving, while we dwell in a House of Clay & when this Earthly Tabernacle, shall be disolv'd may we receive an I[n]herittance Incoruptable undefiled & will neavour fade away were the Wicked will cease from troubling and were our Soul shall for ever Rest *Amen*

Spt 21st 1773

NB this My Son Charles is written for thy & thy litle Sisters Instruction that thou be not [High] Minded but remember the Rock from whence [thy?] was hewn and in [   ] time [when?] I & thy Mother shall be calld home & laid in the Silent Grave You may remember for your sakes we Crosd the Ocean so that you out strip us in Purity of Heart and Holiness of life and always let your words be ye Picture of your hearts Studie to adorn the Doctrine and Gospell of God your Saviour, and Aquaint Your selfs with God and be at peace, at peace with your Selfs & with all Men, and may ye God of peace be with you Ever More *Amen*

17 I Samuel 4:19–22.

James Metcalf to Ann Gill, Maccan River, Nova Scotia, August 1772[18]

JAMES Metcalf, a Methodist like Charles Dixon, was also among the first group of Yorkshire emigrants who came to Nova Scotia on the *Duke of York*, which was filled almost entirely with families. But not all families came intact. Of the eight members of the Metcalf family, for instance, only the 66-year-old father, James Sr., and his eldest child, James Jr., age 27, were on board. The mother, Mary Pebus Metcalf, had died in 1760, and the other six children, who ranged in age from 12 to 26, stayed behind and only some of them came over later. James Jr. had also left his fiancée, Ann Gill, to whom he wrote this letter, begging her to join him. He seemed enthusiastic about his new home and was full of optimism as he described life in the Cumberland area, perhaps because he was trying not to discourage her. He was certainly aware that others were unhappy with Nova Scotia, and so he may have been trying to prepare her for any negative reports she might hear.[19]

Born in Yorkshire to Anthony Gill and Elizabeth Sutton Gill, Ann was 26 in 1772 and living on the farm of Metcalf's old master, Thomas Wilkinson. She kept her promise to James, and sailed to Nova Scotia the next spring. James met her at Ft. Cumberland, where they were married. They settled on the farm on Maccan River, and stayed there for the rest of their lives, raising four daughters, two of whom died in childhood. The Metcalfs prospered. When James died in late 1819 or 1820, he left his 520-acre homestead farm worth £1425 and an estate worth £3880 to his two grandsons.[20]

---

[18] *Source*: Parks Canada, Webster Chignecto Collection, Accession 7001/336, Mt. Allison University Archives, Sackville, New Brunswick. *Courtesy*: Mount Allison University Archives. The letter was addressed "To Mrs. Ann Gill with Mr. Thomas Wilkinson at Martin Lordship near Easingwould in Yorkshire England." The letter is a recipient copy. It was dated simply "august 1772" without a place of writing; however, the last sentence of the letter implies that he was living at Maccan River, Cumberland County.

[19] Webster Chignecto Collection, Accession 7001/347.

[20] Register of Marriages, MG1, vol. 427, folder 1, Public Archives of Nova Scotia, Halifax (hereafter PANS); Webster Chignecto Collection, Accession 7001/347.

august 1772

My Dear this Coms to Let you know that I am in Good helth as these Lines I hope Shall find you wee are meaney Leagues parted but Distance or Lenth of time Since we parted hath not made mee to forgit you I have Got 207 acers of Land[21] 33 acers of Clear Land Very Good Land a Good part of it will bee Easly Clear'd because it hath been formerly Cut by the French[22] I and other two have 45 Acers more for 5 years and orchards that Grow plenty of Appels we Desire to plow ye [45?] Acers and to Sow it with wheat and other Grane it is a pleasant and will be a frutefull place with Cultivation I need not Say much of my place nor of the Countery by this Letter for I have Describ'd it in the other Letter to my Master[23] only one thing I would tell you and that is a Little flye Cald a misketo that is troblesom in Somer time and Bites Like a midg But I am told by the peopel that Came to the place 8 or 9 years Since that there is becom much fewer of them it is oweing to ye want of inhabitance and Cattel to eat up the gras this is the only thing I have to Say against the Country and now I put you to your promis that you promis'd mee Saying I will Surely Come to you well my Dear I Shall be very Glad to See you fulfill your promiss to mee and I will fulfill mine to you if you Come I will be a kind Husband to you and will take you before aney other for I must Marry for I Cannot Live well as I am and as to your passage you need not bee affrade nor to Let your thoughts to trouble you or to think how Shal I under take Such a Journey only try Come and be not affraid I Sopose that you will have plenty from yorkshire to acompaney you   O would I wear in the place of these Lines and that I might be your Companion but that must not be I have Great besiness to Do and Cattle to Look after So I Cannot I Can only pray to our God to protect and be your Soport and Guard when I was at Sea I was Sick but 2 half days half a

[21] When Metcalf first arrived in Nova Scotia, he rented land from J. F. W. DesBarres, a Nova Scotia landowner and speculator, who was able to attract 15 of these newly arrived Yorkshire families to his lands, renting each family 200 acres. In 1785, Metcalf and 19 others received a grant of 10,000 acres on the Maccan River. Webster Chignecto Collection, Accession 7001/347; Report of John Macdonald on the DesBarres Estates, 1795, Papers of J. F. W. DesBarres (hereafter DesBarres Papers), Series 2, Public Archives of Canada, Ottawa (hereafter PAC); Draft of Grant to William Pipes and 19 others, RG 20, ser. "A," vols. 13–15, Nova Scotia Land Papers, PANS.

[22] Acadians. In 1755 the Acadians were deported from Nova Scotia, but in 1764 they were allowed to return and settle there under the condition that they settle in small scattered groups. DesBarres, having lost his Acadian tenants, was able to offer their cultivated lands to new tenants. G. N. D. Evans, *Uncommon Obdurate: The Several Public Careers of J. F. W. DesBarres* (Toronto, 1969), 29, n. 30.

[23] Thomas Wilkinson, to whose residence he addressed this letter. See p. 44, this volume.

Day ye Day that we imbark'd and again Somtime after when the Sea was very Ruff and we all had a very good passage and were very helthfull

the peopel hear are of Differant perswations in Religon they are mostly prisbyterians and Baptists ye Church of England are fewer then eather I believe that if one of our Methodist preachers wear hear he would be gladly Recived by people of all perswations[24] they are Very Strict in Regard to ye Lords Day and Consious of family Dutys but as to the mane thing in Religon would it were more known among all peopel I trust that Religon in its purity will be preached Hear allso people Hear are naterly kind one to another Even the Indian when a Country man Coms to their wigwams [. . . ses] if they have aney meat at all they will Give him Some with them. Spining wheels are Very Dear Hear for they are twenty Shilins a peece English money pays for more then in England ye Guney pays for thre and twenty and fower pence[25] but all ye money in ye place is not English there is the Doller that is 5s the pisterene[26] that Goes for a Shiling Every Countrys Money goes if peopel know its worth all Lin[en] Cloth and woolen Cloth is very Dear hear but they almost all Grow thir own Line[n] and Dres it themselves and the french and New Englands peopel the women are mostly weavers and work their own both Linen and wolen if you Come pray be so Good is to bring about a bushel of wheat if you Can of 4 differant kinds for Seed let yallow Kent be one and hampishire brown anothir for it will be of Great Servis Hear be Carefull to keepe it from Salt water you may if you please lay it Like a pillow in your Bed or in aney place where ye Salt water does not Come provide a little tea or somthing that is nurishing provided you Should be SeaSick I Should be Glad to See my master Wilkison Hear but altho ye Countrys Good I would not advise him to Come Lest things Should not do well So I might be blamed but if he Should I think he might do well Hear is Nothing but the misketoes that is trobelsom and they are Bad So that they make a smook [smoke] at ye door Somtines in the Evening to keep them out of their Houses they are more trobelsom then you may imagin but as I Said before it is for want of the Gras being mowed or eaten or burnt

this is ye only thing that I have to Say against the place all things I think

<hr>

[24] The Yorkshire Methodist settlers wanted John Wesley to send them a preacher, but Wesley answered that he could not do that, unless someone volunteered. In the meantime they held their own prayer meetings. Francis Allen to his niece, December 18, 1774, Webster Chignecto Collection, Accession 7001/337.

[25] A guinea was worth £1.3.4 in Nova Scotia currency (£1.1.0 sterling).

[26] A pistareen (peseta de vellon of four reales) was a Spanish silver coin.

will be made up when inhabitance Comes and trade increases if you Come
be not Discoriged by aney thing in ye Country for it is Good if you Come
you will Sail up to fort Cumberland and when you are there write a line or
tow to me and Send it to me to macann River by aney man and I will pay
him and Come for you but as Soon as you Receive my Letter Let me know
your mind by a letter and I will Be as Good as my word the passage is paid
at Liver pool before you go on bord but if you Should not be abel to pay
make friends to Some that Come and I will to pay write to Mr James
Shanks[27] at Leverpool about it I must Conclude for this time   may ye Lord
bles you and Conduct you Safe hither from

James Metcalf

if you write to mee you must Derect to me at Macan River near fort
Cumberland to ye Care of Governer Franklin at Hallifax Novascotia

Luke Harrison to William Harrison, River Hébert, near Fort Cumberland, Nova Scotia, June 30, 1774[28]

TWO years after the *Duke of York* brought the first Yorkshire settlers to Cumberland in 1772, the Harrison family gave up their
overrented farm in Rillington, Yorkshire, and made their way to Scarborough, about 20 miles to the east, where they found hundreds of
other families like themselves scrambling for passage on one of the
three ships bound for Nova Scotia during the second week of April.[29]
Much had changed in two years. In 1772, the Dixons had to travel from
the northeast corner of Yorkshire near the east coast of England to
Liverpool, on the west coast, and arrived two weeks early to board the
only ship bound for Nova Scotia that was to carry just 62 people. In
1774, emigrant ships were leaving Yorkshire ports in order to accom-

---

[27] For James Shanks, see p. 41, n. 12, this volume.

[28] *Source*: MG 1, vol. 427, #187, Public Archives of Nova Scotia, Halifax. *Courtesy*: Public Archives of Nova Scotia. The letter was addressed to William Harrison of Rillington Nigh Malton, Yorkshire. The letter is a recipient copy. It has no place of writing; however, directions at the end of the letter indicate that Luke Harrison was living at the River Hébert.

[29] The Harrison family left Scarborough the second week of April on a ship with 182 passengers. T47/9/121–123, PRO.

modate hundreds each season. Shipowners competed fiercely by appointing agents all over Yorkshire, and by printing advertisements giving the details of freight costs and accommodations, and sometimes even negative publicity about other ships. The owner of the *Prince George*, for example, had agents in at least eight towns. Some agents, like Thomas Nichols, strategically placed in the town of Ruston near Scarborough, had just returned from a visit to Nova Scotia and had a plan of that "famous and flourishing country" and "all particulars" for "all persons . . . desirous of making their fortunes." His eye-catching ad in the *York Courant* drew attention simply with the header NOVA SCOTIA in large block capitals. One witness, caught among a group of emigrants on their way to Hull, reported that they were passing around letters from friends and family in America, promising "great encouragement" and "greater plenty and abundance."[30]

Luke Harrison, the 20-year-old eldest son of John Harrison and his wife, Sarah Lovell, most certainly must have felt the excitement and anticipation that circulated among the crowd of these eager adventurers, with words like plenty and abundance, fortune, liberty, and opportunity buzzing in the air. So the first appearance of Cumberland – a scantily populated and bleak wilderness – must have been a shock. Luke wrote his cousin one month after his arrival, registering his disappointment and his desire to be back in old England. In this very short, one-page letter, Luke writes three times that he does not like the country, lest William miss the point. Nevertheless, the Harrisons settled in quickly, did not go back to England, and finally prospered. Letters written by Luke and his brother John in 1803 and 1810 reveal quite a different story. In the 30 or so intervening years, Luke had received a 500-acre grant on the south side of the Maccan River and had married Tryphena Bent.[31] John, who was only 14 when he arrived in Nova Scotia, had also acquired a 500-acre grant on the Maccan River, married twice, and had eight children.[32] They had developed their own lands in the wilderness of what they then called "Boney Novascotia"; had cut

---

[30] *Etherington's York Chronicle*, January 21, 1774; *York Courant*, December 7, 1773; *Lloyd's Evening Post*, March 15, 1774.

[31] They got married in 1786 and had nine children. Register of Marriages and Births, MG 1, vol. 427, folders 1 & 2, PANS.

[32] He married Diana Lumley in 1781 and they had two children. In 1791, Diana died of dropsy at the age of 31 and the next year John married Charlotte Mills; they had six children. T47/9/121–123, 84–90, PRO; Register of Marriages and Births, MG 1, vol. 427, and John Harrison to John Harrison, Maccan River, Nova Scotia, June 24, 1810, MG 1, vol. 427, #191, PANS.

down the trees; built saw and corn mills; grown plenty of wheat, rye, oats, corn, buckwheat, peas, flax, hemp, and "the best potatoes in the World"; and had stocked their lands with cows, oxen, horses, sheep, and hogs. Their wives also had to work hard. In Nova Scotia, women spun flax grown on their own farms, wove linen and woolen cloth, then bleached the linen, dyed the yarn, and made their own clothes and dressed themselves well, despite the absence of a staymaker to make stays. They also made the household candles, soap, and starch, and did the laundry. They made yeast as well as bread, and a kind of liquor from molasses and the boiled branches of spruce trees.[33]

John Harrison was emphatic when, in 1810, he wrote "if thare is any young men has any Notion of Coming to this Cuntry of an Industress turn of mind there is no despute of making out very well for himself for if he dos not like this part he Can Soon Earn money to Carry him out again." The environment was even good for child-bearing, Luke wrote in 1803, "Some women that had left of[f] bearing in England begun again in Nova Scotia."[34]

Dear Cousin   june the 30the 1774

Hoping these Lines will find you in good helth as we are at present bles god for it and we have all gotten Safe to Nova Scotia but do not Like it at all and a great many besids us and is Coming back to EngLand again all that Can get back[35] we do not Like the Contry nor never Shall besids that the muss keetoes are a terebel plage in this Contry you may think that muss keetoes Cannot hurt a deal but if you do you are mistaken for they will Swell one Legs and [faces?]

---

[33] Luke Harrison to William Harrison, Maccan River, Nova Scotia, January 1, 1803, and John Harrison to John Harrison, Maccan River, June 24, 1810, MG 1, vol. 427, #189, #191, PANS; and see pp. 69 and 76, this volume. In 1803, Luke Harrison wrote his cousin William that "we have more Women weavers than any other. . . ."

[34] Luke Harrison to William Harrison, 1803; and John Harrison to John Harrison, 1810.

[35] A September 1774 issue of the *Scots Magazine* reported: "A letter from Scarborough about the end of September says, 'The ship Prince George, which sailed from hence for Nova Scotia the beginning of April last, with about 150 emigrants, is returned to England with nearly the same number of passengers she carried out. Many more would gladly have returned, but could not pay for their freight, the country not being in any respect equal to the favourable idea they had formed of it.' "

that Some is both blind and Lame for [Some days?] and they grow wors every year and other and they bite the English worst –

we have taken a farm of one Mr Barron Esq[ui]re[36] for one year or Longer if we Like the rent is £20 a year & we have 10 Cows 4 oxon 20 Sheep one Sow and one breeding mare and he will take the rent in butter or Cheese or Cattle the Contry is verey poor there is very Little money at fort Cumberland and there money is not Like ours English money an English ginea is £1..3s..4d in our Contry Nova Scotia money a dolor is 5s – a pistereen is a Shiling in Hay time men hav 3s a day for mowing the muss keetoes will bite them verey often that they will throw down their Syths and run home almost bitten to dead and there is a black fly wors than all the rest every one in this Contry has trowsers and Sevral women for they fly up their petecoats and bits them terabely one is tormented all the summer with mus keetoes and almost frozen to dead in the winter Last winter they had [6?] months winter and was recond to be a fine winter the frost was not gone out of the ground the 20 day of june which I will afirm for truth –

Mr Mathew Cook I Could wish to be with you again Loving friend for I do not Like the Contry we are in now Remember my Love to your Sister and your father and mother – Mr William Harrison & Mr Mathew Cook your Humble Servant

Luke Harrison

I Shall Let you know the afairs of the Contry another year if god Spare Life and helth but Shall rite no more at present

dear Cusin remember me to my unkle and Ant and to all that aske after me So no more at preasen from your well wisher Luke Harrison

Mr Harper[37] wil be Coming over and you may Send Letters with him all that wants to rite

---

[36] According to a family genealogy, the Harrisons rented their land from Colonel (Edward) Barron of Barronsfield on River Hébert, Cumberland County. (Webster Chignecto Collection, Accession 7001/347.) However, he later moved to lands on the Maccan River and in 1785, with 19 others, received a grant of 500 acres there. (Memorial of John Terris and others for lands on the River Maccan, Nova Scotia Land Papers, RG 20, Series A, PANS.)

[37] Christopher Harper, a 45-year-old farmer, was from Barthorpe-Bottoms, a few miles south of Rillington. He had come to Nova Scotia in 1774 on the *Two Friends* in order to buy an estate. After finding land in Cumberland belonging to John Huston, he negotiated a purchase of 143 acres, including a house, cattle, furniture and other items, for £530. He then returned to Yorkshire to get his family (wife and seven children) and came back to Nova Scotia on the *Jenny* in April 1775. T47/9/77-79, T47/10/59-60, PRO; Christopher Harper to Lord William Campbell, March 4, 1775, DesBarres Papers, ser. 5, vol. 18, PAC; Deed of

Direct them John Harrison or Luke at the river a bare[38] nigh fort CumberLand Nova Scotia[39]

John Robinson and Thomas Rispin, *A Journey Through Nova Scotia*, York, 1774[40]

JOHN Robinson was a farmer from Bewholm, in Holderness, Yorkshire, who was forced off his rented farm when it was sold. He looked around for another farm, but realized he could not afford the recent increase in rents. So he and his friend Thomas Rispin, a farmer from Fangfoss, decided to go to Nova Scotia in order to investigate the opportunities there. If Robinson liked what he saw, he intended to buy property and return to Yorkshire to get his family. When Robinson and Rispin arrived at the port of Scarborough during the second week of April 1774 to board the *Prince George* for Nova Scotia, they found the town "almost full of emigrants" – hundreds of discontented farmers and their families, all hoping to find a better place to live in America.[41]

After their arrival at Halifax, Nova Scotia, Robinson and Rispin started making careful and detailed notes about places suitable for settlement for themselves and their friends – particularly areas around

land, John Huston to Christopher Harper, June 6, 1775, Book C, Deed Book 24, Registry of Deeds, Amherst, New Brunswick. And see pp. 65–66, this volume.

[38] River Hébert.

[39] One letter exists from cousin William Harrison to Luke dated March 25, 1775 (MG1, vol. 427, folder 12, PANS):

> I Recieved Your Letter Dated June the 30th and am Glad to hear of Your safe a Rival in Nova Scotia But as the Country is not so Good as You Expected so if You think of Retorning back to old England You must let us know and we will do all in our [Power to?] help you and [as?] We have had such Various accounts of the Country I Desire You Would send us an account of all the Curosities that you have seen and the Produce of the Country and what Sort of a Winter You have had and if their is any Prospect of Making a Good Settlement You Must Let us know and as to the Transactions of our Contry I must Refar it to Mr Cooks Letter So no More at Present From Your Loveing Cousin W. Harrison This is with my Love to my Uncle and Aunt and all Loving Cousins

[40] *Source*: A copy of the original pamphlet is in Houghton Library, Harvard University. The pamphlet has been printed in the Public Archives of Nova Scotia, *Report for the year 1944* (Halifax, 1945), 27–53.

[41] *Virginia Gazette, or Norfolk Intelligencer*, June 9, 1774. The Harrisons were in Scarborough the same week. See p. 47, this volume.

Cumberland County, where most of the Yorkshire people were clustered. They traveled overland from Halifax to Cumberland, chronicling their journey mile by mile, meticulously reporting almost every subject of interest to prospective emigrants like themselves. They described towns, forests, rivers, marshes, soil types, flora and fauna, different European ethnic groups, the native Micmacs, women's work, methods of clearing land, livestock, construction of houses and barns, descriptions of property for sale, and much more.

When they returned to Yorkshire at the end of 1774, they were encouraged to publish their report by those who insisted that "[t]he opinions and reports respecting that Continent [were] so various. . . ." This was a sentiment expressed by many, like Luke Harrison's cousin William, whose return letter showed his confusion. On the one hand, William was sorry that Luke was miserable: "if You think of Retorning back to old England You must let us know and we will do all in our [Power to?] help you." But William and his friends and family on the other side of the Atlantic had received "Various accounts of the Country." What his cousin had written one month after his arrival was evidently not what he had heard from others, who perhaps had been there longer and were more optimistic. So now that Luke had lived there a year, William wanted new information: "if their is any Prospect of Making a Good Settlement You Must Let us know. . . ."[42]

The pamphlet would certainly be classified as promotional literature, yet it is nevertheless an "on site" report, full of rich details about Nova Scotia, most of which can be verified by other sources. And what must have lent considerable credibility to this pamphlet were the scattered references to farmers from Yorkshire who had found good settlements in Nova Scotia: Mr. Forster from Newcastle, who had "made a purchase" at Ft. Lawrence "last year"; Robert Wilson from Helperby, who had recently bought "an estate at Granville"; and, of course, Charles Dixon from Hutton Rudby, who had bought a 2500-acre estate, half of which he rented to "an Englishman." Robinson wasted no time getting the 47-page pamphlet into print for his wide and eager audience. It was published before the end of the year, and advertised for sale at Mr. Etherington's in York.[43]

---

[42] See p. 51, n. 39, this volume.
[43] *Etherington's York Chronicle*, February 24, 1775.

A
JOURNEY
Through
NOVA-SCOTIA

Containing,
A particular ACCOUNT of the
Country and its Inhabitants:

With Observations on their Management in Husbandry; the Breed of Horses and other Cattle,
and every Thing material relating to Farming.

To which is added,
An Account of several Estates for Sale in different
Townships of NOVA-SCOTIA, with
their Number of Acres, and the Price at which
each is set.

By JOHN ROBINSON, Farmer at
Bewholm, in Holderness
AND
THOMAS RISPIN, Farmer at Fangfoss,
both in the County of YORK,

Who sailed for NOVA-SCOTIA, the 8th of April,
1774, from Scarbrough, on Board the Ship PRINCE-
GEORGE.

YORK:

Printed for the Authors, by C. Etherington,
M,DCC,LXXIV.
[Price: SIXPENCE]

This Pamphlet is entered at
Stationers Hall, so that whoever
presumes to pirate it will be prose-
cuted.

INTRODUCTION

THE Farm lately occupied by John Robinson, Farmer at Bewholm in Holderness, in the County of York, having been sold, he was under the necessity
of leaving it: Being desirous of taking another, he visited several, but they
were set at such rents as he thought he could not by any means afford to
pay. – At this time a rumour prevailing of the advantages that were to be
made in NOVA-SCOTIA, especially by such as were in the farming way;[44]
he came to the resolution of taking a view of that Country, and if he found
it as favourable as represented, to make a purchase there, and return to take
his family over.[45] The opinions and reports respecting that Continent being
so various, and the greatest part of them so destitute of truth, he was induced, with the assistance of Thomas Rispin, Farmer at Fangfoss, who accompanied him in the Voyage and Journey, to take a short account of the
places through which they passed, as well for their own amusement as for
the satisfaction and information of their friends: Many of whom, since their
return to this Country, have strongly solicited them to publish the remarks
and observations they have made, thinking that they would be useful to
those, who, notwithstanding some late unfavourable accounts have been
propagated,[46] are still inclined to become Adventurers in that Land of LIB-
ERTY and FREEDOM. In compliance therefore with the wishes of their
friends, and a desire of being useful to mankind, they commit the following
sheets to the press; and at the same time inform their readers, that they

[44] Thomas Nichols, who had recently returned to Yorkshire from Nova Scotia, had copies of
plans of that province to show prospective settlers, "particularly those skilled in the husbandry business." *York Courant*, December 7, 1773. Michael Francklin also advertised for
farmers, see p. 38 and p. 41, n. 12.

[45] Of the 9364 emigrants who left Britain for America in 1774–1775, 21 stated that they were
going to Nova Scotia to "purchase and return." T47/9–12, PRO. If a person could afford to
make an exploratory trip to America to see what it was like before making a commitment,
this was one of the safest ways to emigrate.

[46] For false reports, see the Introduction to this volume, pp. xvi–xvii, 25–26.

contain a faithful description of that Country, and its produce, without a desire of representing it in any other view, or making it either better or worse, than it appeared to them on their most mature judgment of it. They have besides added an account of several estates in the different Townships through which they passed, that are to be sold, specifying the number of acres each contains, and the prices at which they are set.

A JOURNEY, &c.

ON Friday the eighth of April, one thousand seven hundred and seventy-four, we took shipping at Scarborough, along with about one hundred and seventy other passengers, on board the Prince George, and sailed out of the harbour the same day; and, on the fifteenth of May following, at eight in the morning, we landed at Halifax, in Nova-Scotia, after a pleasant passage of five weeks and one day.[47] Neither of us had an hour's sickness during the whole voyage, though the greatest part of the passengers were sick for near a fortnight; after which they acquired what the sailors called a sea-brain, and became very stout and healthy. A child that was in a bad state of health when it was put on board, died when we came near the coast of Nova-Scotia, a few days after which, its mother was safely delivered of another, and recovered exceedingly well.

We landed at Halifax just the same number we were when we took shipping at Scarborough, all in good health. It may not be amiss to recommend to such as go to America, to provide for themselves; ship provisions are not agreeable to those who have been used to live in a very different way. Every passenger had a certain allowance per day, viz. a pound of beef, and the same weight of bread. This, perhaps, would be thought a scanty allowance by many. Passengers would, therefore, render the voyage much more comfortable, were they to lay in a proper stock of provisions for their own use.

Before our landing at Halifax, the prospect appeared very discouraging and disagreeable; nothing but barren rocks and hills presented themselves to

---

[47] The *York Chronicle and Weekly Advertiser*, April 15, 1774, reported that the ship left on April 9 with "at least 150 emigrants." The *Prince George* arrived in Halifax with 142 passengers on May 15. *Nova Scotia Gazette* Supplement, May 17, 1774. It is unclear whether or not this ship was registered in the registry of ships that left Britain in 1774–1775. It was not named in the registry, but could have been one of the unnamed ships from Yorkshire. However, Rispin's name does not appear on any ship list, and the John Robinson who appears on one of these unnamed ships (the same one the Harrisons were on) left because his farm had been overrented, not because it had been sold.

our view along the coast. This unfavourable appearance greatly damped the spirits of most of the passengers, and several of them begun to wish themselves in Old England, before they had set foot in Nova-Scotia.[48] We cast anchor in the bay, just before the town of Halifax, which has a very good appearance, though the houses are all built of wood. They are painted to look just like freestone, and are covered with blue slate. Most of us took boat and landed, and dispersed to several inns. We went to an old countryman's house, where we were civilly entertained, though we thought their charges high enough. They charged us eighteenpence each for dinner, a shilling for supper, and a shilling breakfast; also, sixpence a night for a bed. They had old English beer at twelvepence a bottle, and their own country cyder at fourpence.

Halifax is situated on the side of a hill, with a fine river and commodious bay, where ships of any burthen come up close to a key, and deliver their cargoes.[49] Ships of large burthen may go up above Halifax eight or ten miles, so that it is extremely well situated for trade. It has been greatly improved within these few years. It was formerly divided into three towns, but they have within these twenty years so encreased and extended their buildings, that they are all joined into one. It was called Chebucto Bay, but when the English took possession of the country, they changed its name to that of Halifax. The inhabitants are a civilized, well-behaved people, of different countries, English, Irish, Scotch and Dutch. They have a neat English church, with handsome pews and lofts, and a fine organ; a Presbyterian meeting-house as neat as the church, and a Methodist preaching-house. They have a weekly market on Saturdays. Their provisions sold rather high, viz. beef fivepence a pound; mutton eighteenpence; veal fourpence, and salmon fourpence a pound; eggs a penny a piece; butter eighteenpence a pound. They have exceedingly fine flour, which they sell at eighteen shillings per hundred. Halifax is the capital town in the province, and the principal place of trade.

[48] Many of the emigrants who came over on the *Prince George* did not wait around to see if they would like Nova Scotia as Dixon and Harrison had done; they returned to England on the *Prince George's* homeward voyage. See p. 49, n. 35, this volume.

[49] Patrick M'Robert, a Scotsman who was also in America looking for a place to settle, arrived in Halifax in September 1774, four months after Robinson and Rispin made these observations; the two accounts of Halifax are quite similar. However, after leaving Halifax, M'Robert took a different route. He went to Pictou and the island of St. John's (Prince Edward Island). Together these two accounts provide an excellent description of Nova Scotia in 1774. Patrick M'Robert, *A Tour through Part of the North Provinces of America: Being, a Series of Letters Wrote on the Spot, in the Years 1774, & 1775* (1776, offprint Philadelphia, 1935), edited by Carl Bridenbaugh, 17–22. This edition is an offprint from the *Pennsylvania Magazine of History and Biography*, 59(April 1935).

They have a fine dock yard, and a garrison of soldiers. Several merchants, of great fortune and eminence, reside there. There are four butchers, and the same number of bakers, who furnish the town and garrison with provisions; and also supply the ships trading to the coast with what they can spare, which occasions a great demand for cattle at this place. The ground near this town is rocky, which makes it tedious and chargeable to clear, so that it will cost from eight to twelve pounds per acre, but when cleared, brings good grass, and will let, for conveniency of the town, from four to five pounds an acre. The trees are all burnt down for three or four miles round the town, though a great many of the stumps are yet standing. We staid here three days, and then set forward for Fort Sackville.[50] For eight or nine miles we passed through nothing but dreary wastes, or forests of rocks and wood. Trees here seem to grow out of solid rocks. We observed one tree in particular, which grew upon a rock that was upwards of eight feet above ground. For want of soil this ground never can be brought under cultivation. Fort Sackville is distant from Halifax about twelve miles, situated upon a navigable river[51] that empties itself into Halifax Bay. At this place is a corn and a saw mill. A fort was kept here during the late war.[52] We thought to have lodged here all night, but their entertainment seemed so indifferent that we resolved to continue our journey until we could meet with better accommodation. At Wellman's Hall, about five miles distant from the last-mentioned place, we staid all night, six of us in number. The mistress of the house was a German. Upon our inquiring for supper, she told us we must pay ninepence a-piece for it, and that she could fry us some eggs and bacon: Accordingly she fried us every one an egg, and as many more collaps. Upon our desiring more, she told us she could not afford us any, but if we had any thing more we must pay for it. However we got two quarts of milk; she gave us one, and the other we paid threepence for. In the morning we set forward for Eglington, nine miles distant from Wellman's Hall; here we breakfasted, and were exceedingly well entertained with chocolate, coffee, and tea, in china, with silver spoons, and every thing very elegant. The butter (the mistress, a clean, neat, notable woman, told us) was a year old, having been put down in May, 1773, and was as good butter as any person could wish to eat. The mistress told us she sowed two bushels of wheat in the year

---

[50] Ft. Sackville (now Bedford) should not be confused with the town of Sackville, the destination of many of the Yorkshire settlers. Sackville was located more than 100 miles to the northwest in Cumberland county (now Sackville, New Brunswick).

[51] Sackville River.

[52] The French and Indian War (1755–1763).

1772, which produced twenty bushels; she sowed two the year following, but it being an unfavourable year, she had not above ten. The soil here began to look much better, clearer of rocks, and where it was cultivated wore a promising aspect. From hence we came to a place called Halfway House, betwixt Halifax, and Windsor, distant from Eglington nine miles; these people were Dutch, but very civil. We then went nine miles further to Montague, where we dined; after which we arrived at Windsor, ten miles from the last place. This is a fine township, and contains a deal of cleared land, which seems very good. Here is a large marsh, all diked in, called the King's Meadow: Part of it is plowed out, and grows good wheat, barley, oats, and peas. The gentlemen of Halifax keep their Courts here. This town is situated upon a fine navigable river,[53] where they can export or import goods to any part of Europe. Some gentlemen keep stores here to receive butter, cheese, or any other produce of the country, which they send to Halifax. It is supposed this will be a market-town; there is already a fair kept at it. We went from hence to Newport, three miles distant, situated upon the same river, and from thence to Falmouth, four miles from Newport, on the other side of the river. Here are large tracts of marsh land bordering upon the river, also great quantities of upland, cleared, but it is very uneven and poor; though what is under cultivation is pretty good. We then went through a large track of wood land, which seems mostly pretty good, and well supplied with running brooks. We only passed two houses till we came to Horton, twelve miles distant from Windsor, which is situated under the north side of a hill, upon a navigable river, which runs up twelve or thirteen miles into the country. Along the side of this river is an extensive marsh, called the Gramperre,[54] (but by the French the Plain of Minas) all diked in, which contains two thousand six hundred acres; here are also other marshes undiked in, with great quantities of upland, though little of it cleared, which seems of a reddish colour, and is chiefly sown with rye, Indian corn, pumpkins, potatoes, and other roots: We saw fine wheat upon their marshes, and as fine winter rye as ever England produced. On their upland, on the south side of the town, is another river, called the Gasperroc,[55] but is not far navigable, except for small boats. The township extends for seventeen miles in length, and twelve in breadth. They are as bad managers in this town as any we came amongst: They value their marsh land at two pounds an acre, their cleared upland at one pound an acre, and their wood land at sixpence. From

[53] Pisiquid River (Avon).
[54] Grand Pré.
[55] Gaspereau.

hence we went over the river to Cornwallis, two miles distant, but it is nineteen from the further end of Horton by land. This is an extensive township, thirty miles long, and twelve broad, and contains upwards of a hundred thousand acres. It is well situated, having four rivers[56] which run into the Bay of Minas; three of them are navigable for ships, where they can import or export any sorts of goods. These rivers abound also with plenty of fish of different kinds. They caught at one tide, during our stay there, forty barrels of fish, which they call shad, and which they sell for four dollars per barrel, of thirty-two gallons; (each dollar is four shillings and sixpence sterling) but when they export them, they sell for twenty five shillings per barrel. Shad is the best poor man's fish of any, for they are so fat of themselves, that they need nothing to make them ready for eating: There is likewise plenty of batt [butt], boss [bass], and cod, which come in their seasons. Here are also large marshes, which are diked in: They have diked over one river, and stopped the tide, which they call the grand dike, and which, they say, cost two thousand pounds. At this time they are diking over another river, which will cost a great sum. They have very good wheat growing upon the marshes, also peas, barley, and oats, and very good grass: Their upland grows good winter rye, potatoes, Indian corn, and pumpkins; also other kinds of garden roots. The upland, when cleared and cultivated, makes very fine pasturing for cattle: The soil is of a reddish mixture, in some places red sand, and in other places a whitish loam; but in so extensive a lordship we may undoubtedly expect to find different kind of soil. About two feet from the surface is a very fine clay, that will make any sort of bricks, but their method of making them is exceedingly tedious. They never cast up their clay before spring, and give it one turn: When it is ready for making, they employ only two men to make them. They have a mould that holds three bricks, which the one carries off, whilst the other moulds them. They burn their bricks with wood, and the bricks have a good appearance; but they sell them at twenty shillings per thousand, which is a very high price. They have good lime stone in several parts of the country, which they might burn to sell very cheap. At Cape Dorre,[57] about thirty miles from Cornwallis, there is a copper mine, and a lead mine near Annapolis, neither of which is worked at present. In this township they keep good stocks both of beasts and sheep, but not many horses; and the Halifax butchers come hither to buy their fat, pay ready money, and take them away from their own doors. Their tillage seems very good, and in general they are the best managers of any in the province. Mr.

[56] The Pereau, Canard, Habitant, and Cornwallis rivers.
[57] Cape D'Or.

Burbridge told us he sowed down two acres of swarth upon the marsh, with wheat, which produced, the first year it was plowed, eighty bushels, though it stood rather too long, and a great deal of it was shaken, which he plowed in again, and had a pretty good crop the year following. He has built a malt kiln, with an intention to set up a common brewhouse, so that they expect to have good ale in Nova Scotia. They value their marsh land that is diked in, and their best cleared upland, at three pounds an acre; their undiked marshes at one pound, and their wood land at sixpence. In this town is a Protestant church, a Presbyterian meeting-house, and two school houses.

We next came to Wilmet,[58] a new-settled place, twenty-two miles from Cornwallis. Here is a large track of wood land, not so good as in some places, and abundance of brooks and small rivers, very suitable for fixing water mills. About sixty years ago, in a very dry season, the wood ground in this township was by some means set on fire, which spread itself almost through the whole of it, and has done so much damage to the soil, that it seems to be of very little value. A hurricane almost immediately succeeded this conflagration, which threw down an immense number of trees, the roots of which had been bared by the fire, so that they lay at this time in heaps, something resembling a timber yard. Here is part good interval land, not much inferior to the marsh, when properly cultivated. What they call interval land, lays by the brooks, which, in the spring of the year, at the melting of the snow, is frequently overflowed, which greatly enriches the ground. The upland about this town is mostly pretty good, and clear of rocks, and they have good clay for bricks. Here is a large track of ground, called Mouse Plains, but very barren and swampy, which grows nothing but ling and moss. They grow in this township winter rye, Indian corn, potatoes, and other roots. The soil is of a reddish mixture, some red, and some a white sand. They say the lighter the earth, the better for the grain they grow here. They chiefly sow in the spring, as in other places. A small river runs through the township, which extends for above twelve miles.

Adjoining to it is the township of Granville, which extends for about twenty-five miles in length, and eight miles in breadth, and runs down Annpolis [sic] Gut, where there is a bason, which separates the township of Granville from that of Annapolis, which is navigable for upwards of twenty miles: On the banks of this river is a fine marsh diked in, also a large marsh, the dikes of which are broken down, containing about nine hundred acres,

---

[58] Wilmot. By 1770 New Englanders who had settled in Annapolis were moving up the Annapolis River to Wilmot. J. Brian Bird, "Settlement Patterns in Maritime Canada, 1687–1786," *Geographical Review*, 45(1955), 399.

called Bell Isle. When the French[59] possessed this province, they had it all
diked in, and grew corn in such plenty that they sold wheat for one shilling
a bushel; but when they were dispossessed of it, they destroyed the crops,
and cut down the banks, which were never repaired to this day. The French
worked all upon their marshes, and did little on the upland, except plant a
few potatoes, other roots, and a little Indian corn. But since the English
came in, they have been so backward in repairing the banks, and so negligent
of their tillage, that they have not grown wheat sufficient for themselves.
This town lies at the foot of a mountain, which extends from Annapolis
Gut into Fundy Bay, abounding with many fine lakes well stocked with
trout, and affords great store of fine timber, such as oak of different kinds;
white and black ash; white mapple; rock mapple, (a very fine wood for
houshold [sic] furniture) birch, white, yellow, and black, but the black is best
for furniture; also spruce fir; pine; cedar; tackamahacka, or juniper; white
thorn; eller [elder or alder], and wild cherry trees, with strawberries, rasp-
berries, gooseberries, cramberries [sic], and many other fruits. There are fine
orchards belonging this town. The soil seems rather of a stronger clay than
any we have yet seen, and some places rather rocky.

ANNAPOLIS ROYAL, adjoining the township of Granville, lies West
from Halifax one hundred and thirty miles; and when in the possession of
the French (who kept a garrison in it) was the capital of Nova-Scotia, and
in a very flourishing condition; a great trade being carried on, and money
and provisions were in great plenty. About seventy years ago it fell into the
hands of the English. When Halifax was built, which is about twenty years
ago, they removed the soldiers from the garrison at Annapolis, to the fort
at that place: The trade went along with them, and has ever since been on
the decline. The forts seem to be tumbling to ruins. This town is as finely
situated for trade as any in the country: It stands at the head of a fine bason,
six miles over; where ships of any burden may ride in the greatest safety: It
runs for above fifteen miles through a narrow passage betwixt two mountains,
called Annapolis Gut, and empties itself into Fundy Bay, where it is about
a mile wide; so that the township extends fifteen miles down the bason, four
the bay, and upwards of twenty miles above the town, through which runs
a fine navigable river,[60] which comes upwards of seventy miles out of the
country. On both sides of the river several families are settled, chiefly from
New-England. They were sent by the government, most of them were soldiers and very poor. On their first settling they were supplied with a years

59 Acadians.
60 Annapolis River.

provisions. They were entire strangers to cultivation, and are very bad farmers. They plough here a little, and there a little, and sow it with the same grain, without ever a fallow, till it will grow nothing but twitch grass; then they cast it aside and go to a fresh place. The French, when in possession of this place, had their marshes diked in and ploughed, which grew wheat in such abundance that they sold it for one shilling a bushel; however, the present inhabitants do not grow so much as is sufficient for themselves, but are obliged to buy Indian corn at four and sixpence, rye at five, and wheat at six shillings a bushel; which they would have no occasion to do, would they but properly cultivate their own lands, leave off the use of rum, which they drink in common, even before breakfast; and to which, in a great measure they owe their poverty – By the growth of a sufficient quantity of barley, which by a little industry they might accomplish, and the brewing of malt liquor, the many fatal disorders which are the consequence of too liberal a use of rum would not be known amongst them, and the sums of money would be kept at home, to their very great advantage, which they now send out for the purchasing that liquor. If this river was settled by English farmers of substance, a very advantageous trade to the West-Indies might be carried on, by the exporting of horses, beef, butter, cheese, timber, deals, and corn; and in return, receive rum, rice, sugar, mollasses, and other spices; which at present they have through so many hands, that they cost them more than one hundred and fifty per cent above prime cost. They likewise want a trade to England, for at present they have all their English goods from Boston, which comes at a very great disadvantage. If this could once be effected, the town would abound in plenty, and perhaps quickly regain more than its primitive lustre. The township is thirty five miles long, and seven broad. They have fine marshes bordering all along the river and mostly diked in. The town is situated at the foot of a mountain, which runs up into the country upwards of twenty miles, upon which grows excellent timber of different sorts. The upland near the mountain is in some places very rocky, but where it is clear of stones the soil is pretty good, and where properly cultivated grows good corn. The land is of a reddish mixture, some red and white sand, some clay, but none so strong as we have in England: It naturally, when laid down, turns to white clover, and looks very suitable for turnips and clover. In the middle of the bason is an island, called Goat Island, containing about sixty acres, now under cultivation; it has a family upon it, and seems a pretty good soil: It belongs a Captain Prince, who asks sixty pounds for it.

PARTRIDGE ISLAND situated North-West from Windsor thirty miles; twenty four from Horton; eighteen from the township of Cornwallis, upon the mouth of the bay of Minas, which runs betwixt two mountains into Fundy Bay, and divides the county of Cumberland and King's county. It is a little round island, lies very high, and almost covered with wood, except a small part under cultivation, which grows wheat, rye, pease, and Indian corn, with pumpkins and other kinds of garden roots. Near this island, which is only surrounded with water in a high tide, are two houses kept as Taverns for the reception of passengers that cross, from any part of the country, the bason of Minas to Cumberland; three persons pay fifteen shillings for their passage, and one passenger pays the same, from this place to the head of the river Bare,[61] which runs to Cumberland. It is about twenty four miles N.E. chiefly woodland, very uneven travelling, but grows very fine timber of different kinds. A small river runs through the woods from Minas Bay to the river Bare: Along the river is a fine interval land and fine meadows: There are likewise many fine running brooks, very convenient for fixing nets. The hills seem rocky, but there is good land in the level parts. Here is a mountain rises with a narrow ridge, called the Boars-Back, running for eight miles till it comes to the head of the river Bare, where Mr. Franklin[62] has settled two English familes [*sic*], who keep Taverns for the convenience of passengers going to Cumberland, they keep a boat, and likewise horses to let to any part of the country.

Mr. FRANKLIN has very extensive tracts of land upon both sides of this river, where he is settling farmers. A man may have as much land as he pleases; the first year he pays nothing; for the next five years, a penny an acre; the next five, threepence; for five years after that sixpence, and then one shilling an acre for ever to him and his heirs. He has another large track of land, called Petticoat Jack,[63] ten leagues N.W. from Cumberland, where he has settled six Old England farmers, men of substance.[64] One, it is said, left an estate of seventy pounds a year in England, where he has left two daughters, and has taken over a house-keeper and men servants, and settled six miles from any other inhabitant.[65]

---

[61] River Hébert.
[62] Michael Francklin. See p. 38, this volume.
[63] Petitcodiac.
[64] Hillsborough Township. Two-thirds of the 40 families who lived in the area around Hillsborough (Hillsborough, Monckton, and Hopewell) in 1775 were Acadians. "Abstract of the number of Families Settled in Nova Scotia, August, 1775," Dartmouth Papers, MG 23, A 1, vol. 1, 349–352, PAC.
[65] This may have been Joshua Gildart, who came to Nova Scotia with his nephew and three servants, and was the first to buy land (500 acres) at Monckton, upriver from Hillsborough on the Petitcodiac. See Bailyn, *Voyagers to the West*, 413–414.

Coppergate[66] lies N.E. from Halifax, about forty-five miles, and N. from Windsor about forty-five miles, is situated upon a large river,[67] which runs about sixty miles, until it comes to Windsor, from thence empties itself into the bason of Minas. It has four townships belonging to it,[68] chiefly inhabited by Irish, who carry on a linen manufactory. They have fine marshes, their upland is chiefly good, and the Irish are the best farmers we have seen in the country. They keep large stocks of cattle, which the Halifax butchers fetch from their own houses. They grow good wheat, barley, rye, pease, Indian corn, flax, plenty of garden roots, and abundance of cucumbers, the largest we ever saw.

Amherst is about twenty miles from the head of the river Bare,[69] well situated for trade, has a fine navigable river within half a mile of it,[70] which runs through large tracts of marsh land, and extends for about fifteen miles in length, and two in breadth. A small quantity of the marsh land is at present diked in, and they are proceeding with great spirit to dike the remainder, which will be of great advantage to the owners, as it may be done at a very inconsiderable expence, a four-foot bank being sufficient to secure it from being overflowed. This land will then produce great quantities of good grass, which, before diked, being constantly overflowed by the tide, brought nothing but flag-grass and reeds. A few years after being properly diked and dried, it will bring good corn. Their upland is mostly level and good, though in some parts it is rocky. We called at the house of one Thomas Robinson,[71] who has got a very fine estate here, and which he has improved to the best advantage. All his marsh, of one hundred acres diked in, he had some tolerably good corn, wheat and oats, growing thereon, though it was sown a year or two over soon, as the salts were not sufficiently out of the soil. He had some good-like barley and oats growing upon his upland, only they seemed to be too thick. He was summer-tilling a small quantity of land for turnips; the only person we remember to have seen in the country, who cultivated that root. This town lies six miles S.E. from

---

[66] Cobequid.

[67] Kennetcook River.

[68] There were actually three townships settled by people from Northern Ireland, Scotland, and New England: Londonderry, which in 1775 had 100 families from northern Ireland; Truro, where 50 families lived; and Onslow, with 30 families. About 20 families lived in scattered settlements on the northern side of Cobequid Basin. "Abstract of the Number of Families settled in Nova Scotia," August 1775, Dartmouth Papers, MG 23, A 1, vol. 1, 349–352, PAC.

[69] River Hébert.

[70] La Planche River.

[71] See the end of this pamphlet for the value of Robinson's property in Amherst Township.

Fort Cumberland, and five from Fort Lawrence, is much exposed to N. and N.W. winds, which blows severe and cold. The moschelloes,[72] small flies, resembling gnats, are exceedingly troublesome here. Their bite is venomous, and occasions blisters to rise, something like the smallpox.

FORT LAWRENCE is situated upon a hill, five miles from Amherst, and a mile and half from Cumberland, and is much exposed to winds and weather. Here are large marshes, but few of them are diked in. They have a deal of upland cleared upon a fine dry hill. The inhabitants are chiefly English farmers. Mr. Forster, from Newcastle, made a purchase here last year. We saw him with eight men setting potatoes within a week of midsummer.

CUMBERLAND is distant from Halifax, which is their chief market town, one hundred and twenty-four miles; but they are cutting a road through the woods, by Coppergate,[73] that will make it much nearer. It is situated upon the point of a hill, facing the bay of Fundy: Near it are three navigable rivers;[74] one about a mile from the town, runs N. for upwards of twenty miles into the country, between Cumberland and Tanteramare; another runs S. and the third, betwixt Fort Lawrence and Cumberland. This town lies entirely open to every quarter, and is much annoyed by winds from the sea. No considerable trade is carried on here, it not being a market town. Such of their produce as they have to spare, they ship off to Halifax, Boston, or any other port upon the continent; and, in return, receive rum, molasses, and other kinds of merchandize, suitable to this country. They have very good pasturing on extensive commons and marshes, some of them thirty miles long and ten broad. Few of the marshes are diked, though a four-foot bank would stem the tide, and preserve them dry, notwithstanding it flows sixty or seventy feet perpendicular. It is a very fine place for breeding cattle, but does not seem equally favourable for producing corn, the grain being often mildued, occasioned by the fogs which so frequently come from the bay. We were told, that at this place the spring is a fortnight later, and the winter a fortnight sooner, than in some other places of the country. Moschelloes are very troublesome here, especially to strangers. Several English farmers are settled near this town, but from the want of time, we had not an opportunity of visiting any of their houses. One Mr. Harper[75] has made

---

[72] Mosquitoes. Complaints about the mosquitoes were universal. See, for example, the letters of James Metcalf and Luke Harrison, this volume.

[73] Cobequid.

[74] The Aulac, Misaquash, and La Planche rivers.

[75] See p. 50, n. 37, this volume.

a purchase here of a considerable quantity of fine cleared land, with a good house upon it, elegantly furnished, with barns, and other conveniences, besides woodland at a distance, and twenty cows, with other cattle, &c. for which, we were told, he gave five hundred and fifty pounds. He lets out as many cows as bring him in twelve pounds a year.

TANTRAMARE[76] lies N.E. from Cumberland fourteen miles by land, but by water, not above five. There is also a little town called Westcock, situated upon the mouth of the bay, and another called Sackville, both in the parish of Tantramare. They have large marshes belonging to them, with a great deal of upland, which we thought as good as any we had seen in the country, and it lays under the south-side of a hill, in a warmer situation than Cumberland. There are fine navigable rivers running thro' their marshes. Moschelloes are as troublesome here as at any place we were in. Thomas Bowser[77] has taken a farm here of five hundred acres, forty-five of which are marsh, diked; twenty upland, cleared; which is a good pasture, and four hundred and thirty-five woodland. He took a lease for six years, at the rate of four pounds ten shillings a year, and is to work out his rent every year, at four shillings a day. He has only three cows, though he might keep ten, with other stock in proportion. He has not bought a farm as he wrote he had to his friends in England. Charles Dixon, about two years ago, when he first went over, purchased an estate at this place, containing twenty-five hundred acres.[78] He has one hundred acres of marsh diked in, one hundred acres of upland cleared, a good house and barn, twelve cows, four oxen, and other cattle, for which he paid four hundred and seventy pounds. Half of his farm he has lately let to an Englishman for thirty pounds eight shillings a year, and lets him have six cows, two oxen, and a brood mare: The like in number and value he is to leave when he quits the farm. He seems to have fallen in very well. He was this year appointed a justice of the peace.

In clearing their woodland, they cut down the trees two or three feet from the ground, and let them lay until summer, about which time they are dry, and they set them on fire as they lay. At the back end of the year they sow the land down with rye, harrowing it in amongst the ashes without any plowing; where the stumps are thick, they hoe it in. The first year's crop generally pays them all the expence of cutting and burning; the next year

---

[76] Tantramar.

[77] Thomas Bowser was 28 when he came to Nova Scotia in 1772 with his wife and two sisters on the *Duke of York*, the ship that also brought Charles Dixon and James Metcalf. W. C. Milner, *History of Sackville, New Brunswick* (Sackville, N.B., 1934), 129.

[78] See p. 42, this volume.

they plant potatoes; and so continue three or four years, while the stumps are rotten, when they pull them up with a yoak of oxen. There are men in the country who take the land to clear, and will cut down and burn it for twenty shillings an acre. Some let their ground lie, after the first crop, for pasturing, until all the stumps are decayed, which appears to be the best way. Where the trees have grown are little hills which take some time to level, and make ready for laying down; but when it is properly laid down, it makes excellent pasture, and naturally grows a fine white clover.

When they break up the swarth land in the marshes, they plow it about the fall, and sow it in the spring with wheat, which grows very well. We saw fine wheat growing upon the marshes, and as thick as it could stand. The soil is exceedingly good, and several yards deep. The French have sown wheat for fourteen or fifteen years together without a fallow, and the land brought good crops to the last. The French had such plenty of manure, and so little occasion to use it, that they suffered it to lay about their barns in such quantities, that it became so troublesome, they were obliged to remove their barns to other places: And it is observable at this day, that there is always a piece of good ground where their houses have stood. The soil in general is of a lightish, warm nature, though in some parts of a reddish sand, mixed with a little gravel; in others, a whitish, loamy earth, and in some places a strong clay. The soil is, generally, a foot or two deep, where you come to an exceeding fine clay, that makes good handsome bricks; Some parts of the country are rough and rocky.

Their cattle are but small, much like our Lancashire beasts, but not quite so large: They are lively-looking cattle, with fine horns. They keep many oxen, with which they till their lands, and use them in all their draughts. We have seen from one to four pair of oxen at one team, both at plow and at a wain, which they call carts, without any horse at them. They are in general good draught beasts, and are as tractable, and observe the driver's word as well as our horses in England. They work their oxen until they are eight or ten years old before they feed them, and they in general grow to be good beasts. During our stay at Cornwallis, we saw a pair which had been fed, sold to a butcher at Halifax for thirty-three pounds fifteen shillings. They do not use whips in driving. We never saw any in the country, instead of which they make use of long rods. The French used to yoak their cattle by the horns; but in those parts they yoak them now after the English method.

The horses are small, chiefly of the French breed, about fourteen hands and a half high, plain made, but good in nature. They seldom draw with any, so that few keep more than one or two for their own riding; they all naturally pace, and will travel a long way in a day: They are very dear; a horse that would sell for about six pounds in England, would fetch ten with them. Their method of breaking them is very extraordinary: They yoke a pair of oxen to a cart, and tie the horse to it, and drive away till they have rendered him quite gentle. They then put on the bridle, and he is mounted without more to do.

Their cows like the oxen, are but a smallish breed, and their management of them so bad, that they give but a small quantity of milk; for they fetch them up early every evening to milk, and let them fast till seven or eight o'clock the next morning. Mr. Robert Wilson,[79] who went this year from Helperby, nigh Boroughbridge, in the county of York, bought an estate at Granville: He let his cows lie out all night in their pastures, and the little time he had them when we were there, which was about three weeks, they gave near double quantity. A pretty good cow and calf will sell at Cumberland for about five pounds ten, or six pounds; but at Annapolis, and other parts of the country, as good may be bought for four pounds ten or five pounds. It is very common amongst the wealthy farmers, to let out to the poorer sort of people their cows for twenty shillings a-year. There are some that have from ten to twenty let out in this manner. They generally value the cow when they lend her out, and if any improvement is made, the borrower has a proper consideration; but if she be any worse he must make a suitable satisfaction. They let out brood mares and sows after the same manner.

Their method of rearing calves is somewhat singular; as soon as they go to milk, they turn out their calves which suck one side of the cows, as the women milk on the other, and when they have done they are put up again, and continued to be fed in this manner till they are three or four months old, when they are turned out to grass: They never hopple their cows, but milk them into a pail, which they call a bucket, with a wooden bowl; and as soon as they have milked file it into stone dublers or bowls before it cools, that it turns sower in six or eight hours. It is common to let it stand eight and forty hours, when they can take the cream off and double it up like a pancake. The milk is so very sower and stiff that it turns out of the bowl like a cake of flummery: They say the sowerer it is they get the more cream and butter. The Irish have still a different way, for they put their milk into a barrel churn as soon as it is milked, for five or six days together, and when

<hr />

[79] Robert Wilson and his family were probably on the same ship as the Harrison family. Wilson left Yorkshire with his wife and seven children because his rent was raised too high. T47/9/121–123, PRO.

they think it is a proper time, they let off the milk and churn for butter. However different their method of managing the dairy is from that used with us, yet we must do them the justice to say, that we have eaten as good butter of their manufacturing, as ever we eat in England: It seems too their butter will keep well, for we met with some that was exceedingly good, which had been kept (as we were informed) a whole year.

The women are very industrious house-wives, and spin the flax, the growth of their own farms, and weave both their linen and woollen cloth; they also bleach their linen and dye their yarn themselves. Though they will not descend to work out of doors, either in time of hay or harvest, yet they are exceedingly diligent in every domestic employment. The candles, soap and starch, which are used in their families, are of their own manufacturing. They also make their own yeast, and make a kind of liquor, by boiling the branches of the spruce tree, to which they add molasses, and cause it to ferment in the manner we do treacle beer in England.

The sheep appear to be of the Spanish breed, are long legged, loose made, and have short, but fine wooll. They clip four, five, and some six pounds, which they sell for eighteen pence a pound.

The pigs are of a very indifferent breed, much inferior to any we ever saw in England: They feed them very fat with Indian corn, pompkins [sic], or potatoes. They keep their pork and beef always in pickle, and never dry it as is customary in England.

They have abundance of game in the woods. The mouse-deer is also in great plenty; they are very large, some of them weighing eighty stone; their flesh is much like that of an English ox, and is very good eating. They have also rein-deer, which they call carraboes, and numbers of bears, both of which they reckon good eating; the latter are very ravenous, and frequently kill sheep, calves, and swine, wherever they fall in their way. In the township of Granville, one of these animals killed thirty sheep in a night, eleven of which were together in a barn, and the property of one man. Those bears are usually as large as a calf of a year old, and have a head like that of a mastiff, with legs as thick and strong as a horse. Notwithstanding their ferocity, they will not attack the human species.

The beaver, which is about the size of a small Guinea-pig, is reckoned good eating; their furs are very valuable, and sell for six shillings a pound; they live upon fish, the bark of trees, and large roots that grow in the fens: They have a wonderful manner of making conveniencies for themselves; they cut down large trees with their teeth, which they build houses with three stories high, by the side of lakes, for the convenience both of securing themselves and catching fish: If the water rises, they go into the second or third story, and when it falls they come lower; as they always sit with their tails in the water. They breed only once a-year from two to five at a litter.

The porcupine, of which they have great numbers in this country, is shaped like an hedge hog, but near five times as large; they are used for food, and the Indians ornament their boxes with their quills.

The land turtle, or tortoise, is also common in Nova Scotia. Its belly and back are covered with a remarkably strong shell, the colour much resembling that of a frog, under which it can draw itself in times of danger, and be entirely secure from any injury from without; its head is like that of a snake; and it goes very swift upon four legs. Some persons esteem them good eating.

The lucovie, or wild cat, is also an inhabitant of this country; it is a fierce animal, and frequently does much damage amongst sheep. Their skins are of a light hazzle colour, and are valued as a good fur. Here are also otters, minks, sables, martens, tiskers, musquashs,[80] squirrels, and flying squirrels; the last of which has a small body and a loose skin, which it extends like wings, and is borne up in the air a considerable time. The skins of all those animals, as furs, are esteemed very valuable. In this country there are no lions, tigers, or wolves, as has been reported. They have snakes of different kinds and colours, but they are very harmless, and the destructive rattle-snake is not know [sic] amongst them.

They have wild fowl and game in great plenty, such as geese and ducks, of which they have two sorts, and teal. Their partridges are of two colours, brown and black; the brown sort are esteemed the best; the black are not so sweet, occasioned by their eating spruce, which is their chief food in the winter. They are as large as a Guinea-hen, and so tame and plentiful, that we killed several of them with our sticks as we passed through the woods. The wood-pigeons resemble our stock doves, but are not quite so large, and have longer tails. Black-birds, thrushes, and a small bird, called the hum-ming-bird, not much larger than a drone-bee, are in great plenty; also several kinds of small birds, of which we have not any in England. They have eagles, gleads, hawks, buzzards, ravens, and water-crows; but neither sparrows, mountain-larks, cuckows, or rooks.

The rivers abound with salmon, trout, and various kinds of fish; great plenty of sea-fish, as cod, ling, butt, &c. is brought up by the tide into the rivers; also abundance of shell-fish; as crabs, lobsters, &c. the latter of which were the largest we ever had seen.

Their houses are generally built square, and chiefly of wood, with chimneys of brick in the centre, so contrived as to convey the smoke from all the

---

[80] Muskrats.

different fire places. The windows are all sash'd, and as they pay no duty for them, they are very numerous, and render their houses light and pleasant. They all build with post and pan;[81] when they get about three yards high they take it in a little; about two yards higher they fix their chamber windows, and above them their roofs; some build a story higher. After being boarded, they appear very neat and compleat houses. They board the outside up to the roof, with what they call clapboards, which are about four inches broad, a quarter of an inch thick on the lower side, and exceedingly thin on the upper, so as to lay on each other's edge. They wainscot the inside and make it very neat. Their roofs are covered with planks, on these they fix what they call shingles, which are pieces of board, about eight inches long, four broad, and a quarter of an inch thick at the bottom, and thin at the top, and are used much in the same manner as we do slate in England. All their houses have cellars under them, and are in general very convenient.

Their barns are built of wood, some of them with clap-boards and shingles in the manner of their houses. They contain different apartments for their horses, cows, and sheep; and have a floor above for their hay and corn, which is for the most part deposited in their barns, as they do not seem fond of stacking. The entrance of their barns is so large as to admit a loaded waggon.

The climate seems to be pretty near that of England, but rather warmer in summer. We were not there at the hotest [sic] season of the year, which is during August and September. The weather is finer and milder at the back end of the year than it generally is in England; and their winter does not commence till the latter end of December. It generally begins with hoar frosts, succeeded by snow, which usually falls in great quantities for a few days, and is followed by clear settled frosty weather; so that the snow frequently covers the ground for near three months. The farmers take this opportunity to lead home what hay they have stacked, or rather made up into pikes for loading in winter, which is generally in their more distant closes, and of supplying themselves with fire-wood, and for building; the roads, at this season, after being beat are exceedingly good. Great numbers of the inhabitants employ much of their time in hunting in the woods, where they will frequently continue for a week, taking a quantity of provisions with them; and at any time when there [sic] store is exhausted, they can readily make a fire and dress part of the game they have taken, for which purpose they constantly carry a steel and tinder-box, with matches, &c. in their pockets. At night they make large fires, near which they wrap themselves up in

---

[81] Post and pane construction consisted of timber framing, with plaster or brick used to fill in the spaces in between the timber.

blankets, and lay down to sleep with as much composure as if they were in their own houses: From such a practice we are led to think that this climate is never so cold as it has often been represented. When the snows are very deep, they have what they call snow shoes to walk in, which keep them from sinking. On the outside of those shoes is a wood rim, about the thickness of a good walking stick, turned like an ox-bow, the back part is almost close, they are near a foot broad in the middle, and a foot and a half long; worked at the bottom like a sieve with thongs of the mouse-deer's skin. pieces [sic] of wood are fixed across, which make a place for the feet, and they are fastened on with straps. The snow usually begins to go about the beginning of March. Their spring is generally cold, and something later than in England. When their vegetables of any kind once begin to grow, they make a more rapid progress than any we ever observed in England; and it is really astonishing how a close of grass or corn will spring up in a few days.

Money is indeed very scarce in this part of the world,[82] so that trade is chiefly carried on by the bartering of their goods, which is undoubtedly a great disadvantage to the country, and on account of which they labour under the greatest inconveniencies. What they purchase at present, is for the most part on a year's credit, and they do not pay less than a hundred per cent. interest. Their payments are made at the end of the year, with wheat, butter, cheese, beasts and horses, or whatever is convenient for them. There are merchants, whom they call store-keepers, who derive great advantage, by supplying them with all sorts of cloths, linen as well as woollen, and wearing apparel; also rum, sugar, molasses, &c. imported from Boston and the West Indies; for which they receive the produce of the country, and export it in return for the merchandize they receive from abroad. By this profitable traffic, many of them concerned in it have made fortunes in a few years. We knew some that had not been in business above four or five years, and begun trade with a mere trifle, at this time worth fourteen or fifteen hundred pounds; notwithstanding they did not seem to be acquainted with the best markets either to buy or sell at. Were a few substantial men, who understand business of this kind, to engage in the above branch; the articles in which the above persons trade might be imported at half the price that is paid for them at present, and their money kept at home.

It is the due improvement of the land in this country, on which its best and most lasting interest depends, and without which it can never be wealthy or flourishing; the exportation of its crops would bring in a return of money, that, at present, as was observed before, is much wanted.

[82] See p. 50, this volume.

It is, indeed, surprising what chemerical notions many persons entertained of Nova-Scotia, previous to their leaving this country, with a view of settling at that place. They imagined that they should find lands cultivated, fields sown, and houses built ready to their hands; and that they would have nothing to do, but to take possession, and reap.[83] Not finding things in quite so favourable a situation as they foolishly expected, and having no inclination, by diligence and industry, to render them so, they return, and, by way of excuse for themselves, represent it as a miserable country, and the inhabitants in a starving condition.[84] However, the truth is, it is a very extensive country, abounding with fine navigable rivers, and is as well situated for trade as any place in the world. At present they consume the greatest part of their produce at home; but, by a judicious improvement of their lands, which might easily be effected, they would raise such stocks of cattle, and crops of grain, as would enable them to supply the West India markets, from whence they would have their return in ready money.

They have good land that will grow any sort of corn, flax and hemp, and pastures that will feed any kinds of cattle. Their woods produce timber, fit both for ship and house building, and supply them with pitch and tar; also, with fire wood: And they have coals for getting. They have great plenty of iron in New England. In short, they have all kinds of naval stores, as well as every necessary of life within themselves, without being beholden to any power upon earth.

The greatest disadvantage this country at present labours under is, that its inhabitants are few;[85] and those in general, ignorant, indolent, bad man-

---

[83] As one account described their fanciful notions, the prospective emigrants would "every day have the pleasure of climbing up large mountains of Roast Beef and after that to swim in oceans of wine and rivers of rum." *Leeds Mercury*, April 26, 1774.

[84] One of the authors' purposes for writing this pamphlet was to tell the truth about Nova Scotia, so that prospective emigrants would not believe exaggerated accounts. Some emigrants did have unrealistic expectations and returned immediately to England. In addition to those who returned on the *Prince George*, emigrants also returned to Yorkshire in 1774 on the *Providence*, and to Port Glasgow in 1775 on the *Cochran*, the *Peter*, and the *Blandford*. *York Courant*, October 11, 1774, and *London Chronicle*, May 16–18, 1775. Negative propaganda often took the form of publication of news of these returning emigrants or of accounts of unhappy settlers who could not afford the return passage. One such report of misery sent by a young woman in Halifax, Nova Scotia, to her parents in Hull, Yorkshire, was quickly published in a York paper. She complained that "the inhabitants in general seem to be poor miserable beings, which was very mortifying to me. . . . It is a desolate, oppressed and almost uninhabited country." *York Courant*, August 30, 1774.

[85] An abstract of the number of families in Nova Scotia in 1775 enumerated 2488 families, and estimated the total population based on a family size of six (taken from the family size in

agers, and what is the natural consequence of such qualities, the greatest part of them are poor: They have neither inclination nor industry to make great improvements.[86] Can it then be wondered at, that a country so poorly, so thinly, and so lately inhabited, should have rather an unfavourable appearance, especially to those who have lived in the finest and best cultivated counties in England, where neither pains nor expence has been spared to improve their lands to the utmost advantage? Besides, where there is a want of proper management, have we not seen, even in our own country, men that occupied estates of their own, and could not make a living of them; but when the same farm has fallen into the hands of a skilful [sic], industrious farmer, he has both paid the rent, and lived better on it than the owner could.

John Robinson, one of the persons by whom the foregoing remarks and observations were made, is of opinion, that not any of the persons who have returned from Nova-Scotia, whether farmers or labourers, but had a better opportunity of supporting themselves more comfortably there, than they are ever likely to have in England. With respect to himself, he has not the least doubt of making a much better provision for his family upon the land which he has purchased in Nova-Scotia, than it is possible to make on the best farm in the county of York. Who then, as he observes, would continue here to be racked up till bread[87] can scarce be got to supply the wants of their children? A large sum of money would not induce him to stay any longer in this country; nor does he doubt, should it please God to continue his life twenty years longer, of seeing as great improvements in the uncultivated lands of Nova-Scotia, as has been made within these few years in the barren, winney commons of England, and at as small an expence; the land being equally as good and as capable of improvement. Besides, the improvers of

Lunenburg) as 14,928. The estimate given two years earlier in 1773 was 17,752. In the county of Cumberland, where most of the Yorkshire emigrants settled, 220 families were counted among the settlers from New England and Northern England, as well as 30 Acadian families. "Abstract of the Number of Families settled in Nova Scotia," August 1775, Dartmouth Papers, MG 23, A 1, vol. 1, 349–352, PAC.

[86] Charles Dixon also noted that the New England settlers were indolent and ignorant. This is perhaps an unfair assessment. The farmers in the Cumberland Basin area were far from a market where they could sell their surplus, and in an area where land was cheap and labor expensive. They had little incentive to farm intensively and therefore did little more than subsistence farming to take care of their own needs. The Yorkshire emigrants, on the other hand, came from an area where land was expensive (if available at all), labor cheap, and markets accessible. Wynn, "Late Eighteenth-Century Agriculture . . . ," 86, 88–89; Snowdon, "Footprints in the Marsh Mud," 57.

[87] Bread here is defined as "means of subsistence."

land in Nova-Scotia have greatly the advantage of those in England, as the land cleared and improved by the former, is generally their own property, while the latter are for the most part tenants, and, as is too frequently the case, after all the pains and expence they have been at for the improvement of their farms, are deprived of the enjoyment of the fruits of their industry.

Many persons seem desirous to know the reason why some of the inhabitants of Nova-Scotia are selling their lands; and several of those who were not satisfied with that country, on their arrival there, and immediately returned, have given out, that such land-sellers were also about to quit it. The real truth of the matter is, that large tracks of ground, chiefly woodland, were granted to the first settlers, who, in general, were very poor; yet, by a persevering industry and good management, they have cleared great quantities, which they occasionally sell off, in order that they may be the better enabled to proceed in the improvement and stocking of the remainder of their lands.

A poor man may take a farm, stocked by the landlord, for which the latter receives for the rent, half its produce; or, for every cow, thirty pounds of butter, half the cheese; and so in proportion of whatever else the farm produces.

NOVA-SCOTIA extends five hundred miles in length, and four hundred in breadth. There are vast tracks of land at present unoccupied; and, in general, their large marshes are but thinly peopled. As mentioned before, it is extremely well situated for trade; and the number of navigable rivers that run through it, renders land carriage unnecessary.

The inhabitants are of different countries, though chiefly from New England, Ireland and Scotland. The New Englanders are a stout, tall, well-made people, extremely fluent of speech, and are remarkably courteous to strangers. Indeed the inhabitants, in general, poor as well as rich, possess much complacence [sic] and good manners, with which they treat each other as well as foreigners. To the honour of this country, we may say, that abusive language, swearing and profaneness, is hardly known amongst them, which is the great scandal and reproach of Britain.

The Sabbath is most religiously observed; none of them will do any business, or travel, on that day; and all kinds of sports, plays and revels, are strictly prohibited.[88] They take great care to educate their children in the fear of the Lord, and early to implant in them a right notion of religion, and the great duty they owe to God and their parents. The children have a

---

[88] James Metcalf noted that the Yorkshire settlers "are Very Strict in Regard to ye Lords Day." See his letter, this volume.

very engaging address, and always accompany their answers, with "Yes, Sir; or, No, Sir;" or, "Yes, Ma'am; or, No, Ma'am," &c. to any questions that are asked them; and, on passing their superiors, always move the hat and foot.

The men wear their hair queu'd, and their cloathing, except on Sundays, is generally home-made, with checked shirts; and, in winter, they wear linsey woolsey shirts, also breeches, stockings and shoes: instead of which, in summer, they have long trowsers, that reach down to their feet. They dress exceedingly gay on a Sunday, and then wear the finest cloth and linen. Many of them wear ruffled shirts, who, during the rest of the week, go without shoes or stockings; and there is so great a difference in their dress, that you would scarce know them to be the same people.

The women, in general, (except on Sundays) wear woolseys both for petticoats and aprons; and, instead of stays, they wear a loose jacket, like a bedgown. It is owing to the high price of stays, and not to any dislike they have to them, that they are not worn in common. The few that are used, are imported either from New or Old England, as they have not any staymakers amongst them. The women, in summer, in imitation of the men, usually go without stockings or shoes, and many without caps. They take much pains with their hair, which they tie in their necks, and fix it to the crown of their heads. Nor are they on the Sabbath less gay than the men, dressing for the most part in silks and callicoes, with long ruffles; their hair dressed high, and many without caps. When at Church, or Meeting, from the mistress to the scullion girl, they have all their fans. We even thought, in the article of dress, they outdid the good women of England.

Nothing can be said in favour of the inhabitants, as to their management in farming. They neither discover judgment or industry. Such of the New Englanders, into whose manners and characters we particularly inspected, appeared to us to be a lazy, indolent people. In general, they continue in bed till seven or eight o'clock in the morning; and the first thing they do, after quitting it, is to get a glass of rum, after which they prepare for breakfast, before they go out to work, and return to dinner by eleven: They go out again about two, and at four return to tea. Sometimes they work an hour, or two after, and then return home, both masters and their servants, amongst whom there seems to be no distinction; and you scarce can know one from the other. They are all Misters and Sirs, and their maidens all Misses; so that you never hear a Christian name mentioned. They usually all eat together at one table, except amongst a few of the wealthier sort.

The original inhabitants of Nova-Scotia, as well as the other provinces of

America, were Indians,[89] and there are now several tribes of them dispersed about the country. Each tribe has a sort of King or Chief, with other inferior Officers. They have no settled place of abode, but ramble about in the woods, and support themselves by hunting or fishing: Wherever they kill a mouse-deer or carroboe, they fix their tent, or as they call it a wigwham, and continue as long as they can find any game near the place. After which they remove their quarters in quest of fresh game. They are very expert in hunting, and excellent marksmen with the gun, and spare no kind of wild beasts or fowl they meet with. They are a friendly, harmless, well-behaved people, and are ready to do any little service for you they can, such as assisting you in the crossing a river, directing you on the road, &c. but they cannot by any means be prevailed on to assist in any sort of labour.[90] They are stout and active, well made, of a yellow complexion, their face and nose are broad, their eyes usually black, and their teeth remarkably white, and have long black hair: They rub their bodies with bears grease to prevent the muschetoes from biting them. They for the most part wear a piece of cloth, generally blue, something resembling a wide riding-coat, with a kind of sleeves, but have neither buttons or button-holes: This they tie round them with a piece of the skin of some animal or the root of a tree. In general they wear neither breeches, stockings, or shoes; some indeed, wrap a piece of blue cloth round their legs, and others wear a kind of shoes made of mouse-deer's skin, which they call moggisons. They seem mightily fond of dress, and we saw a few who had ruffled shirts on, which they never wash or pull off so long as they will hold together; but they generally go without shirts. The women are much of the same shape and complexion with the men, and wear their long black hair loose about their shoulders. They do not wear either shoes, stockings, or shifts, but a sort of petticoat that reaches from their middle to the knee, and a loose piece of cloth like a cloak thrown about their shoulders. Each man has his own wife, and they are very faithful to each other. We were told that as soon as their children are born they are laid in a streight [sic] cradle made of the bark of a tree, where they suffer them to lay till they can walk without assistance. The streightness in stature for which these people are so remarkable, it is thought is owing to this means. The affection

[89] These were Micmacs, whose territory before contact covered over fifty thousand square miles, including all of present-day Nova Scotia, Prince Edward Island, most of New Brunswick, and the southern Gaspé penninsula in the province of Quebec. L. F. S. Upton, *Micmacs and Colonists: Indian–White Relations in the Maritimes, 1713–1867* (Vancouver, 1979), 1.

[90] James Metcalf also reported on the friendliness of the Indians.

that reigns amongst them is somewhat singular, for when they meet after being some little time absent, they salute each other with a kiss on each side of the face, and then on the lips.

Their canoes are very ingeniously made, mostly of the bark of the birch tree, without eitheir [sic] nails, pins, leather or hemp; instead of which, they sew them up with roots of trees, dyed different colours, and line them with ashwood slit thin like the girth wood used for milk pails, &c. in England: They are sharp at each end, about two feet wide in the middle, and will carry four or five men; with the use of a small paddle, they make their way very expeditiously on the water. We crossed Annapolis river twice with an Indian in one of those canoes.

The Indian women are very ingenious in making boxes and hat cases of birch bark, which they sew with the roots of trees, and work in upon the lids and sides porcupine quills, dyed various colours; these boxes are very neat and curious.

As they are great hunters they get many valuable furs, which they exchange for blue and scarlet cloth, checks, &c. also for rum, and other spirituous liquors, to these they have become much addicted, and to which the great decrease amongst them is principally owing: They frequently drink to intoxication, when many of them are drowned, or perish with cold by laying on the damp ground.

The English, at such places as the Indians frequent, sell their goods to them at very extravagant prices; we have seen the Indians purchase scarlet cloth at the rate of forty shillings per yard, which has not cost fifteen in England; hatts at five dollars each, that have not cost above one dollar; checks for two shillings, that has not cost above tenpence or a shilling; and other articles equally dear.

The Indians in those parts seem to cleave much to the French, and have a French Priest amongst them, who making his religion subservient to his interest, and a cloak for the most unrighteous practices, defrauds these poor credulous people of their property, by teaching them to confess their sins unto him, at the same time making them believe that he cannot give them absolution unless they present him with a certain number of furs. Some of them speak the English language tolerably well. When intoxicated with liquor they are rather quarrelsome, but are soon appeased by speaking to them in harsh terms.

An Account of several Estates with their Number of Acres, &c. and Prices, that were to be Sold, which we viewed as we passed through the following Towns.

The Reader must observe, that the Prices of those Estates are reckoned at the Currency of Halifax in Nova Scotia, which is upwards of Eleven per Cent. less than English money.

At HORTON, which the French called MINAS.

Belonging to JOHN ATWELL.

	Acres.
Marsh land – –	30
Dike land – –	17
Upland cleared –	22
Ditto uncleared –	31
Wood land – –	400
Total	500

With a house and barn, which was sold to a Yorkshire man for 99£.

MARY ELDERKIN.

Marsh – –	40
Broken dike land –	19
Upland cleared –	80
Upland uncleared –	150
Dike upon the gram	30
Woodland – –	1000
Total	1319

With a log-house, the price 300£.

DANIEL WHIPPLE.

Upland cleared –	17
Ditto uncleared –	18
Dike land – –	2
Marsh – –	5
Woodland – –	10
Total	52

With a new house sold for 90£.

SAMUEL D'WOLF.

	Acres.
Marsh – – –	22
Broken dike land –	17
Upland improved –	40
Uncleared – –	60
Common share lot –	6
Woodland – –	400
Total	545

With a good house, barn, and stable, the price is 200£.

Mr. CHIPMAN.

Upland cleared –	60
Ditto uncleared –	30
Marsh undiked –	30
Total	120

With a log-house, which was sold to John Atwell of Horton, for 100£.

BEN. BECKWORTH.

Upland cleared –	50
Marsh diked – –	20
Ditto undiked – –	60
Uncleared home lot	50
Wood land – –	1000
Total	1180

With two houses and a barn.

Mr. JOSEPH GRAY, at
Halifax.

		Acres.
Upland cleared –		40
Ditto uncleared –		60
Dike broken – –		60
Marsh undiked –		30
Wood land – –		400
	Total	590

CHARLES PROCTOR
at Halifax, but the
land at Horton.

Upland cleared –		30
Ditto uncleared –		12
Marsh undiked –		20
	Total	62

Mr. FORSTER.

		Acres.
Upland cleared –		200
Marsh diked –		15
Wood land – –		1785
	Total	2000

With a good house and barn, price
400£.

Estates to be Sold in the Township of CORNWALLIS

Mr. CHIPMAN's
near the Meeting.

		Acres.
Upland cleared –		20
Marsh diked – –		12
Wood land – –		230
	Total	262

With two log-houses and a
log-barn, price 200£.

Mr. CHIPMAN's
near the Church.

Upland cleared –		10
Marsh undiked –		31
Wood land – –		60
	Total	101

With a good house and barn, price
100£.

Mr. CHIPMAN's

		Acres.
Marsh diked –		23
Upland cleared –		23
Wood land – –		20
	Total	66

With three houses and a barn.

Mr. PHILIPS's.

Upland cleared –		90
Marsh diked – –		2
Ditto undiked –		6
Wood land – –		27
Wood land undivided		600
– –	Total	725

Sold to John Robinson of Bewholm,
for 350£.

JOHN WIDDON's

	Acres.
Upland cleared –	90
Ditto uncleared –	90
Marsh diked – –	20
Ditto undiked –	15
Upon Canna marsh	12
Total	227

With a good house and barn, price 300£.

Mr. CHIPMAN's, upon Prerois river.

Marsh land – –	150
Wood land – –	1750
Total	1900

Price 300£.

Mr. CHIPMAN's where he lives.

Upland cleared –	50
Marsh diked – –	20
Ditto undiked –	25
Wood land – –	80
Total	175

With a good house and barn, price 500£.

Mr. PORTER's.

	Acres.
Upland cleared –	50
Wood land – –	80
Marsh diked –	16
Undiked – –	5
Wood land at a distance	570
Total	721

With a house and barn, eight cows, four four-year old oxen, six calves, three horses, twenty five sheep, five pigs, six acres of Wheat, three acres of oats, one and an half of rye, half an acre of flax, and two of roots, price 350£.

Dr. WILLOUGHBY's.

Upland cleared –	100
Marsh diked – –	38
Ditto undiked – –	26
Wood land – –	300
Ditto at a distance	500
Total	964

With a good house and barn, price 850£.

Mr. LONGFELLOW's.

Upland cleared –	138
Ditto uncleared –	130
Marsh diked – –	50
Ditto undiked – –	15
Total	333

With a house, price 350£.

Estates to be Sold in the Township of GRANVILLE.

Mr. PRINCE's, called
Mount Pleasant.

	Acres.
Marsh Land – –	52
Upland cleared –	120
Wood land –	1328
Total	1500

Sold to Mr. Wilson of Helperby,
with a good house and barn, for
350£.

Mr. HAMLINGTON's
farm, the owner Mr.
Wallis at New-York.

Marsh diked – –	70
Upland cleared –	70
Marsh undiked –	56
Wood land – –	2394
Total	2590

With a house and good barn, price
400 guineas.

Mr. MORRISON's.

Marsh undiked –	28
Upland cleared –	70
Wood land – –	902
Total	1000

With a house and barn, price
400£.

Mr. PRINCE's, called
Crochers.

	Acres.
Marsh diked – –	20
Upland cleared – –	50
Wood land – –	930
Total	1000

With a house, sold to a
Yorkshireman for 120£.

Mr. HAMLINGTON's.

Marsh undiked –	14
Upland cleared –	40
Wood land – –	446
Total	500

With a house, price 100£.

Mr. PRINCE's, at Belisle.

Marsh diked – –	28
Upland cleared –	80
Wood land – –	992
Total	1000

With two houses and two barns,
price 300£.

Mr. WILLIAMS's.

Marsh undiked –	70
Under improvement	120
Wood land – –	1810
Total	2000

With a house, barn, and stable,
price 400 guineas.

Mr. LEONARD's

	Acres.
Marsh diked – –	7
Ditto undiked –	14
Upland cleared –	10
Wood land – –	3̱1̱7̱
Total	348

With a house, price 70£

Mr. LEONARD's.
 where he lives.

	Acres.
Marsh undiked – –	12
Upland cleared –	30
Wood land – –	4̱5̱8̱
Total	500

With a house and good barn, price 200£.

Mr. GREGORY's.

	Acres.
Marsh undiked –	28
Upland cleared –	30
Wood land –	9̱4̱2̱
Total	1000

With a good house and barn, 250£.

Capt. YOUNG's.

	Acres.
Marsh undiked –	14
Upland cleared –	10
Wood land – –	4̱7̱6̱
Total	500

Price 40£.

Mr. FARNSWORTH's.

	Acres.
Marsh undiked –	14
Upland cleared –	8
Wood land –	4̱7̱8̱
Total	500

With a house sold to Jonathan Milner.

Estates to be sold in the Township of ANNAPOLIS.

Mr. TIMOTHY RICE's.

	Acres.
Marsh undiked –	5
Upland cleared –	150
Wood land –	1350
Total	1505

With a good house and barn, 13 cows, 2 oxen, 15 young cattle, 30 sheep, one mare, one cart, and other implements to the value of 224£. The whole 550£. Here is the finest orchard in the province.

Capt. WHEELOCK's.

Marsh diked –	70
Improved lands –	80
Wood land –	500
Total	650

With a house and good barn, 300£.

Mr. SIMPSON's

Marsh undiked –	3
Improved land –	2
Wood land –	500
Total	505

With a log house, three cows, a new boat, two tons burthen, 50£.

Mr. COLBORT's.

	Acres.
Marsh diked –	12
Ditto, undiked –	30
Improved land –	60
Wood land –	450
Total	552

With a house and new barn, six cows, four oxen, three three years old, and four two years old, three calves, one mare, one cart, one plough, two sledges, one harrow, 20 sheep. Sold to Thomas Skelton, of Market-Weighton, for 220£.

Capt. WINSLOW's.

Marsh diked –	30
Improved land –	40
Wood land –	930
Total	1000

With a house, 250£.

Mr. HARDY's.

Marsh diked –	15
Undiked –	7
Upland improved	78
Wood land –	700
Total	800

With a house and bad barn, 300£.

Mr. CLARK's.

	Acres.
Marsh diked –	12
Ditto undiked –	24
Improved land –	20
Wood land –	1000
Total	1056

With a house and barn, five cows, one mare, one cart, one harrow, and one plough, 200£.

Mr. BASS's.

Marsh undiked –	20
Improved land –	40
Wood land –	340
Total	400

With a house and barn, 200£.

Mr. LOVETT's, at
Round Hill.

Marsh diked –	100
Ditto undiked –	70
Upland cleared –	150
Wood land –	1680
Total	2000

With two houses and two barns, 1200£.

Mr. LOVETT's.

	Acres.
Marsh undiked –	14
Improved land –	40
Wood land –	446
Total	500

With a bad house, 200£.

Capt. W. GROW's.

Marsh diked –	22
Improved –	20
Wood land –	150
Total	192

With a house, 150£.

Estates to be sold in the Township of AMHERST.

Mr. PIPE's.

	Acres.
Marsh undiked –	220
Upland improved –	20
Wood land. which he bought this year	1760
Total	2000

With a bad house, and stock, in value 120£. He paid for the whole 350£.

Mr. FREEMAN's.

	Acres.
Marsh diked –	100
Upland cleared –	20
Wood land –	880

With a bad house and log barn, 250£.

Capt. FEETH's.

	Acres.
Marsh, diked and fenced –	200
Upland cleared –	70
Wood land –	900
Total	1170

With a house and log barn, 400£.

M. DICKER's

Marsh diked –	45
Improved land –	10
Wood land –	500
Total	555

With a bad house, 130£.

THOMAS ROBINSON's, that he bought two years ago.

	Acres.
Marsh undiked –	100
Upland cleared –	20
Wood land –	425
Total	545

With a bad house, 80£.

Mr. LUSBY's, that he bought.

Marsh undiked –	50
Wood land –	450
Total	508

The price 50£.
They have both got their marshes diked and fenced since they got them.

Estates to be sold in the Township of TANTERAMARE.

Mr. COOK's.

	Acres.
Marsh diked –	54
Ditto undiked –	62
Upland cleared –	20
Wood land –	1650
Total	1786

Mr. CALLEN's.

Marsh diked –	80
Upland cleared –	20
Wood land –	1650
Total	1750

With a house and barn, 300£.

Mr. MAXWELL's.

	Acres.
Marsh diked –	60
Upland cleared –	20
Wood land –	1170
Total	1250

With a house, 200£.

Mr. HAWKINS's

Marsh diked –	60
Upland cleared –	20
Wood land –	1170
Total	1250

With a house and barn, 250£.

GEORGE FAWKIE.

	Acres.
Marsh land –	45
Upland cleared –	10
Wood land –	445
Total	500

And a log house. He bought this farm two years since.

Wm. FAWCITT's.

	Acres.
Marsh land –	45
Upland cleared –	15
Wood land –	440
Total	500

With a house. This he has had two years. His brother John Fawcitt made a purchase this year in the same neighbourhood.

FINIS.

MIDDLE COLONIES

Letters of James Whitelaw, Philadelphia, New York, and Ryegate, Vermont, 1773–1783[1]

ONE of the ways that people could minimize the risk of emigrating was to subscribe to an emigration company, in which members each bought shares that entitled them to a certain amount of land in America. Agents were sent to the colonies to scout for good land, and when a tract large enough for all company members was found and purchased, the shareholders could then come to America to settle. If the prospective emigrants could afford the passage to America, this system provided them with their own land, a familiar community, and assistance in getting settled.

James Whitelaw, a 27-year-old surveyor from Lanarkshire, was one of the agents for such an organization founded in Paisley, Scotland, as the Scots American Company of Farmers, or the Inchinnan Company. He and David Allen went to America in 1773 in order to locate and purchase a tract of land that would be suitable for the settlement of all 138 members. They traveled some 2700 miles on horseback before deciding to buy half of the township of Ryegate, New York (now Vermont), from John Witherspoon.[2] Similarly, Barnet, the town directly north of Ryegate, was settled by the United Company of Farmers for the Shires of Perth and Stirling.[3] The following letters

---

[1] *Source:* James Whitelaw Papers, MSS 25, 29, 32, Vermont Historical Society, Montpelier. *Courtesy:* Vermont Historical Society. The letters are all retained copies. Ryegate was located in territory, claimed by both New York and New Hampshire, that later became the state of Vermont (see p. 94, n. 18, this volume).

[2] For John Witherspoon, see p. 23, n. 89, this volume.

[3] See "Journal of Colonel Alexander Harvey of Scotland and Barnet, Vermont," *Proceedings of the Vermont Historical Society for the Years 1921, 1922, and 1923* (Montpelier, VT, 1924), and

describe in some detail how this subscription method worked from the American side and how it eased the emigrants' transition from the old environment to the new.

Six of the many Whitelaw letters are printed here. They cover the first two years of the Company, when the settlement was founded, through the end of the war, by which time Ryegate was firmly established and operating as a more or less independent entity. They are more revealing about the process of emigration than most other letters in this book. Resources were abundant and land was cheap and plentiful, but emigration and risk-taking were not as easy, cheap, or profitable as those abroad had hoped and expected. When Whitelaw and Allen arrived in Ryegate, they found an empty tract of wilderness land without even a shelter. It took the entire year for Whitelaw, David Allen, and one other member, James Henderson, to clear four acres of land, construct a few log houses, survey the lots, and bring in provisions from the nearest seaport, 100 miles away. And all of this was very costly. By 1774, only one year after the Company was founded, it was in debt and Whitelaw realized he could no longer draw on the Company for needed expenses, no matter how necessary they were. So in order to build mills that the Ryegaters needed, they had to come up with most of the money themselves. When the Revolution cut off communication with the Board in Paisley, Whitelaw and the company members in Ryegate governed themselves. At this time Ryegate contained about 30 households. They held town meetings (to which the noncompany town residents were invited), elected officers, organized a militia, signed a mill bond, and found ways to keep afloat financially. By the time communication had resumed after the war, the town was firmly established and able to advise the Board on what was best for the settlement, rather than having to take advice and direction from an absentee governing body.[4]

The last two letters, written toward the end of the Revolution, clearly show Whitelaw's more realistic view of wilderness settlement. He knew that the community was successful and a good risk, but he

Frederic P. Wells, *History of Barnet, Vermont . . .* (Burlington, VT, 1923). For a general account of the Scots American Company and the settlement of Ryegate, see Bernard Bailyn, *Voyagers to the West: A Passage in the Peopling of America on the Eve of the Revolution* (New York, 1986), 604–634.

4 Eugene R. Fingerhut, "From Scots to Americans: Ryegate's Immigrants in the 1770s," *Vermont History*, 35(1967), 195–197, 200–202.

also knew that the company members could not expect to improve their lands if they did not come over and work hard themselves. He knew that it took effort and would not be cheap – at the very least one had to come up with passage money. Settlers in Ryegate also found out that they needed more land than their original allotment gave them, and so they tried to buy lots from those who did not intend to emigrate.

Members of the Inchinnan Company who settled in America all had different experiences. Some came over at the Company's expense in exchange for a year's worth of labor, after which they received land. Many had enough money to bring themselves and their families to America, and to find temporary lodgings, usually in Newbury, until their houses were built. A few, like David Allen, returned to Scotland and never came back to Ryegate, or never left Scotland at all. Others who arrived at Ryegate with the intention of settling there moved on to other places.[5]

But, of the early Ryegate settlers, perhaps Whitelaw has left the most complete record of his life in America, where he had a long and prosperous career, and remained in Ryegate until his death in 1829. He continued as agent for the Company until 1794, held many town offices including clerk and treasurer, was the Surveyor-General of Vermont from 1787 to 1804, and opened and operated a land office. He was also active in the Associate Presbyterian Church of Ryegate. He married three times. His first wife was Abigail Johnston from the adjacent town of Newbury, whom he married in 1778. In 1790, he married Susannah Rogers of Bradford, Vermont, and in 1815, 14 years before his death, he married Janet Harvey, the widow of Alexander Harvey, the agent for the United Company of Farmers.[6]

Though Whitelaw appears to be the author of these letters, he occasionally refers to himself in the third person or as "we," probably to present the letters as impersonal reports from the Ryegate settlers to the Company at home. For this reason, Whitelaw's own subjective sentiments may have been bleached out, leaving these rather matter-of-fact accounts. However, much rich detail is contained in these letters. They also reveal Whitelaw's values and concerns, and here and there something of his personal feelings: his gratitude at the "health-

[5] Fingerhut, "From Scots to Americans," 197–198.
[6] Thomas Goodwillie, "Life of General James Whitelaw," Vermont Historical Society, *Proceedings* (1905–1906), 111, 112, 117, 118.

ful" climate and his disappointment that the crops were not as good as he expected.

James Whitelaw to the Company, Philadelphia, Pennsylvania, May 26, 1773[7]

Gentlemen

We arrived here the 24th Inst. in good health thank god our passage you'll observe was 60 days being from the 25th of march to the 24 of may the length of our passage was more owing to little than to contrary wind for we had exceeding pleasant weather for the most part of the voyage we send you nothing particular concerning our voyage only on saturday the 27 of march we had the last view of scotland about 6 oClock at night & on sunday we had a pretty hard gale of wind from the south west which beat us some Leagues back the wind continuing from the same art on munday our Captain thought proper to take [tack] about in order to go by the north of Ireland but on the same day about 7 oClock at night the wind shifted to N.E. obliged us to tacke about to our former course on Wedinsday the 31 we left the land upon which day the wind shifted N.W. from whence it continued till the 8 of aprile by which time we were in Lat 40° Lon 18° the wind continuing mostly from the same quarter we continued sailing to the S.W. till the 25th of Aprile when we was in Lat. 30° Lon 4°6..3'o we continued between the Lat of 30° and 33° till the 14th of may when we was in Lon. 68, after which we continued north west till the 20 when we made cape hinlopen[8] about 2 oClock that day we had the first view of America and about 9 at night we came to an anchor within the cape in order to wait for a Pilot which we got about 7 oClock next morning so we were 2 days in going up the river the banks of which are very pleasant particularly upon the Pensilvania side upon our arrival here we immediatly went to Mr William Semple[9] his brother

---

[7] The letter is undated and gives no place of writing. Whitelaw wrote that he and Allen arrived in Philadelphia on May 24, where they stayed until the morning of May 27. He mentioned at the end of this letter that he wrote it the day before he left for New York, hence it was written on May 26. See James Whitelaw, "Journal of General James Whitelaw, Surveyor General of Vermont," Vermont Historical Society, *Proceedings* (1905–1906), 123.

[8] Cape Henlopen is on the coast of Delaware at the mouth of the Delaware Bay.

[9] William Semple was a Philadelphia merchant.

being on the wharf read to receive us in order to conduct us to the place where accidentaly we met with Doctor Witherspoon[10] who appointd 6 oClock at night to have some conversation with us we delivered him the letters we had for him he promised to do every thing in his power to serve us in the affair we were come about. in the mean time let us know that he along with some other Gentlemen had a township of Land consisting of about 23,000 acres on Connecticut river in the province of new york which he was willing to dispose of. Mr. Semple has promised to serve us in the article of Credit and every other way that lies in his power. We have met with many people in this place who has given us good hopes that we will not need to return without our errand. we intend to set out for New York to morrow in the morning from which place we Intend again to write you by the first opportunity Gentlemen

James Whitelaw to William Whitelaw, New York, July 15, 1773[11]

Dear father

Having an opportunity of being once more in this place and of two ships being ready to sail for England I again write you that I am in good health and I have reason to thank God that I never was so well in my life as since I came to this country for to the best of my remembrance I never gave a single cough since I left Greenock.

As we have now been through all the places which we intend to visit in this Province I will give you a short account of what we have seen since we left this place.[12]

On wedinsday the 9th of June we set out from this place for Albany in a sloop and arrived there on saturday the 12 at night the distance being 165 miles, we met with worse weather going up this River than we did in all our passage from Europe one nigh it blew so hard that I was obliged to stand for a sailor the whole night. the land on the banks of this river is very

---

[10] For John Witherspoon, see p. 23 n. 89, this volume. John Witherspoon was also a land speculator who owned property in Nova Scotia and in the part of New York that later became Vermont. See Bailyn, *Voyagers to the West*, 390–392, 397, 610–611.

[11] William Whitelaw was James Whitelaw's father, who lived in Whiteinch, Lanarkshire, Scotland.

[12] See also Whitelaw's "Journal," 123–133, for a similar account of the journey through the northern provinces. See Bailyn, *Voyagers to the West*, 615, for a map of their 2700-mile trip.

steep and rockey most part of the way between this and Albany but when you come near albany it becomes flat and very pleasant. Albany is a handsom little toun about twice as large as Anderstoun[13] and the inhabitants mostly dutch we set out from this for Johnsonhall where Sir William Johnson[14] lives which is on the banks of the Mohawk river and about 44 miles west from Albany where we went to view some lands which he had to sell. the lands are very good but the situation not so good being over a high Mountain and through a large swamp and there is no navigation nearer than albany.[15] here we saw great numbers of Indians of which there are always plenty about this place they are of a tauny complexion with long streight black hair which their squas (or women) wear long and tied behind and the men wear theirs short their shape is handsom for the most part and of an ordinary size they wear no cloaths except a kind of blanket which they wrap about their shoulders and two pieces of skin which they hang one before and another behind to cover their nakedness they seem to be very fond of Jewels as the most part of them have braclets ear rings and nose Jewels which is an ear ring which they hang between their mouth and nose the gristle of their nose being pierced for that purpose, we saw one in particular which besides the forementioned Jewels had a round piece of lather hung before his breast which was all drove full of white headed nails and a great number of buttons and other trinkets hung round it and he wore a cap made of some beasts skin with the hair on it and a long tail down to his waist at the end of which hung about 20 or 30 womens thimbles you may easily conjecture what a noise these trinkets made as he walked along what makes them look most remarkable is the painting of their faces which they colour all over with red and black strokes.[16]

[13] One estimate for the number of houses in Albany County in 1776 was 350. Evarts B. Greene and Virginia D. Harrington, *American Population before the Federal Census of 1790* (New York, 1932), 102. Anderston is a district and ward of Glasgow, near Whiteinch, where Whitelaw's father lived.

[14] Sir William Johnson had lived in New York since 1738 and had become a land baron in the region of upstate New York. His manor house was Johnson Hall, north of the Mohawk River, from which place he presided over Indian conferences. He was an avid recruiter of settlers for his lands, and was responsible for helping many new arrivals get established. His experience with lands and settlement was the reason that Whitelaw and Allen paid him a visit. See Milton W. Hamilton, *Sir William Johnson: Colonial American, 1715–1763* (Port Washington, NY, 1976).

[15] Johnson's price for these lands was a dollar an acre. Whitelaw, "Journal," 126.

[16] The Indians referred to here are probably Mohawks, whom Sir William Johnson knew well. The Mohawks, with the Oneidas, Onondagas, Cayugas, Senecas, and Tuscaroras constituted the Six Nations of the Iroquois.

We bought two horses here and set out from this place for new perth where one Doctor Clark[17] lives who was to inform us about lands and he told us that he had some small lotts but none large enough for us from this we was to have gone to Crown point but he told us that all the lands about lake Champlain were in dispute between the two Governors of york and new hampshire and indeed all the best lands in the province.[18] so we went from this to Charlestoun in new hampshire where Mr Church lives who is partner with Doctor wotherspoon and Mr Pagan in their tounship on Connecticut river[19] and he went along with us and showed it to us and it seems to be good land but very far back being more than 300 miles from New york and tho it lies along the banks of Connecticut river it is 200 miles above Hartford which is the highest that sloops come up that river the nearest seaport to it is portsmouth which lies about 100 miles east from it.

In our way to this place we lodged one night where Doctor Wheelock has his Indian Academy or Colledge[20] when we went and called for him and as it was night he invited us in to prayers in his Colledge when he prayed very earnestly for all the people that had contributed to the building and mentaining of his Colledge he told us that now he had in his Colledge 80 students of which upwards of 30 was on Charity and 17 of these were Indians.

In our way from Doctor Clarks to Charlestoun we had a very bad road being over some very steep Mountains and one morning we set out from a house at 6 oClock and did not see another till 12 our road being through the woods where we had no way to direct our selves but by marks on the trees as the road was not cut from Charlestoun to new york the road is pretty

[17] Thomas Clark, a Presbyterian minister from Ulster, led about 300 of his parishioners to New York in 1764 and settled in White Creek, a remote tract north of Albany, where only three families of New Englanders lived. Clark renamed this settlement New Perth. See William L. Stone, *Washington County, New York* . . . (New York, 1901), 385–386, 391–393.

[18] New Hampshire claimed it had a right to grant lands as far west as a 20-mile boundary east of the Hudson River. The Duke of York's grant fixed New York's eastern boundary at the Connecticut River. In 1764 the king decided in favor of New York, but Ryegate had been granted in 1763 to 94 proprietors by the government of New Hampshire. These proprietors later sold Ryegate to John Church and associates, but Church had to obtain title from New York. Full title was not granted until 1775. Fingerhut, "From Scots to Americans," 187–188.

[19] The 20,000-acre township of Ryegate was jointly owned by four speculators: John Church, Witherspoon, John Pagan (a Glasgow merchant), and Pagan's brother William (a merchant in New York). Bailyn, *Voyagers to the West*, 610.

[20] For Eleazar Wheelocks Indian Charity School for the education of Indians and for those white children who wanted to be missionaries, see p. 126, n. 83, this volume.

good as it is mostly through an old inhabited Country the Hay harvest is all finished along the road and now they are busy with their wheat and Rye harvest ~~the Common way they have of Cutting down their victual is with what they call a crad[le] which is a scythe with a bow on the [end?] for catching the~~ they have here a curious way of managing their stacks so that as soon as they are up they are thatched and it is this they have 4 long trees which they set up at the 4 corners of the place where they are to build the stack and they make a frame on which they erect a roof[21]

the Crops in this Country are not so good as I expected to find them as their wheat does not commonly produce above 6 or 7 bolls an acre and their Rye about the same their barly looks to be pretty good but their oats are but very indifferent the Indian Corn will produce 12 or 14 bolls an acre and they have several methods of Cooking it so as to make excellent food they have plenty of white peas and a kind of beans but none of our scotch peas or beans. if the Country were properly Cultivate they might perhapes have larger Crops for they do nothing but just plow & sow and some places they summer fallow their wheat land which turns out greatly to their advantage There are several ways of Clearing used in this Country such as Girdling, Cutting, and Grubbing. Girdling is only Cutting a notch about an inch deep and two inches broad round the root of the tree which makes it die their method of Cutting is to stand upright and cut the tree about two or three feet from the ground and for grubbing it is very little practised tho it is surely the best way Where they want only pasture the only Cut the small brush and girdles all the trees and for tillage they cut all except the very large ones which they girdle and then they set fire to them and burns them and with the leaves lying on the ground burn the whole surface then without ~~ever grubbing or~~ plowing doing any thing else they harrow through among the roots with a three Cornered brake then sow their Grain which will grow tolerable good this they continue for three or four years after which they use the plough.

The weather they tell us has been warmer than ordinary for two weeks past and though it is warmer than at home it is no way intolerable and the people in this country seem to be very healthy. I never expected to have stood my Journy so well for though we have rode since we bought our horses above five hundred miles I have never been the least weary

Pray Remember me to my Mother and to all my brothers and sisters and all other friends and aquaintances I have no more but remain yours &c. New York July 15th 1773

---

[21] In the original manuscript, a line was drawn across the page after this paragraph.

James Whitelaw to the Company, Ryegate, February 11, 1774

Gentlemen

We wrote you from Princetoun New Jersy the 4th of Octr.[22] in which we gave you an account of our tour to the south country as also of our purchase of one half of the Tounship of Ryegate from Doctor Wotherspoon we sent you a copy of our Minute of agreement with him[23] and likewise some of the best proposals made us in the south country from New York by Capt. Hastie. Having found a sloop to Carry James Henderson[24] with our Chests and what Tools we had purchased to Hartford on Connecticut river and having discused what other bussiness we had to do we left New York on the 19th of Octr. and arrived at Newberry or Kohass on the first of Novr and put up with Jacob Byley Esqr.[25] to whom we was recommend by John Church Esqr. one of the proprietors of Ryegate and James henderson arrived about a week after us with our Chests and tools and some provisions we had bought down the Country such as Rum salt Molasses &c. in a Canoe about the 10th of the Month Mr Church came up and we divided the toun the south part whereof has falln to us which in our own opinion and in the opinion [of] all that knows it has the advantage of the North in many respects 1stly it is the best land, 2dly nearest to provisions which we have in plenty within 3 or 4 Miles and likewise within 6 Miles of a grist and two of a saw Miln, 3dly we have several brooks with good seats for Milns and

---

[22] This letter appears to be missing from the Whitelaw Papers, but a full description of the southern journey can be found in Whitelaw's "Journal," 138–145.

[23] Whitelaw and Allen agreed to pay £666.13.4 sterling (c. 16 pence per acre) in four installments for the southern half of Ryegate. "Minute of Agreement between David Allan & James Whytlaw as Commissioners for the Scots American Company and John Witherspoon of Princeton in New Jersey," Whitelaw Papers, MS 29, folder 3.

[24] James Henderson was a wright from Kilbarchan and Inchinnan, Renfrewshire, who left Greenock on March 25, 1773, and arrived in Philadelphia on May 24. He was one of the first members of the Scots American Company to settle in Ryegate. On August 1, 1774, he contracted with David Allen and James Whitelaw to work one year (from October 1774 to October 1775) for the Company in Ryegate for a salary of £17.10 plus food, lodging, and washing. "Certificate of James Henderson," The Session Book for the Township of Ryegate, Town Clerk's Office, Ryegate, Vermont; Whitelaw Papers, MS 29, August 1, 1774; Whitelaw, "Journal," 146.

[25] Colonel Jacob Bayley, later a Brigadier General, was a prominent resident of Newbury, Vermont. See Frederic P. Wells, *History of Newbury, Vermont* (St. Johnsbury, VT, 1902), 434–436.

likewise Welds[26] river which has water enough for 2 milns at the driest season of the year of which the north part is entirely destitute, 4ly there is a fall in Connecticut River a little below our uppermost line which causeth a carrying place for goods going up or down the river. 5ly we are within 6 miles of a good Presbyterian Meeting and there is no other Minister above that place.[27] The Ground here produces Indian Corn and all kinds of English Grain in perfection likewise Garden stuff of all kinds in the Greatest plenty and perfection Onions Goosberrys and hops being the Natural produce of the Ground and the place is very fit for orchards We can have market for the produce of the ground at the following prices viz wheat from 3/6 to 4/6 Pr English Bushel Peas 4/6 Oats and Indian Corn from 1/6 to 2 shill. Potatoes 9d butter 6d the English pound Cheese 4 1/2d Beef 2d Pork 4 1/2d all sterling Money this Country produceth excellent flax which sells when swingled from 41/2d to 6d Pr pound there are likewise a great many other things grows here in the open fields which the Climate in scotland will not produce such as Water and Musk Melons Cucumbers Pumpkins &c. sugar can be made here in aboundance in March and Aprile from the Mapple tree which we have in great plenty Salmon and trout and several other kinds of fishes are Caught in plenty in Connecticut river, in short no place that we have seen is better furnishd with grain, flesh, fish, sugar, melons, roots, and other Garden stuffs than this considering its newness, here can be had all the necessarys of life and several of the luxuries and we think any that hath joined this plan and comes here and settles and is industrious may have a very genteel and comfortable way of living in a few years. Clearing seems to be no great hardship as it is commonly done for from 5 to 8 Dollars Pr acre, and if proper Methods be taken those that stay at home may reap considerable advantage, when we arrived here we expected that John Hyndman[28] who moved up with his family in July last in order to settle here would have had a house built where we intended to have lodged till we built one of our own but contrary to our expectations we found his family at Kohass[29] and his house not half up as he had spent the summer labouring to other people

---

[26] Wells River.

[27] Whitelaw is probably referring to the Presbyterian Church in Newbury, the town directly south of Ryegate. The minister there was Rev. Peter Powers. Edward Miller and Frederic P. Wells, *History of Ryegate, Vermont* . . . (St. Johnsbury, VT, 1913), 40.

[28] John Hyndman, his wife, and son William came to America in 1771 from Kilallen, Scotland. They settled first in Baltimore, but moved to Ryegate in 1773 after hearing about settlement possibilities there from John Witherspoon. Miller and Wells, *Ryegate*, 394. Hyndman was not a member of the Scots American Company.

[29] Newbury.

and neglected building his house till that time and as you will observe by the foregoing part of the letter that Mr Church was not then come up to divide the toun we did not know what part of the toun was ours and so could not build for ourselves we though proudent to assist John Hyndman in finishing his house that we might get him again to assist in building ours and likewise that we might lodge the more comodiously while it was abuilding and we got his finished and likewise one built for ourselves by about new years day wherein we now live pretty comfortably.

James Whitelaw intends next week to go to Portsmouth with two horses in a Slea (which is the common carriage they use in this country in the winter) to bring up some of the necessarys we yet want as also to settle a corespondence with his aquaintance Thomas Achincloss Merchant there to whos care any of the Company writing to us will please to direct you will also perceive by the sequal of the letter that the money we have got is almost exhausted and we will be obliged to draw upon you for the sum of twenty pounds ster. which we expect to get from said Achincloss and to draw no more on you till David Allan goes down the Country on his way home after the lands is surveyed and laid off which business we intend to fall about as soon as the season will permit which conform to the information we have of the country will be about the beginning of may for though the snow goes away by the end of March or beginning of Aprile, the month of Aprile is said to be the wettest weather of the whole year which makes it very unfit for traviling in the woods and we can forsee that this job will require a good deal of time as the lots are very numerous and the most that a surveyor can travile is about five miles a day.

The winter here is not neigh so severe as is commonly reported for though it sometimes freezes very hard for two or three days at a time yet it always goes off again and the weather becomes very Moderate though it always freezes some and we have had a more pleasant winter than ever we saw at home for the weather is always settled and though the ground is always covered with snow on the account of having no thaw yet it did not fall till near the end of Decr. and it has not been above 8 or 10 inches deep this winter and the people here says that this winter has been none of the warmest

We now conclude with sending you an account of the way and manner we have used your money as also a rout of the road from the sea coast to this place.

We have received of the Coys. money in Lieu of Expences by cash in hand and draughts upon you £100 ster. which we have expended as follows viz.

	£	S	D
To Traviling Expences before purchasing	38	9	3
To Ditto after purchasing.	10	3	4
To Expence of James Henderson his and Coys. tools and his and our chests from Philada. to Ryegate	9	9	11 1/2
To Horses, tools, House, and houshold furniture.	23	1	7 1/2
To loss [Pr?] Exchange on our last draught to William Semple of 35£ ster	00	15	4 1/2
To provisions	15	00	0
To Balance remaining in our hands.	3	00	5 1/2

£100...00... 0[0/4?]

When David Allan returns home he will bring an inventory of what tools
and utensils the Company has here and as for provisions we have not as yet
used above one fourth part of them and if the two horses were to be sold
they will bring more money than what they cost but we find we cannot want
them

If any of the company be coming to us, Portsmouth is the neighest landing being about 110 miles 40 of which you have water carriage but part of
the road is not yet well opened. Newberry port is the next being 126 miles
and a good waggon road all the way   Boston is the next the distance of
which we do not positively know but would advise none to go to any port
farther south of all the three Newberry port seems at present to be the most
commodious on account of the goodness of the road and waggons commonly
going and you may have a passage to it from any of the other two almost
any day as the distance from either is only 4 or 5 hours sailing with a good
wind and vessels always going. when you come to Newberry you will enquire
for Capt. Moses Little Mercht. with whom Jas Whitelaw hath made himself
aquaint and tell him you are coming to us at Ryegate on Connecticut River
and he will give what directions you need for conveying yourselves and
Chests hither the road is as follows viz.[30]

Whoever of the Company comes over this season need not be here before

---

[30] Description of road seems to be missing. The part of the letter that follows was separated
from the first part in the manuscript collection, but a letter that Whitelaw wrote to the
Company on May 9, 1774, implies that the two parts belong together.

the beginning or middle of July as we expect it will be that time before the lands can be surveyed and laid off and you know till that be done we can neither show them their own lots nor can we employ them for the Company but if any young persons chooses to come over sooner and chooses to labour for their bread they may have plenty of employment and good wages in the neighbourhood, but against the aforesaid time five or six good hands would be very necessary and it will be convenient for each of them to bring a cutting ax and a hoe like one of the largest you hoe potatoes with and some bed cloaths along with them and any thing else they think fit and if any think to be here before the middle of June you will send with them a few of your best common beans and a few of your best English potatoes, as the potatoes here are of a very bad kind and the soil is exceeding good for them

A beding of Cloaths must be had here for the Manager or Managers before next winter and as you can purchase them cheaper at home than here it will perhapes be convenient to send them with some of the people that come over

you'll please let both our folks know that we are in good health at present you'll likewise let James Henderson['s] people know that he is well we have no more but remains your most obed. huml. servts.

febr. 11 1774

James Whitelaw to the Company, Ryegate, December 26, 1774

Gentlemen   Ryegate Decr 26th 1774

I wrote you Octr. the 14th[31] when I advised you of the arrival of Severals of the Compy they are all in good health at present and have all built houses on their own lots wherein they now live and they generally seem to be well pleased with their situation

A few days after I wrote you Andrew Smith[32] died of a Cholic but as I

---

[31] In this letter, Whitelaw is mainly concerned with reporting new arrivals of company members, and is anxious to know how many members are planning to come to Ryegate in the spring, so that he can get provisions and grain for them. He writes that company members are busy building a two-story frame house 16' x 36' to shelter new arrivals as they come in, but they have had to do without a shoemaker, and need one who can tan and curry leather. Whitelaw Papers, MS 25.

[32] Andrew Smith, a member of the Company, arrived in Ryegate on October 8, 1774, with his

wrote concerning that in my fathers letter I suppose you have already heard of it

About 2 weeks agoe I had a letter from Archibald Taylor[33] informing me that he was at Newbury port and intended to stay there till I sent him word which way to come here   I hear that there are several others of the company in the country which have not as yet come here.

I wrote you formerly about building of Milns and since that time we have had several people experienced in building Milns to see our stream and they think that it will not answer very well as it is too small to carry the miln for the greatest part of the year but there is a fall in wells's river about a mile and a half from the toun spot which is seventy feet high and several very convenient places on it for building but it is in Newbury though within 100 yards of our line and I expect to buy the Lot (which contains 100 Acres) for about 7 or 8 pounds ster. and as there will be very little dam to build and almost no race to cut we can both buy the lot and build the Milns for a good deal less money than we can have them built on our own stream as we will need a dam at the mouth of the pond at least 150 feet long to raise the water 3 feet and it will require a race 300 yards long and in some places 5 feet deep to drain it 3 feet which will all be to cut through rocky ground and will cost almost double the price of the lot on wells river and the people that are here are determined to have them built next summer and to have them placed on wells river and if the Company do not agree to have them in that place they will keep them for themselves but I am certain that build[ing] them there will be of great advantage to the company as there is no miln within 12 miles of this place that has water above one quarter of the year and here will always be water for two or three milns at the driest season.[34]

---

brother James. Both were from Douglas, Lanarkshire. Andrew was the first of the group to die in Ryegate. Whitelaw, "Journal," 149.

[33] Taylor and his family arrived in Ryegate on February 1, 1775. He became constable of the town in 1776. Whitelaw, "Journal," 150.

[34] On December 27, 1774, the Company wrote Whitelaw giving him permission to build the mills "provided that the Settlers who are, or Shall be on Rayegate bear their respective Quotas of Charges proportional to their Shares as well as the Members here: in Case the Assesment just levied be not Sufeicient to Compleat the Same, this we think most reasonable as Such Machinerie is more for their Conveniance then ours: And their obligations therto you will preremporly require as also the assistan[ce] the people with you have promised." Whitelaw received these orders on May 15, 1775, and wrote (May 29, 1775) that at a meeting of members, all "Signed an obligation to bear their proportional share of whatever assesment may be found necessary for compleating the miln and have likewise promised as much work gratis among them as makes 50 days of one man." Whitelaw Papers, MS 29.

John Waddle is in good health and is desirous that you would send over his wife and family to him as he told me you had promised to help him in case that he thought he could find any way to pay you back your money and as he can turn his hand to several kinds of work I put no doubt but he may find plenty of employment in the Country and may be very usefull to the Company and if he be spared in health I doubt not but in a few years he may be able to pay to the Company what he cost them in bringing over his family and if you do not send over his family to him he will be obliged to return home again

Last time I wrote you I told you that David Ferry[35] was desirous you should let his wife know that if she could find any way among her friends to bring her over that he thought they could make out a great deal better here than at home but he is doubtfull that their friends will think it too much to lay out for them and he says that if you will [bear?] the expence of sending them here he will bind and oblige himself and Heirs to pay to the Manager here what Money it costs the company to bring them over and Interst for the same either in labour or Money as shall be found most convenient he has one daughter 17 years old and another 15 and a boy between 10 and 11 so his family will be more than fit to mentain themselves as Womens work is very valuable in this place[36] and as he is now hired with the Company part of the money will be due him before they come over

James Whitelaw to the Company, Ryegate, December 11, 1780

Gentlemen   Ryegate Decr. 11th 1780

I wrote you last July[37] in answer to yours of the 21st of Octr. 1779 but had no opportunity of sending of the letter till about 10 days agoe when I sent it by a gentleman bound from this place for Holland. The Bill that you

---

[35] Ferry arrived in Ryegate on May 23, 1774, and on July 30, he contracted to work for the Company for a year for £10 sterling "with board and washing only." Whitelaw, "Journal," 147, 148; Whitelaw to the Company, Ryegate, October 14, 1774, Whitelaw Papers, MS 25.

[36] On October 14, 1774, Whitelaw had written the Company that the colony was "at a loss for young women as we have here about a dozen of young fellows and only one girl and we shall never Multiply and replenish this wooden world as we ought without helps meet for us and as this is an excellent flax country a parcel of good spinners would be the very making of the place." Whitelaw Papers, MS 25.

[37] This letter seems to be missing from the collection.

mention to have protested I have never yet heard of Though I have had letters from Doctor Wotherspoon lately he says that he will never take up the bill as the persons he sold it to were too long in negotiating it so I hope I shall never hear more of it.

The letter you mention to have sent on the protest being taken I have never received.

The people here think Strange to hear that they are liable to two asessments as they were freed from all future asessments when they left you except for building the mills and they think it cannot be for that as the bill that was drawn on you for that purpose was protested by you, and as for the improvements being all made in general we never heard of it before nor do not understand it and so would be glad to have it explained.

The account of interest you mention to be an overcharge you must reacon Compound Interest as that was what the Doctor charged.

I have Sent you with my last letter a Copy of the Deeds of Ryegate and also a copy of my letter of a Aprile 26th 1777 Containing an account of Disbursments to the time that letter

I also wrote you that the people here had agreed to let John Scot[38] have the use of the Common ten years to finish the house and barn and the Clearing up what was cut down in the Common which ten years Commenced the first of may last.

Severals of the people here wants to enlarge their farms if it is agreeable to the Company or to the partners that may own them Archbald Taylor wants to have lots 107, 108, 109, 110, 111, and 112, and James Henderson wants to have lots 125, 126, 127, 128, and 104, and 105. John Scot wants to have lots 136, 137, 138, 139, 140, 141, and 142. John Orr wants to have lots 143, 158, and all from that to 150 inclusive Robert Orr wants 144, 145, and 146 and John Gray wants to have lots 147, 148 and 149 William Neilson wants to have lots 245 and 278 and all north of them James Neilson wants to take up lots 302 and 328 and all north of them James Henderson 301 and 329 and all south of them to wells river John Shaw 351 and 377 and all north of them James Smith wants 89 and 103 and all between them David Reid 78 and 79 and I want 77, and 129, 130, 131 and 132 all the above named persons will give the

---

[38] John Scot arrived in Ryegate April 16, 1775, and the next year became collector of the town, and in 1780 selectman. In May 1780 he offered to finish clearing the common and to board the sides and cover the roof of the barn, to lay in a good floor, finish the house, make a cellar, and keep the fences in repair, at his own expense in return for ten years' use of the common. If the Company decided to use the common during those ten years, they would have to pay him the amount he expended for repairs, etc. Whitelaw, "Journal," 150–153.

whole for these lots that they Cost the Company or their particular owners for prime Cost and asessments which they expect to be about £3 or £3:5/ Sterling I can have 200 pounds Sterling for the Common land in the middle of the town including 300 Acres in the Square and 90 Acres on the west side and foot of the pond part of said 90 Acres was intended for mill seats but is entirely unfit for that purpose as the mills would never go except about two months in the Spring and as we have mills on Wells's river within half a mile of that place which have plenty of water through the driest seasons there will never be the least need for mills there and that 90 Acres of land is most part of it good for almost nothing   the pay will be at three different terms the first on the first of febry. 1784 of fifty pounds ster. the next on the first of feby. 1785 and the last on the first of febry. 1786 of 75 pound ster. each with Interest at 6 Pr Centt from this time till paid and the purchaser will leave 20 acres Covering the present burying ground for building a meeting house or any other public use or if you will let the purchaser have the mill lot between lots 52 and 62 Containing 19 acres he will leave 40 acres Covering the burying ground which will be a considerable farm for a minister or will serve for some other public purpose it is my opinion that it would be best for the Company to sell it as it will never bring above half the Interest of that money in the way it is at present as it was Set at vendue in the year 1779 for £2..14/ ster. and now as I have mentioned before John Scot has got the whole of it for ten years for only finishing the house and barn and a little Clearing and no body else would do it so Cheap as it was set up to him that would do it cheapest -- As for building a town here to have a house on every lot it will never answer as the houses will never have any inhabitants at least not above one fiftieth part of them and so it would be foolish or even rediculous to build them, and to carry on a public farm there will be no advantage to the Company, as a farm will never be of any advantage here except the owner goes on it and improves it himself and those that thinks to live in Scotland and reap advantage from a farm in this new Country will find themselves entirely mistaken and the reason is this, the land is so cheap, and so plenty here that there is no person but will rather improve a farm of his own than work for any other person if you have any mind to Sell the Common I should think it best to sell the mill lot between lots 52 and 62 and so reserve 40 acres in the Common as that stream is too Small for a mill It would be a very great advantage to us who are here if you would all sell your lands to such as would improve them except such of you that intends to come here soon as we are obliged to make roads through your land to accomodate the towns beyond and to do every other public thing which has already caused one third of the inhabitants to purchase in other towns and almost all the rest will leave the town in two or three years from this time unless you either come to settle your lands or sell to those that will, and indeed the law of the land obliges us to Clear roads through your land and pay public rates for it or if we refuse to do it they will sell your land and take the price of it for that purpose. I should be glad to hear what lots are drawn above No. 70 and who has drawn them as there has none of the company come here that has lots above that number except Thomas Clark and Archbald Taylor.

[Note at end of Whitelaw's copy of letter:] The letter that was sent was the same as the within only the payment proposed for the Common was in three equal portions or if the Company rather choose the payment is to be all made in one sum on the first of febry 1785 with interest from this date. the terms for the three payments are the same as within

James Whitelaw to the Company, Ryegate, October 16, 1783

Gentlemen   Ryegate Octr. 16th 1783

I received a letter from Mr Wm Houston dated June 26th[39] a few days ago informing me that he had sent me two letters a few weeks before that neither of which have yet come to my hand I also received your letter of the 10th August 1781[40] in June last when I sent you an answer informing you that instead of selling the milns I had with the advice of the Coy members here Sold the two westermost ranges of lots and the lands South of wells's river at half a dollar Pr acre after I had waited till last January for your advice and with the price of said lands took up the [protested?] bills as I thought you would rather sell that land than the mills (understanding by your advice of Decr. 27th 1774 that you had about 60 lots thrown into Coys. hands) I also informed you that I still thought it more for the Coys. advantage to sell the mills and Common than to keep them but that the person was gone that proposed to buy the Common and that I thought it would not bring quite so much money now as it would then as money is now much scarcer than it was then and that people at present rather incline to settle on Lake Champlain and the river falling into the same which makes the price of land lower here now than it was then though I hope lands will in a short time

39 Whitelaw Papers, MS 29.
40 Ibid.

Sell as well here as formerly I therefor told you that I would not sell them till farther advice was received from you unless I could get the price formerly mentioned and the terms of payment the same – the above is part of my letter to you of June 18th.[41] which I hope you have received before this time. I understand by Mr Houstouns letter of June 26th and Several others received here Pr favour of Mr Stewart[42] that there is a considerable Spirit of Emigration among you at present[43] and I am glad to hear it and would advise all that are so minded to come as I think it will be much for their advantage as I understand you labour under much greater hardships now than you did when I left Scotland which was then almost intolerable in some cases.

As I understand that there are numbers of the members of the company that have either forfited their lots or are willing to sell I think it would be much the best for those that intend to come here to purchase as many lots contiguous to their own as would make at least 100 Acres as it is not worth while to begin on a smaller farm but if larger so much the better it would likewise be better if a farm consist of 200 or 300 acres to have it in two ranges as it would be too long and narrow in one – I should likewise advise that if the Company have any lots in their own hand that it would be much better to sell them to people there who would come and settle them and take the money there than put them into my hands for sale, for money being at present very scarce here the pay must be chiefly made in Cows Oxen horses Grain &c which answers here as well as money though it would not answer a draught near so well I should even advise the Coy. to Sell the milns and Common to some person who is coming over and wants a farm. I have already told you that they must be sold cheaper now than they might have been a few years agoe, but take both together they are well worth 300 pounds sterling and I could now take cattle and produce for them to that amount here though if they were to be sold for money I know of no body that could advance near so much Cash at present. it is likely that if any person was coming over that had money enough to purchase the Common and mills he would want first to see them before he bargined which I should think right. if that was the case he might lodge his money in Some Secure place

---

41 This letter seems to be missing.

42 Walter Stewart settled in Barnet, where members of the United Company of Farmers for the Shires of Perth and Stirling established a Scottish immigrant society similar to the Scots American Company of Ryegate. Whitelaw Papers, MS 29, June 26, 1783; see Bailyn, *Voyagers to the West*, 635–636.

43 Mr. Houstoun wrote in his June 26, 1783, letter that as land values increase in America, they decrease in Scotland "on Account of emigration from this burthened part of the World with taxes; which I dare Say is more than doubled Since you left your Native cuntry–"

in Scotland and if he liked the place after seeing it he could give you a draught on the person with whom he left his money or if he did not like it but choose Some other land Some where else he might draw for his money here as bills of Exchange are generally as good here as money and Sometimes better and for my own part if I was in Scotland and coming here and had a large Sum of money I should bring no more along with me than enough for necessary expences and draw for the rest after I came here.

With respect to balanceing the accounts between the members of Coy. on both sides of the Sea I Suppose you meant in case of the Commons being Sold as to the other accounts I have Sent them Several times to you and there is very little difference in them now from what was then.

As I understand that there are numbers of the company & others of the mind to come here if the advices from us are agreeable I will give you a short account of the country from the experience I have had of it and first with respect to the face of the country it is in Some places pretty level in others hilly and uneven but even in the most uneven places the Soil is generally fertile and fit for produceing all kinds of grain you have in Scotland but Mr Allan can give you as good an account of these things as I can, with respect to the quantity of grain produced on an acre wheat at an average will produce fifteen bushels or better Rye as much and pease about the same Indian Corn and oats about double but with good improvement wheat will produce more and there are people in this town who have never had under 20 [bushels?] and often above 25 on an acre and their land naturally no better than their neighbours [the?] prices of grain are much the same as when Mr Allan was here viz wheat & pease a dollar Pr bushel Corn $^1/_2$ and Oats $^1/_3$ flax we can raise in great plenty and it sells at 6 pence ster. a pound butter & pork the same price Cheese 4 pence and beef about 2 pence and we can always have a good market for all the above articles once in the year without carrying them over the [barn?] door and though we seldom have our pay in money we can have Something of [the same?] Value and which will answer the same and, though after the country comes to be fully settled the price[s] may perhaps be some lower. but even if that is the case I think it is much better living here than in Scotland. the people here are all in pretty good circumstances the[re] are none has less than [15?] acres clear and Some have near [20?] the lowest can raise enough to make a comfortable living and the rest in proportion. the country is very healthy and agreeable to british constitutions there having been scarcely any sickness in the town since it was settled and only [3?] of the people that came from Scotland and [2?] children born here have died at present all the people are in good health [&] the Constitution and laws of this state (viz Vermont) are generally allowed to be the best on the Continent and the taxes very light though in the other states they are very high.

Alexander Thomson, *News from America* (Glasgow, 1774)[44]

ALEXANDER Thomson was a 49-year-old farmer in Cork-erhill, near Glasgow, Scotland, when he and his family decided to move to America in 1771. He was married to Elizabeth Edmonstone, 43, with whom, at that time, he had had 13 children. The eldest, Robert, did not go with them. The rest of the family arrived in America in September 1771, and the following April Thomson bought a 430-acre plantation located on both sides of the Conecocheague Creek near Chambersburg, Pennsylvania, where he lived for the rest of his life. There, the Thomsons had two more children and lived a prosperous life. They were members of the Reformed Presbyterian Church and for many years held services at their farm, Corkerhill. When war broke out with the British, Thomson and his sons supported the American cause, and three of his sons joined the American army. Thomson died on February 26, 1800, and was buried at the Presbyterian Church in Rocky Spring, near Chambersburg.[45]

This pamphlet, dated August 16, 1773, and written in letter format, was published in Glasgow in 1774 at the request of the author, Alexander Thomson. In some respects it is typical of promotional literature of the time: It was written with a bias toward encouraging people to emigrate to America and is overly optimistic. But it is nevertheless fundamentally accurate. The people and places he mentions are real. Thomson, like Robinson and Rispin, was motivated to write the letters in order to dispel rumors that he was unhappy and had made a bad decision in going to America. He appeared to have had no other reason for publishing this pamphlet; the sales would not make him rich, nor did he have any lands that he wished to sell to prospective emigrants.

[44] A copy of the original pamphlet is in the Princeton University Library, Princeton, New Jersey. For another recent edition of this pamphlet, see Mina R. Bryan, ed., "News from America," *Princeton University Library Chronicle*, 43(1982), 221–233.

[45] T. W. J. Wylie, "Franklin County One Hundred Years Ago," *Pennsylvania Magazine of History and Biography*, 8(1884), 313–314.

Unfortunately, spelling and grammar have been edited, and some of the passages have been deleted, but what remains is a straightforward, though rosy, account of what Thomson knew to be true of his experiences in America.

At the time Thomson was writing these letters, James Whitelaw and David Allen, the agents for the Scots American Company of Farmers,[46] were visiting him while on their tour of America. They had brought him a letter from Thomson's "Gentleman" friend, the Rev. Mr. Thom, to whom the following pamphlet was addressed. Thomson was familiar with the Scots American Company, as he had been advised before leaving Scotland to join the society, so he had probably known Whitelaw and Allen in Scotland, or had at least heard of them. And all three knew John Witherspoon,[47] himself a recent emigrant from Paisley, who was an active supporter of emigration and did everything in his power to help new arrivals like Thomson and Whitelaw find land and get settled. Thomson was also able to help Witherspoon: Witherspoon owned a copy of Thomson's pamphlet, which was no doubt useful to him in instructing new arrivals.

NEWS
FROM
AMERICA.

LETTER I.

FROM

ALEXANDER THOMSON, late Tenant at CORKERHILL
in the Parish of PAISLEY, now Proprietor
of a considerable Estate in PENSILVANIA.

TO

A GENTLEMAN near GLASGOW.[48]

---

[46] See p. 88, this volume.
[47] See p. 23, n. 89 this volume.
[48] Thomson's correspondent was William Thom, minister of Govan. (William Whitelaw to James Whitelaw, March 25, 1774, Whitelaw Papers, MS 29.) According to Ned Landsman,

GLASGOW:
Printed and Sold by JOHN BRYCE, at his Shop
opposite the New-Church, SALT-MARKET.
M,DCC,LXXIV.

****

N.B. In the following letter, the ideas of Mr. Thomson are strictly adhered
to; his own words and even the turn of his diction are preserved; ——the
spelling and grammar are mostly corrected, because he desired this to be
done; ——some expressions, in which he seemed to ascribe to much to the
merit of his correspondent, are either altered or suppressed. His friends having heard of this letter were impatient to see it,——and as they understood
he had desired it to be printed, it was no longer possible to resist their
importunity.

****

CORKERHILL[49] in PENSILVANIA, August 16th, 1773.

DEAR SIR,
I KNOW well that after the promises I made you, you could not
have thought that so much time would pass, before you had any letter

at least five of the promotional pamphlets published in Britain during the early 1770s, including *Informations Concerning the Province of North Carolina, Addressed to Emigrants from
the Highlands and Western Isles of Scotland. By an Impartial Hand* (Glasgow, 1773), were
written by William Thom. (Ned C. Landsman, "Witherspoon and the Problem of Provincial
Identity in Scottish Evangelical Culture," in Richard B. Sher and Jeffrey R. Smitten, eds.,
Scotland and America in the Age of the Enlightenment [Edinburgh, 1990], 39, and see p. 45,
n. 25.) However, Alexander Murdoch suggests that the author of *Informations Concerning
. . . North Carolina* may be Alexander Campbell of Balole. A comparison of Balole's letter
(in this volume) with the pamphlet reveals marked similarities. For example, compare pp.
185, 186, of Balole's letter, and pp. 446, 441 of the pamphlet, printed in William K. Boyd,
Some Eighteenth Century Tracts Concerning North Carolina (Raleigh, NC, 1927). Murdoch
also points out that Scotus Americanus, the anonymous author of the pamphlet, writes from
Portaskaig, which is five miles from Balole on Islay. (See Alexander Murdoch, "A Scottish
Document concerning Emigration to North Carolina in 1772," *North Carolina Historical
Review*, 67[1990], 445.) In some cases, at least, William Thom may have facilitated the
publication of certain pamphlets, as he did Thomson's *News from America*, instead of having
written them.

[49] Corkerhill, which Thomson named for his father's farm near Glasgow, Scotland, was located
about seven miles from Shippensburgh, Pennsylvania, on both sides of the Conecocheague
Creek. Wylie, "Franklin County . . . ," 313; Whitelaw, "Journal," 136–137.

from me. Indeed I did not forget my promise, but after I had got an agreeable settlement to myself, I was desirous to have some particular knowledge of this country, before I should undertake to write any account of it to you.

In July 1771, I and my wife and twelve of our children went aboard the Friendship in the harbour of Greenock: It was after the middle of that month when we set sail for North-America, and happily we arrived at the city Boston on the tenth of September, all in perfect health.

I believe that some of my neighbours and acquaintance thought it strange, that one of my age should forsake his native country: but I thought I had but too much reason to do as I have done: as I was blessed with a numerous family, (and I have had another child since I left Scotland) I was very desirous to provide for them: All my sons who were able to work were brought up to the business of farming, and it was by their labour that I was assisted to gain any money I have: I therefore endeavoured to have one or two of the eldest of my sons settled in farms at home; and with that view I employed myself for the space of five years, in looking out for such farms as might answer my purpose. I travelled through the country for twenty miles round the place where I lived; but tho' I found plenty of vacant farms, I told you before, and I declare it again on the word of an honest man, that I could see no farm for which the laird did not ask more than double the rent it was worth; so that if I had meddled with any of them I say well that my sons would never be able to pay the rent, and that in three or four years I would not have had one shilling to rub upon another.

After I had spent so much time and labour to no purpose, I confess that at length I conceived a sort of distaste for the lairds: I imagined that as they knew I had a little money, they wanted to get it from me as fast as they could; and in truth some of my neighbours observed a change in my temper, and alledged that I was turned so obstinate that I would not stay in the country, even though some laird should offer me a farm or two on reasonable terms: and I dare not say they were altogether in the wrong.

As I was going to America not for merchandizing but as a farmer; several of my acquaintance and well-wishers told me that I would save both time and money by landing at New York or Philadelphia, but I had a great curiosity to see Boston, especially as I understood that some of my father's friends had settled there long ago, and some from Paisley very lately. However I stayed at Boston but a few days; for I made all the haste I could to wait on Dr. Witherspoon at Princeton in West-Jersey, and when I had gone there, I was sorry to hear that he had gone away a day or two before, to convoy some of his pupils home to their parents who lived in Virginia; but

I had the good luck to come up with him in the city of Philadelphia. I delivered to him the letters I had from Scotland, and he received me very kindly: When he understood my errand he was very earnest to assist me to get a right farm. He advised me to take patience, and that I should not be hasty in making a bargain. But that as he was upon a journey, I should wait at Princeton till his return, when he would do all he could to get me settled in a comfortable manner: He also advised me to rent a farm for some time, but as I had so great a family with me, I was desirous to have a house of my own as soon as I could conveniently get it: and I also thought it would be better for me to improve land that was my own than any rented farm; and as I had heard so much said about the goodness of land upon the Ohio,[50] both at home and since I had come here, I would fain have settled there at first, but as I could not conveniently do so, I bargained for the plantation on which I now live, before Dr. Witherspoon returned from Virginia; and if it had not been for the reason I have told you, I would have conducted myself entirely by his advice. But I have much cause to rejoice and none to repent that I made this purchase.

I had stayed about seven months in the country before I took possession of the purchase, during which time my family were not idle, but cheerfully applied themselves to such labour as they were employed in by the Planters about Princeton and Philadelphia; by this means it happened that my landing at Boston was not as great a disadvantage as you may think: my stock of money was not much impaired thereby, and my children learned the work of the country; they had never till then worked to any but myself: But I thought nothing of this alteration; when I had been obliged to enter on such an enterprize, I was willing to submit to greater inconveniencies than any I have met with.

It was in April 1772, that I settled on this plantation: It is situate at the distance of 150 miles from Philadelphia, and it is just as far from Fort-pit; it lies in a large and beautiful valley which runs thro' all Pensylvania, Maryland, and Virginia[51] it consists of about 430 acres, and there was a house of two stories high, and office-houses upon it: The house is built of square blocks of wood nocked or indented into one another; it is well plaistered, so that it is warm enough, and I have six convenient rooms in it.

My plantation which I have called Corkerhill, after the name of the farm where my father lived and died, and where I lived so long; My plantation consists wholly of limestone-land, and in general limestone-land is reckoned

---

[50] See also p. 117, n. 58, and John Campbell to William Sinclair, p. 157, this volume.
[51] The Cumberland Valley in Pennsylvania and the Shenandoah Valley in Virginia.

the best in this country. There is plenty of limestone for manure in every
field, and it doth not cost much labour or expence to come at it; and it can
be burned with the wood which we grub out when we clear the ground.
Our greatest labour is to cut the wood into small pieces when we are to burn
the lime.

Dear Sir, I do assure you I am well pleased with the country, and with
my situation in it. I bless God that I came here, and I heartily thank every
man who encouraged me and helped me to get the better of that fear which
a man is under when he is to venture over so wide a sea, and indeed when,
excepting my eldest son, I was to carry along with me all that was dear to
me in the world, I could not but be anxious about them; but I was determined in my mind, and providence hath been very favourable to us. We are
all at present in good health; and blessed be God, we have always been so
since we came into this country. They say here, that the air and climate of
Pensilvania agrees better with European constitutions, than even the air of
Europe itself, and I am inclined to think that this is true, from that constant
health which my family have enjoyed.

The man from whom I bought this plantation had lived upon it for the
space of eleven years, and in all that time he had cleared no more but fifty
acres, and I have got other fifty acres cleared since I came to it in April 1772:
upon ten acres of which I had a good crop that very season. I and my three
sons cleared these fifty acres without any other assistance but that of one
man, whom I hired for half a crown a-day of our currency besides his victuals. The clearing of these fifty acres cost me in whole, about ten pounds of
our currency, which is about six pounds Sterling, besides the labour that was
done by my own family; and in truth I was very well pleased to find that
the clearing of ground was so easy; for before I left you, some of my neighbours were like to fright me, when they told me, that several sensible gentlemen had assured them, that it would take ten or twelve pounds Sterling
to clear a single acre; but these gentlemen were mistaken, for that is not the
truth: Three men will clear three acres in six days just for the plough; and
in general over all the country hereabout, a man will do forty rood a-day,
for which he gets half a crown currency and his victuals. I gave 300 pounds
Sterling for this plantation, and I could sell it already for double that money.

We who are country people used always to think it a great matter, that
the gentlemen in Scotland had orchards, we thought this a fine thing; but
here, almost every farmer hath a good orchard, and indeed squashes, pimp-
kins [sic], gourds, cucumbers, melons, and all other garden-stuff grow in the
open fields: But unluckily through the slothfulness of my predecessor, there
was no orchard on the plantation when I came to it; To supply this defect,

I have already planted two hundred fruit trees, and I was pleased to see that one of the trees had three apples upon it this year, though it was not planted till march last.

Dear Sir, I have said so much about my industry and labour upon the plantation, but I have said it on purpose, because I know that a vile and false report hath been published at home, that it is only lazy persons who come over here. Now you know well, and I need not tell you that the very contrary is true; the lazy are motionless, and like snails abide on the spot where they are, till they either starve, or are compelled by hunger to go a begging: whereas the industrious strive to maintain themselves by their labour without being troublesome to any body, and many of them finding it difficult to live by their labour at home, they are so far from being lazy, that they have activity and spirit to venture over to America: but I pity many of your poor people who are indeed very lazy; and it is impossible but they must be lazy, because they have found by long experience that by all their labour they can make no profit to themselves.

My stock of cattle is not hitherto very great; however I have enough of horses, and I have cows, and hogs, and sheep, and by proper care they will soon multiply. I did not think it prudent to exhaust too much of my stock in buying cattle all at once; for as I have many children I design to purchase more land for them.

Dear Sir, notwithstanding my promise, I am yet very unfit to write you a description of the country; and indeed it is needless, as you know so much and so well about it already: but for the sake of my promise, and for your satisfaction, I will tell you the truth about it as far as I can, and I shall begin with the climate.

Till I came into this country I did not, I could not imagine the climate was so fine and so healthy: The air is sweet and clear, and we find an agreeable smell; one would think that the sky is much farther distant from us than it seems to be at home. The south-west-wind rules the summer seasons, and the north-west the winter. The winters which are very agreeable continue from December till March; and we have no such black foul weather as at home, but a fine pure sky and bright heavens; no storms as at home, but fine small breezes; no winds to shake or rains to rot the corn.

Sir, I cannot express the beauty of the summer season, it is so fine, so pleasing, and healthy. While I and my sons are clearing ground, and go for a while to walk, or rest ourselves in the forest among the tall oaks on a summer day, the sight of the heavens and the smell of the air give me a pleasure which I cannot tell you how great it is. When we sit down to rest, the breezes of the south-west wind, and the whispering noise it makes on the top of the trees, together with the fine smell of the plants and flowers pleases us so exceedingly, that we are almost enchanted and unwilling to part with such a pleasure. If my dear countrymen knew the beauty and healthiness of the climate, they would not be so afraid to come to North-America. There are a good number of old people just about where I live, some sixty, some seventy, and some eighty years of age. I thought it right to tell you all this, because I know that much pains have been taken to spread abroad a bad opinion of the country and climate, as if it were unhealthy: I will not say why this hath been done, but I suspect it hath taken its rise from some designing men among you, who though they saw many people in great straits, and many next door to starving, have for some views of their own, endeavoured to terrify them from coming here.

In truth, I am sorry to hear of the great distress of farmers and tradesmen in your country. You mention this in your letter, but I have heard much more from some folks I lately met with when I was at Philadelphia; and so far as I understand, the weavers and other tradesmen, as also many farmers are in a far worse condition than they were when I came away in the year 1771, for it seems the tradesmen cannot get employment, and the meal continues to be as dear as it was.[52] If the tradesmen and farmers would come here, they would soon find themselves in a better condition; and there is plenty of room for them all, yea for all the people that are in the three kingdoms. And this is the best poor man's country in the world, for the price of provisions is cheap, and the price of labour is dear; and there are many people in Pensilvania and the neighbouring provinces, who had to work here to pay their freight, who have good plantations and are in wealthy circumstances: But this country is chiefly profitable to those farmers who bring along with them one, two, or three hundred pounds; such farmers can afford to eat good pork, beef, or mutton, as often as those who have one, two, or three hundred pounds of yearly rent in Scotland; that is to say, if they have some tolerable skill in farming, and live upon the land they take up here; and I believe there are no farmers in the world who live on so coarse and so poor food as do the generality of farmers in poor Scotland.

With respect to the soil of this province, some parts of it are rich and some poor just as at home: if it is well improved and manured, it will bear good crops just as the land does in other countries: but so far as I have yet seen or heard, the farmers here are really lazy: they make no improvement on their land but just what they do with the plough, in which they are not very expert; many of them do not so much as draw out to the land the dung

[52] See also Hugh Simm to Andrew Simm, September 27, 1774, p. 143, this volume.

which is made by their cattle. When I came to this farm there was lying in several heaps at the house all the dung that had been made in the space of eleven years. I was glad to find I had so much ready manure, so I drew it out to the land, and the crops were answerable to my pains and expectations; for I had this year a rich crop of wheat and rye and of Indian corn.

But the richest soil in all North America is on the rivers Ohio and Misissippi [*sic*], and I intended to have gone and settled there at the first, but my wife did not incline to go so far back at that time, and that was the reason I made a purchase so soon and did not take Dr. Wotherspoon's advice; but I made the purchase on the road that leads to the Ohio river and as I have told you, I am just 150 miles from Fortpit: and as soon as we have this plantation put into some order, I and one of my sons will go back and take up a large tract for the rest of my children.

Mr. Lewis Evans who travelled over the middle provinces and most of the country that lies on the Ohio and Misissippi, wrote a geographical description of these territories. I know he speaks the truth with respect to the many parts I have seen, and I am thereby the better disposed to believe him concerning the rest especially as I have conversed with several of our own people, who all agree with him in his account of the Ohio and its branches.[53]

The land on the Ohio is a rich deep soil all the way from Fortpit downwards. That river hath many branches which furnish good navigation to the adjacent parts, and there is plenty of limestone and stone-coals in many of the rivers that fall into the Ohio. Mr. Evans, who published his book in the time of the late war,[54] maintains that the territory then in dispute was as great a prize as had ever been contended for between two nations, and that the influence that a state vested with all the wealth and power that will naturally arise from the culture of so great an extent of good land, in a happy climate, will make so great an addition to that nation that wins it, (where there is no third state to hold the balance of power), that the loser must inevitably sink under its rival. He says, That country exceeds in extent and

---

[53] Lewis Evans was an American geographer and surveyor who traveled extensively in the region of America that extended south from Montreal to Virginia and west from Rhode Island to Ohio. His detailed observations enabled him to make the most accurate maps of this area at that time. His most famous map was published in his *Geographical, Historical, Political, Philosophical and Mechanical Essays. The First, Containing an Analysis of a General Map of the Middle British Colonies in America;* . . . (Philadelphia, 1755). A facsimile of the *Analysis of a General Map of the Middle British Colonies* . . . has been printed in L. H. Gipson, *Lewis Evans* (Philadelphia, 1939), 141–176. The following paragraph was taken, in some places verbatim, from Lewis Evans's pamphlet, p. 31 (see Gipson, *Lewis Evans*, p. 175).

[54] The French and Indian War (1755–1763).

good land, all the European dominions of Britain, France, and Spain; and he affirms, that with moderate cultivation it is capable to maintain fifty millions of people. But for a farther account of the land on the Ohio and Mississippi, I refer you to Mr. Lewis Evan's book; and I have desired the Reverend Mr. Marshall[55] of Philadelphia to send you a copy of it.

In your letter you mention the American company of Farmers in the West of Scotland;[56] and I cannot but approve of their sending over skilled men to take up land for them before they bring their families here: they have just taken the method which you and others advised me to take, and I would surely have followed your advice, but I could not prevail on my wife to stay a year behind me.

David Allan and James Whytlaw, the two commissioners from that company, are now in my house and I hope they will rest with me for a week or two, for I can easily accomodate [sic] them and their horses.[57] They are going now for North Carolina to look for a large tract of land agreeably to their commission. A large tract of land to the extent of 16,000 or 20,000 acres, all contiguous and conveniently situated and not yet occupied, is not to be got in the middle provinces; tho' they might hereabout get plenty of single plantations here and there: for the farmers are many of them selling their plantations and going back to take up larger tracts. I therefore advised them all I could to go to the Ohio, but they are afraid the settlers there will be too far from market or a landing place.[58] Since I came to America I have learned to think that those who have got a rich soil, in a favourable climate and who have all the conveniencies of life in great plenty, may be happy

[55] William Marshall (1740–1802) was a minister in the Associate Presbyterian Church of Perth, Scotland, and came to Philadelphia in 1763. His first church was in Deep Run, Bucks County, but in 1769 he moved to Philadelphia, where he was pastor of the Associate congregation. James B. Scouller, *A Manual of the United Presbyterian Church of North America, 1751–1887*, rev. ed. (Pittsburgh, 1887), 484–487.

[56] The Scots American Company of Farmers, also called the Inchinnan Company. See p. 88, this volume.

[57] Allen and Whitelaw arrived at Thomson's plantation on August 5, 1773, and stayed about ten days. For an account of this visit, see Whitelaw, "Journal," 135–138.

[58] Whitelaw's journal entry reads: "[Thomson] told us that all the lands in or nigh [his] place was taken up but he could buy plenty of single plantations with improvements on them for about three pounds sterling an acre, as He told us that many people in that neighborhood was selling their plantations and going back to the Ohio, and he thought that would be the best place for us. But after we made all the enquirey about it that we could, we did not think it a fit place for us. For though it is allowed by all to be the best land in America, yet it lies entirely out of the way of all trade, being 300 miles of land carriage from the nearest navigation . . . ," Whitelaw, "Journal," 137.

enough though they have but little money, and they may carry on a sort of inland trade among themselves by way of barter: but those on the Ohio will not be long under that necessity, for I hear that money is already subscribed to improve the navigation by cuts into the Ohio: and besides the farmers on that rich country may easily get money by rearing large flocks of cows, hogs and sheep which they may drive to Philadelphia, and the market-towns of New-York and Maryland. By my living here I see that much of that fine land on the Ohio and Misissippi will quickly be taken up though no person should come to it from Scotland. I see emigrants in crouds passing this way almost every week; one of my family whom I lately sent to Philadelphia lodged in a house with fifty of them,[59] and within these few days I saw more than threescore all of them hastening to the banks of the Ohio. Some of them come from Ireland, some from England and from Germany; and we hear that several shipfuls are coming from Corsica or Italy. About Fortpit where three considerable rivers fall into the Ohio,[60] the country is pretty well peopled already.[61] We are in no fear that any harm will be done us by the Indians; I have seen many of them and by all I can learn they are a harmless people, except they be affronted or wronged; I hope we shall never have any bickerings with them. But it would not be a small number of enemies that would terrify us or even those about Fortpit, for besides a well-trained militia we have all guns in our hands. For there is no disarming act or game act as with you; which last you know, is considered as part of the disarming act.[62] Our young

[59] Many new arrivals were "warehoused" in private homes before getting settled or finding someone to indent them and pay for their passage. Advertisements appeared in Pennsylvania newspapers for emigrants who were staying at Martin Knoll's, Widow Kreiderin's, and Widow Meyers's. See *Pennsylvania Gazette*, January 12, 1774, and February 9, 1774; *Wochentliche Pensylvanishe Staatsbote*, December 28, 1773.

[60] The Allegheny and Monongahela flow into the Ohio at Pittsburgh (Fort Pitt).

[61] The flood of migration to western Pennsylvania and Ohio started when new lands were opened up in April 1769. These former Indian lands were put on sale at £5 for 100 acres, with easy credit and payment terms. People flocked to the land office, which had 2790 applicants on the opening day and had sold over one million acres in four months. This area was particularly attractive to newcomers, especially Germans and Scotch-Irish, who could find in the west better land buys for the limited amount of capital they brought with them. Jack M. Sosin, *The Revolutionary Frontier, 1763–1783* (Albuquerque, NM, 1967), 56. Pamphlets favoring settlement on the Ohio and Mississippi helped to direct the migration westward. See, for example, *The Advantages of a Settlement Upon the Ohio in North America* (London, 1763).

[62] The Disarming Act for Scotland was passed in 1746, after the ill-fated uprising in 1745 when the supporters of the House of Stuart attempted to depose the Hanoverians. This act in-

men are at full liberty to shoot all sort of game whenever they please: and by frequent exercise are as good marksmen here as any in the world. Indeed by the throngness we have been in, my sons have seldom hitherto had leisure to partake of that diversion: they must first improve the plantation.

I need not tell you, for you know it already, That we have here no tithes, or general taxes, or poors-rates or mill-multers[63] or such other grievances, as tend to relax the diligence or industry of the farmers. We have the privilege of choosing our ministers, schoolmasters, constables and other parish officers for laying and collecting the necessary assessments; these are chosen by a majority of the votes of the inhabitants. In this neighbourhood if any differences are like to arise about roads and churches, they are amicably adjusted without any law-process. We have no characters hereabout which answers to that of a Scotch justice of peace, which we who came from Scotland look upon as a very great blessing; and there is, I believe no part of the world where justice is more impartially administred [sic], than in the province of Pensylvania [sic]: in our law-courts the poor are in no danger of being browbeaten and born down by the rich. With respect to our laws they are made by those who are, not nominally only, but really our representatives; for without any bribes or pensions they are chosen by ourselves, and every freeholder has a vote. In one of the American provinces an honest man who was my acquaintance in Scotland, and who came over some years ago, is already a representative of the House of Burgesses. He had a small but a valuable paternal inheritance; but as the laird in his next neighbourhood fell to work with him about roads and marches and other pretences of contention, he judged it prudent to let that laird have his subject, before it could be wasted with the expence of litigious law-processes, where the laird's friends were the judges. He is now possest of three considerable estates, and is ten times richer than ever he could expect to have been in Scotland.

I might write to you at large about the religious liberty which is enjoyed in this province in the most extensive manner. We have indeed no religious establishment; but Christians of every denomination, as they choose their own ministers, so they also make provision for them, and so far as I know the several sects live in good friendship with one another; if I am spared I may give you some farther account of these several sects, as well as of my intended purchases in another letter.

stituted many restrictions, including a ban on the bearing of arms. D. B. Horn and Mary Ransome, eds., *English Historical Documents* (London, 1957), 10: 656.

63 Mill taxes (mill-mulcters).

Dear Sir, I again beg pardon that I did not write sooner to you according as I had promised, and I am sensible I have not wrote so clearly as I would wish to do when I write to you; for neither the spelling nor the grammar is good, but you must forgive me: And I have another great favour to ask of you, which is, That you would correct the spelling and grammar a little, and send this letter of mine to the press yourself, or else put it into the hands of some member of the American company; for, it may be, some of them will take the pains to get it published, with my name on the title or at the end of it. You may think it strange that I beg this favour of you so earnestly: but there are two reasons which make me wish that this letter were made publick: one of them is because of a report which hath been sent abroad among you that I am discontented, and that I have made an ill bargain, and that I am ruing my race, and wanting to be home again; which are great untruths; and may be there is some malice at the bottom of them; I want therefore that all my friends and acquaintance should know that I am very happily settled, that all is very well with me, that all my family are cheerful and in good spirits, and that I hope I shall soon provide a comfortable settlement to every one of them who is come up to years. The other reason for my desiring that my letter should be published is, That I hope it may be of some use to my dear countrymen. I hear as I have told you, That many farmers and a very great number of labourers and tradesmen are in more distressing circumstances than they were when I came away. Perhaps there are many of them who have some thoughts of coming hither, but are hindered by their fears about the climate or the Indians; now if this letter shall help to remove these groundless fears, it will in so far tend to the relief and encouragement of my dear countrymen; and I am sure that no man who knows me will suspect that I have written any thing here but the truth. If tradesmen, or labourers, or farmers design to come over at all, they ought by all means to come immediately, before they be too old or turn so poor, that they will have no money to bring with them, nor even to pay their freight; and the sooner that farmers come over, they will both buy land the cheaper and also have a wider territory, out of which they may make choice of the richest tracts.

The providence of God hath been wonderfully kind to those who have emigrated from your country. For two or three years past, many vessels freighted with emigrants have yearly sailed from the coast of Scotland; and I never knew of any calamity or grievous accident that befel any of these vessels. This is certainly remarkable, it is ground of thankfulness and confidence. But the same providence that preserves your honest people in their way to America, seems to frown upon them while they remain at home.

Your labourers and tradesmen are in misery by reason of the dearness of the markets, and that dearness is occasioned in part at least by the long course of bad seasons you have had: This is a dispensation of providence which surely hath a language.

I had almost forgot to tell you, That when I was at Philadelphia, I saw some Scotch news-papers in which a great deal was said about the death of emigrants by sea and their wretched state after they have come to the American towns. As I have said already, I never heard of any ill happening to emigrants by sea, and if they suffer any harm here, it will be rather from the hospitality than from the cruelty of this people; no doubt those who are forced to indent must be in a state of dependance till they have served out their time, and I pity their case. But as I have told you, I know several people here who served to pay their freight, who have now good plantations. However, our opinion here is, That both your farmers and tradesmen should come away before they grow so poor that they will have nothing to bring with them, or even to pay their freight.

I sincerely thank you for your last kind letter, which I received from the companys commissioners; I read it over with pleasure, and I thought I was just conversing with you, as I used to do, and that frequently, in your own house. If it is not troublesome, I beg to hear at times from you. If you direct your letter to the care of Mr. Marshall, he will take care of sending them to me.

I do not know if ever I shall see you again, but I am sure I wish you well and all your family, and my hearts desire is that God may ever keep you in all his good ways. I have come over to America, but I hope both you and I are seeking for a better country, and that we shall at last meet in that city which hath the sure foundation.

I am, &c.

ALEXANDER THOMSON.

F I N I S.

Letters of Hugh Simm, New Jersey and
New York, 1769–1774[64]

DISSATISFIED with his trade as a mechanic in Paisley, Scotland, Hugh Simm turned to the study of classics and divinity and sought the tutelage of the renowned Scottish divine John Witherspoon. When Witherspoon and his wife left their home in Paisley in 1768 so that Witherspoon could take up the post of presidency of the College of New Jersey, the 31-year-old Simm followed him in order to continue his studies. On Witherspoon's recommendation, Simm was hired by the college trustees to be the librarian and inspector of rooms at the college, an appointment which came with a salary of £5 currency, plus room and board. However, within the year he found a job as a schoolteacher. Though he was not sure at first whether or not he wanted to stay in America, he soon settled down, got married to Mary Boyd, and became more and more satisfied with each new teaching position.

From his brother Andrew, a weaver in Paisley, he received news about friends and family in Scotland, and in return sent information about the growing Paisley/Glasgow community in America, thereby serving as a vital link in this network by encouraging unemployed Scots to come to America and by giving them advice. At least 25 Scottish emigrants are named in Simm's letters.

The Revolution changed Simm's plans to stay in America and continue his teaching career. As a loyalist, he served as quartermaster in the Loyal American Regiment and after the war, he and his family returned to Paisley, where he pursued his scholarly interests. He died in 1810 at the age of 73.[65]

---

[64] *Source:* Papers of Hugh Simm, 1737–1810 (22 letters and documents, 1748–1810), Princeton University Library, Princeton, New Jersey. Printed with permission of the Princeton University Library. The letters are recipient copies.

[65] L. H. Butterfield, *John Witherspoon Comes to America* (Princeton, NJ, 1953), 83; *Glasgow Sentinel,* July 19, 1810.

Hugh Simm to Andrew Simm, Princeton, New Jersey, December 2, 1768[66]

from my cell princeton college decem 2 *1768*[67]

dear Brother and Sister in law

About eight week before this I wrote a former letter but as that by an unlucky accident was miscaryed before it left america I heave a Suspition that it will not be arrived but Shall not repeate ainything Said there till I know it except on or two things – and first I gaive directions for the making a black goune of bombazeen[68] in this manner it must be long and flouing reaching doun to the heels and draun together at the tope like a womman['s] goun with a little neck like that of a bavaria[69] and if maid of Velvet it will be So much the better its Sleeves are wide and long Reaching to the root of the thumb round which runs a pice of Silk five inches broad the Breasts to tuck Back on each Shulder and to laye below the chin with a ribbon you will recive materials from mr ersking in glasgow and I hope to be able to remit payment next Summer by a law of the college all the Students are obliged to weare them – to this I would add a tower for my head and if you please your little dickionary [I K?] with m'cyouing on the types two or [three] Stiks of pomet[70] a penn knife with an account of the expences and which I forgot half an hundred of qulls [quills] and I wish hou Soon they would arrive – at my first arrival here I was exammened and found qualifyed in all the yousfoul learning that is taught here and heave received the degree of batcheleer of airts on whi[c]h occation I composed and Spoke a latine oration before the trustees of the college which was verey obligingly recived[71] – the doctor

---

[66] The letter was addressed to Andrew Simm "weaver in the tounhead of paisley North Brittain." No. 1 was written on the back page, probably by Andrew Simm, indicating that it was the first letter received by him from his brother.

[67] Hugh Simm and the Witherspoon family arrived in Philadelphia on August 7, 1768, on the *Peggy* from Glasgow. T. J. Wertenbaker, *Princeton 1746–1896* (Princeton, NJ, 1946), 51.

[68] For a picture of a College of New Jersey graduation gown for 1773, see Henry L. Savage, ed., *Nassau Hall, 1756–1956* (Princeton, NJ, 1956), plate x.

[69] Bavaroy (or bavary) is a kind of cloak or surtout.

[70] Pomade was an ointment used to soften skin or to put on hair or wigs, which were pomatumed.

[71] Commencement was on September 28, 1768. Witherspoon wrote to Benjamin Rush that "there was a vast Concourse of People Ministers from all quarters Ladies & Gentlemen from N. York and Philadelphia." Witherspoon delivered his inaugural Oration in Latin. (Witherspoon to Rush, October 8, 1768, N. York while on vacation, John Witherspoon Collection, Folder 14, Princeton University Library.) Hugh Simm actually received an hon-

teaches me divinity privetly and I heave allraidy composed Some Sermons with which he is verey weel pleased – he is very kind to me and I heave Just now Received from him Six pounds of monny – I receive my matinence in the college and heave a room of my oun[72] – the professors are verey obliging to me and I am at presant [the] first Student [in?] the college [and I expect] to [have finished] the who[le] [   ] Session [which] ends in ma[   ] next[73] there are about an hundred and ten ministers in this prysbetry and a hundred vacancies which cannot be Suplyed[74] they are verey urgent with the doctor to Send for ministers from Scotland – but I must Leave these and mack room for the fallouing accounts – when at york[75] about Six weeks ago I enquired for Jennt lang's husband and recived verey distink accounts concerning him and was informed that he listed in the airmy and went to the tacking of quibeck or mouintreal[76] and was ether killed or dayed of Sikness and that the other brother named Alaxender was also dead but they could not tell in what manner – hendry Glen is in halyfax a merchent and I am informed intends to be maryed it being given out that his wife in paisley is dead – Robert Stewert is in Brunsweek a little toun about Sixteen miles from this – John m'cneal may be informed that one of that name cam over here about tuinty years ago but died two years Since and left a wife and Son in long illand but I cannot be informed if it is the Same person he enquires for – I can hear no account of one orr a frind of mathew Stewart the drummer – I hear nothing of petter Bishop – Robert willson your [wincl] Supposes that your good brother is dead – [dear] brother I am verey desirous to hear from you Send me a particular account of my good Sister and every

---

orary degree of Bachelor of Arts; 11 other students received the Bachelor of Arts, and 12 students received the Master of Arts. William Nelson, ed., *Documents Relating to the Colonial History of the State of New Jersey*, (Paterson, NJ, 1904), 26: 286–288 (hereafter *New Jersey Archives*).

[72] Normally three students shared a room. Varnum L. Collins, *President Witherspoon: A Biography* (1925; reprint, New York, 1969), 105.

[73] Bottom of page torn.

[74] Princeton was in the presbytery of New Brunswick, in which there were 10 vacancies as of May 1769. There were 112 vacancies in 12 presbyteries (of which New Brunswick was one) in the Synod of New York and Philadelphia, the highest court of the Presbyterian Church in America at this time. Synod of New York and Philadelphia, *An Account of the Annual Contributions . . . 20th May, 1769* ([Philadelphia, 1769]), 6; William T. Hutchinson and William M. E. Rachal, eds., *The Papers of James Madison* (Chicago, 1962), 1: 87, n. 1 (hereafter *Madison Papers*).

[75] New York.

[76] The British took Quebec from the French in 1759 and a year later took Montreal, forcing the surrender of all of New France.

on of your childring with my mother and brother I hope yet to heave the
comfort of Seeing you tho I cannot hint the time I am not Sorry for my
comming here but do not inclien to Spend all my life in it tho I feind
nothing So dissagreeable as my being at so great a distance from you – Send
me and account of every thing that is particular in the place the death persons
new buildings accidences and occurences with whatever is remarkible everey
thing ainything [will be] news here – I will concloud the letter [with an?]
account of [pub]lick affaires – which may be [prin]ted in the p[ub]lic papers
– and nou my dear [broth]er I recomen[d] you to the g[race?] of god
We are all here in the Greatest confusion and uncertainty and are at last
convinced that the repealing of the Stamp act[77] proceeded nether from fear
nor lenity but was only a recovering of the blow to Strike it again with Surer
aim – at my first arrival here about four monthes Since the insolence of
yondr little isle the increasing power of america and her future empire were
the usual topics of the public news the common Subjects of conversation
and the ordinary themes of theatrical declamation but on the news of the
unexpected arrival of the troops at boston[78] all were Struck at once to Silence
not with fear but indignation and they expressed by their faces the [St . . .]
[. . . nce] of liberty which they posessed in their [hearts?] their first language
was we are we must be free – we were all for a few dayes in the utmost
Suspence expeting to hear that the people of boston would not permit the
troops to land (for hints to that purpose had before been given out if ever
Brittan Should Send a milatary power to enforce duties upon them) but we
were Soon informed that they were not only lande but also received into the
toun to the loss indeed of the troops themselves as it gave them an opertunity
for disserton which greatly prevails amongst them tho prevented as much as
possible by the vigilence of the officers and detered by that most [   ][79] a
misund[er]Standind also prevails between the office[rs] and the leading men
of Boston and we are Just nou informed that there heave been a mob betuixt
the inhabitants [and] the common men in which Som of the former are
kiled I wish it may prove to be without foundation but [Son]thing of that
kind Seems verey likly from [the] presant disposition of the people[80] – they
are taking all proper measures to prevent its evil consequances [by?] encouraging manufactures – and the merchants of new york have entred into

---

[77] The Stamp Tax of 1765 was repealed in February 1766.
[78] The first arrivals in Boston of two regiments from Ireland were on October 1, 1768. By 1769
the troops numbered almost 4000 (over one-quarter the population of Boston).
[79] Four or five words illegible.
[80] This was no doubt a rumor – the Boston Massacre was on March 5, 1770.

an asociation to tack no mor[e] goods from Brittan after the month of march
but they are [d]ivided by this question whither they Shall rece[ive?] non of
ainy kind or only Such as have high [du]ties laide on them – but whatever
fears [pr]evail along [the?] Shoar yet [Blessed] be go[d?] [   ] all queit in
[th]e Back [p . . .] and [   ] [. . . nces] btwixt the indians and [   ]
[. . . ling][81] of Som of them by one ironcutter are nou happyly ajusted We
have Just nou conclouded a new treatty withe them by which we have received a very great extent of land[82] – there were present many of their kings
with great numbres of their Subjects and all expressed their Sincere affection
to and Steady attachment to the Brittsh Goverment – I intended to Send
you an account of the progress Mr Whillock's Scheme for converting the
indiens[83] but must postpon it to Som other oppertunity – Since the writing
of this I am informed that I am to teach in the Grammar Scool[84]

[81] The last line on the page is torn and about three or four words are missing.

[82] The Treaty of Ft. Stanwix was signed on November 5, 1768 at a meeting supervised by Sir
William Johnson, superintendent of Indian affairs for the northern district. At this conference, attended by 3400 Indians, the Iroquois sold 1,800,000 acres of their land for £10,460
worth of goods. This acquisition opened up parts of modern-day western New York, western
Pennsylvania, western Virginia, West Virginia, and Kentucky and created a new boundary
line with the Iroquois. Ray A. Billington, *Westward Expansion: A History of the American
Frontier*, 4th ed. (New York, 1974), 152–153.

[83] Eleazar Wheelock's plan for converting the Indians, which he referred to as "the great
Design," was to educate them for missionary work and then send them back to their home-
lands where they could Christianize their brethren. For this purpose he founded Moor's
Charity School in Lebanon, Connecticut, where he would educate boys and girls from
different Indian groups. The school began with the arrival of two Delaware boys on December 18, 1754. Wheelock moved the charity school to Hanover, New Hampshire in 1770,
where it was incorporated with the newly chartered Dartmouth College. Wheelock became
the first president of Dartmouth College, and continued to supervise the recruitment of
Indians. James Dow McCallum, ed., *The Letters of Eleazar Wheelock's Indians* (Hanover,
NH, 1932), 14–15, 24; Margaret C. Szasz, *Indian Education in the American Colonies, 1607–
1788* (Albuquerque, NM, 1988), 219–220; Bobby Wright, " 'For the Children of the Infidells'?:
American Indian Education in the Colonial Colleges," *American Indian Culture and Research
Journal*, 12(1988), 10–11; Frederick Chase, *A History of Dartmouth College . . .* , 2 vols. (Cam-
bridge, MA, 1891), 1: 88–89, 155.

[84] The grammar school, contained in the same building as the college, was reorganized by
Witherspoon and opened for students on November 7, 1768. *New Jersey Archives*, 26: 383–
384, from a newspaper notice in the *Pennsylvania Journal*, March 2, 1769.

Hugh Simm to Andrew Simm, Freehold, New Jersey, June 8, 1769[85]

Freehold[86] June the 8 *1769*

my Very loving Brother

In my former letters[87] I informed you of the Steaddiness of the Drs[88] favour towards me which in manny instances hath ben more then I Could either expect or deserved I Shall therefor Say no more with respect to that but inform you of another change in my condition which hath latly taken place − After I had taught about Six months in the Colledge a letter came to the Doctor desiring to know if he Could provide a teacher for a grammar Scool about twinty miles from the Colledge − The Doctor thought proper that I Should undertake it which was also my own desire I accordingly received a recommendation and arriving at this place was very kindly received by the trustees of the Scool − Here I teach latine Greek and natural philosophy which is a very agreeable and pleasant emploiment at first indeed it required attention and much diligence but I find it daily growing more and more easy − I am to receive about 50 or 55 pounds of this mony a year 15 of which I pay for boarding − I board in [a] planter's house about a quarter of a mile from the Scoole wh[ere I] am extreamly well yoused − Heare is no kind of toun all is a Continoued wood except in Such places as are Cleared by the planters − The Cuntry is extreamly fine and agreeable we have abowndance of fruits of all kinds nor is the greatest Strainger prevented from going into their orchyeards and pulling as many as he pleaseth − I often take much Satisfaction in traversing the Silent and lonly woods which are all now in their bloom and verdure but am very Sencibly disconsolat in not having any aquantance with whom I might Converse there being none here who have any relation to Scotland except a millar who Came from Killburny about 16 years ago and two families the decendents of one Kerr who was bannished here for being concerned at the affair of Badal Bridge[89] − I youswally go to

[85] Letter addressed to Mr. Andrew Simm, "Weaver in toun head Paisly." No. 2 was written on the front page of the letter, evidently by Andrew Simm, indicating that it was the second letter received by him from his brother. Andrew Simm received the letter January 24, 1770.

[86] Freehold was settled by Scots Presbyterians.

[87] This is the second letter in the surviving Simm Correspondence. In the first letter, Simm mentions having written a letter that may have miscarried.

[88] John Witherspoon.

[89] The Battle of Bothwell Bridge in 1679 was an unsuccessful Scottish rebellion against the imposition of English authority in Scotland. After this, a large number of Scottish prisoners

princeton every 4 or 5 weeks – the last time I was there was on the 3 of June
to See the transite of venus over the Sun's disk it Came on very near the
time marked in the tables and we Could perceive its ingress very distinctly
– I Suppose that with [you?] it was not att all visible nor did we ourselves
See its [   ] not emerge till the Sun was below the horision [   ] the
time of the transi[tion] I received the Box [   ] with the necessaries [al
. . .] – I return [you . . .] Sincerest thanks for your Care and the Contin-
uance of your affection – Be careful to give my Service to all those who have
Sent Books this is a very grateful present in this part of the world where
books are So very Scarce – The goun is extreamly well made but hath about
a 4th part more of Cloath then is necessary – Give my Service to James
Sclatter and Mr Ersking thank him for the News which is a fine complement
and inform them that I hope when my half year is expired to be able to
remite payment – I am glad to hear of the wellfare and increase of your
family tho Sorry that molly's disease Still continowes – Your performance
in the news pleaseth me very much – Could you not procure the news
and Send them every half year – your Journal is extreamly well I hope you
will not fail to Continou it – The list of deathes heath given me Excessive
grife –

As to youre Enquiries – I may afterward draw a mape of Princeton but
cannot at present – I have Seen no Indians Since I Came here they are much
further up in the cuntry – The Serpents are pretty numerous but not very
daingerous they are youswally aboute 3 feet long and often lye in the public
roads to enjoy the heat of the Sun and warmth of the Sand this hath exposed
me to dainger once or twice as I youswally walk from the Scool to where I
boart with a book in my hand I had almost Stumbled upon one or two
before I was aware one of which was 5 feet long – But we are in much more
dainger from a tree which is common in the woods here of Such a pois-
sionable quality that if it chance to Scratch the Skin tho never So little it
will make the person to Swell to turn Sik and break out into blistres as if
he had taken Strong and powerful phisick – and even the Slightest towch
or the Smell of it at a distance is hurtful – Here I Cannot help taking notice
of a little insect which is common amongst the ortcheards and fruite trees
it is Called the lightning bird and is about the Size of a butterflye they are
never Seen but in dark nights when they appear flying from tree to tree
leaving a Stream of Sparkling fire behind them which for an instant Seemeth
to extend from on tree to another

were sent to the colonies. A. E. Smith, *Colonists in Bondage: White Servitude and Convict
Labor in America, 1607–1776* (1947, reprint New York, 1971), 180.

I Suppose by this time you have received my Second letter – [Give?] my Service to James mcmurtary – Inform me if Robert Still inclines to love books – And how J Brown J Mccllilan A Gemmil are inform [them?] Mr Sandiman[90] doth not Succede – James Greenlees is in princeton and Seems to love it – I Suppose I will not See Mr Atking which I am Sorry for – How is Mr [. . . llian] – Direct your letters as formarly – I have had no Sickess except the day before yesterday but am now well – The colledge took fire some time [past?] but was got owt[91] – Is John [Tenahill?] well and yet in the Shope – the Doctor is well his familly and all the Boys

As you hinted in your letter that a Soldier in america had Sent home an account that the Boys were all Sold and otherwise badly yoused I think proper for the Saik of truth and to prevent any thing of that kind again to assure you that it is So fare from being true that they all Confess to me that they are extreamly happy in their Condition and if at home would again desire to be back – Since their first leaving Paisly they have received as kind and obledging yousage as Could be expected from the most indullgent master I wish I Could Say as much with respect to their diligence and fedellity towards him – I know no grownd for the report of their being Sold if it was not that at owr first coming here as theire was not work Suficient for them about the doctor's[92] house one or two of them went to Serve for Some monthes in the Countrey

But I am now to represent the Doctor to you in another point of view which is with respect to his managment of this import imploiment – I may Safely affirm that the colledge of New Jersey ows its preservation from certain ruine to his undertaking the direction of it – At his first arrival here he found it little better then a mere wrek its reputation was gone its funds were exausted and in a little time it had certainly Sunk to the bottom[93] – The

---

[90] Sandimanians (also called Glasites) were a small Scottish sect named for John Glas (1695–1773), and his son-in-law Robert Sandeman (1718–1771). Glas, a Presbyterian minister, was the founder of the sect, but in the early eighteenth century leadership passed to Sandeman, minister of Perth. They established several communities in Scotland and elsewhere, but never gained more than a small following.

[91] On January 30, 1764, *The New York Mercury* reported: "The College at Princeton, took Fire last Week . . . it received little damage thereby." From a newspaper extract in the *New Jersey Archives*, 24: 302.

[92] John Witherspoon.

[93] When Witherspoon took over the presidency, the College of New Jersey was near bankruptcy with total assets of about £2500, including scattered real estate. A large amount had been kept for years by the treasurer without yielding interest and the accounts were in a state of "hopeless confusion." Furthermore, the college had sustained losses of hundreds of

first of these was restored by the reputation of his Character and the high opinion which they had conceived of him especially when they have found that they were not dissapointed but that he hath Com up to their most ellivated Conceptions – To remmidy the Second not long Since he Sett on foot a Subscription in behalf of the Colledge with no less a disine then to mak it altogether independent this hath already met with very great and remarkible Success as an example of whic[h] in the bounds of one Congregation in Philadelphia there was no less then Six hundred pounds Subsribed for[94] – The Doctor Still Carries it on with that Spirit and resolution So peculiar to him that he Seems rather to demand it by authority then intreat it as a favour – He hath ganed the goodwill of all the Students their numbers constantly increas and it is their Constant wish that as he hath been the Support So that he may long Continou to be the ornament of Nasau Hall[95] –

Now that the God of nature the God of all grace and the god of owr father bless you and your little fammily for time and Eternity is the ernest desire of your affectionate brother

Hugh Simm

Hugh Simm to Robert Atken, Freehold, New Jersey, October 13, 1769[96]

Dr Sir   Freehold octob 13 *1769*

'Twas no Smal Surprise to me to hear that you are yet on this Side of the atalantic otherwise I Should certainly have directed a letter to you if not have come to See you – I purposed at the first hearing that you were to be at Princeton to attend on you there but as you are uncertain when you will

---

pounds in bad debts, tuition was in arrears, and trustees were using endowment funds to pay expenses. Wertenbaker, *Princeton,* 52–53.

94 Witherspoon traveled throughout the colonies to raise funds for the college. The fundraising had been so successful that by September 1770 the college had paid off its debts, purchased scientific equipment, and had investments worth £5114.8.3. Wertenbaker, *Princeton,* 55.

95 Nassau Hall, named for William of Nassau (King William III of Great Britain), housed the entire college and grammar school at this time. Wertenbaker, *Princeton,* 39; Ruth L. Woodward, "Dr. Benjamin Rush in Princeton: 1777–78," *Princeton History,* 5(1986), 17.

96 Simm addressed this letter to "Mr Rob Atken mertchent from paisley to be found near Mr Sproat's Shop Philadelphia."

come and that the Dr[97] will not be at home which may prevent your comming I cannot venture for tho it be vacation with me Just now yet I find
Sufficient employment to prepare for the next half year – I have a verry
agreeable employment and Situation heare my incomes are not large indeed
but Sufficient for present mantainence – As a number of the boys will be
fitted for the colledge in the Spring to which Should they go it will render
the Scool not worthy attendence So that it is probable that I will not Stay
here longer then that time – If you come to princeton and would favour me
with a visite nothing could be more desirable It is but about 18 miles and
not much further from Philadelphia if you do not do So I cannot hope to
See you till I call upon you at the Buhannan's head

Hugh Simm

Hugh Simm to Andrew Simm, Freehold, New Jersey, July 20, 1770[98]

Friday Jully the 20 [1770]

So long my letter hath remained with me for want of an oportunity to
Send it away but I am to go up to princeton tomorrow morning where if I
find no private way of Sending it will dissmiss it with the publick post – I
have heard from John Hadden and William Brock on Sunday last they are
both verey well – Last year in agust we had a view of a comet with a very
long tail and this Same year we Saw another about 8 days Since of the
bearded kind I suppose with you they would be both visible – A resolution
a few days Since hath ben taken at york[99] to import goods[100] – The weather
at present is extreamly hot So that all kinds of hard labour is insupportable
and tho I have my health extreamly well yet I would not love to go to a
hotter climate – My recreations are usualy either to go and visit the neighbours who are all extreamly kind or to walk thro the woods in a pensive
manner Somtimes with my gun in my hand the game is either Squirrals or

---

[97] John Witherspoon.

[98] Addressed to Andrew Simm, "Weaver in Townhead Paisley North Braitin." This was the
third letter Andrew Simm received from his brother.

[99] New York.

[100] During the summer of 1770, the New York merchants started buying British goods again,
in violation of the colony-wide nonimportation agreement. When a letter containing this
news arrived in Princeton, the students burned it in front of Nassau Hall. *Madison Papers*,
1: 50–51. See also description in Collins, *Witherspoon*, 132.

pigeons which come in great plenty twice in the year in their going and [return]ing to the South of America but they are much less numerous these few years past then formarly occassioned by this remarkible accident that in their progress from north to South mistaking the Sea for the land in the midst of a great fogg vast numbers of them perished and cam down from the Sky in Such clouds that Som vessels which wer on the coast hadd almost ben Sunk to the bottom – No more at present I intend to keep this letter open till I go to princeton tomorrow that if any thing occure to me there I may hint it in the post Script Farewell

HS

Hugh Simm to Andrew Simm, New York, March 3, 1772[101]

New-york March the 3 1772

My Dear Brother and Sister

It is with unexpressible gladness that after So long a delay I again find another proper oportunity of writing unto you – the various Chainges of life the different Situations in which I have ben placed and the Constant ex-pectations I have had of being able to inform you what would probably be the end of this Strainge course of providence which I have Come [there?] have hetherto prevented me – I have at last I hope arrived at the long wished for period and Cannot but look bak with wonder and astonishment on that amazing labyrinth thro which providence hath led me and before me with Somthing of an agreeable hope – But as I intend no more at present but only to inform you of my present condition I Shall Just name a few of the most remarkible things which have Chanced to me Since the writing of my last letter – That letter dated I think in July 1770 I took to princetown in which Jurny I contracted a Severe fever and tho all dispared of my life yet it pleased god that I recovered in the Space of 8 weeks – I then received an invitation from burlingtown at the Same time another from princetown to teach Hebrew there the first of these I accepted but was So disgusted with the Quakers that I left it in two daies I then went to the College and remained all the last winter – The Teacher who Succeeded me in freehold

---

[101] Letter addressed to "Andrew Simm Weaver in Paisley North Brittian." Andrew Simm noted on the letter that he received it on April 18.

not pleasing the people there they dismissed him and almost constrained me to return – At the end of that half year I received an invitation from New york to teach a Grammar School there where I arrived January the 10 *1772* and have a very agreeable prospect in this place – These are Some of the most material things with have Chanced Since my last letter but many peculiar Circumstances attending and the dispotion of my own mind under them I must pass over in Silence – I Shall only add My Dr Brother that hetherto the lord hath helped me and tho assulted with Some of the most Severe trials which Can attack the humman mind yet he hath preserved my natural and I hope also my Spiritual life – I thank you in the most obleging maner for not neglecting to Send letters to me tho you have not received one from me this long time but you may now expect to receive letters from me very often – privatly tho I must Send this with post – Send by the post as often as you pleas – I wish you would Send me more news papers – Give my Complements to James Tanahil and William Sclater and inform them that I will write letters to them with the first oportunity and I beg to receive letters from them – Give my complements to andrew Russel – Send me an account of all things that are remarkible particulary deaths – fail not to give 2 pence to each of your litle childring in my name and desire them to bless god that I am well – I will write more largly in another letter[102] – my wagges is about 120 pounds of this mony but living extreamly dear to me 50 pounds yearly[103] – John Hadding is dead – I add no more – I ernestly recomend you to the grace of god

Hugh Simm

PS Mr Galbreath Just now Sends me the following lines and desires you to aquant his Sister Mis Galbreath that he hath his Complements to her that his wife was Safly delivered of a Son feb the 26 and recovers very well the childs name is William that he desires her to aquant Mrs freenos of the Same and that he and family are well and love this Cuntry –

give my Complements to my Step mother – Send a letter as Soon as possible direct to me teacher of the grammar School in Fletten Barrick Street[104]

---

[102] About 15 lines at the bottom of this page were written in small print to make them fit on the page.

[103] One hundred and twenty pounds New York currency was equal to about £69 sterling, and 50 pounds currency equal to about £29 sterling. Compare this salary to that of David Duff, the teacher in Maryland, who was making £16 sterling a year in addition to bed, board, and washing and any extra money he could make from other pupils. He hoped to make as much as £40–£50 sterling a year. See below David Duff to James Grant, 1772, p. 161, this volume.

[104] Flatten Barrack Street was south of Wall Street between Broadway and Broad Street.

Hugh Simm to Andrew Simm, New York,
November 14, 1772[105]

N-York Novem the 14=*1772*

My Dr Brother and Sister

In my last I informed you of my Settelment in York where I Still remain –
My Situation at present is in many respects agreable my wages and Credit
both increased and I begin perhaps too fondly to think that this is my rest
for ever and hope in a Short time to Settel in a regular maner – Here I am
well Supplied with books news and company of all kinds which makes Som
kind of recompence for my formar lonly Situation in freehold – I can Say
little about returing to Scotland at present tho nothing could be more de-
sireable that is Still more doubtfull all I Can Say is that perhaps next year I
may Send you as much mony as will purchase a house near you and return
Some time after my Self and will then inform you of many things conserning
America which are to loon for a letter then we Shall take Sweet counsel go
to the house of god in company and live ang die together but these things
belong to god – I have Joyned the Seceding Congregation in this town of
which Mr Mason[106] is minister a corespondent of Mr Elies's – I have Sufficient time to read and walk as I teach only 6 hours in the day and have
one idle day in the week I often then wish to have an oportunity to visite
[you] and your little family but when Shall that time come

A few days ago I accidently met with Hengry Glen In the Streets of york
he was then on his way from Virgin to Boston was well and had his Complements to you and my Sister in law – John Hadding is dead – James
Greenlees is well – James Witherspoon is gon to Jamaica[107] – I Spoke to Dr

---

[105] Letter addressed to Andrew Simm "waver in Paiseley North Britain by the favour of Mr
Galbreath." Andrew Simm received this letter January 16, 1773.

[106] John Mason came to America from Scotland in 1761 and was installed as pastor of the
Associate Congregation of Cedar Street in New York City. Mason's ardent patriotism led
him to serve as chaplain in the Continental army during the Revolution. It is interesting
to note that, though Simm associated with Seceders (Associate Presbyterian Church) like
Witherspoon and Mason, he was never a patriot and enlisted in the British army during
the war. Scouller, *Manual of the United Presbyterian Church*, 490–492, 25.

[107] John Witherspoon's son James had graduated from the College of New Jersey in 1770. In
1772 the board of trustees gave him a commission to go to the West Indies to solicit funds
for the college. The Reverend Charles Beatty, an agent for President Witherspoon, was
also appointed to go to the West Indies, but died shortly after landing in Barbadoes. No
report was ever made on collection of funds from the West Indies. Collins, *Witherspoon*,
143.

Graim a few days ago he is gon to the west indies – I know nothing of any of the Boys – Let me know particularly concerning your Self and every one of your family and as many other aquaintances as you think proper – I was greatly dissapointed in not receiveng a letter with elizabeth Gibson and Mr Galbreath's Servant – I wish you Could Send me more news papers with all the old pamphlets relating to the persecution particularly the blind mans prophcy – Let me know all the Deaths that are remarkable the present State of trade the price of meal and Such other common things – Give my compliments to my Step-mother my Brother Uncl Andrew Russel John Barr – Let me know all that I am owing you in your next letter – I have [wrot to William Sclatter to pay you the mony betuix][108] him and me – I wish you would write every 3 or 4 months I will mak no account of the price – I have Scarcely any oportunity of writing to you except by the post Ships Seldom return to Scotland but either by the west indies or the Straits – The following Books I wish you could Send – 1 Mr muier's Second desertation on the Greek pepositions 2 the Blinds man's propecy with any other old pamphlest relating to the persecution – 3 Satan's Invisable world 4 Spiritual logic 2 Coppies – 5 John Stivenson's life Pediens life Blairs lives – The Millar's nam in freehold is John Craig – The minister's name Mr McClean

I Cannot but take this oportunity to observe that the distance betw[ixt] you and me is So great that it will certainly Subtend an angle Visible to a considerable distance in the heav[en]s if therefor the Solar Spots fall within that angle they will make a regular difference on the disk of the Sun if observed by you and me at the Same time please then to begin to observe the Spots on the Sun on the 1 day of Aprile at 9 in the morning whilst I do the Same here at 1 in the afternoon drawing a Circle of 1 inch in diameter to represent the disk of the Sun marking the Spots as near as possible both in their Size and Situation and Send your observations with your first letter by this method if at all it may be discovered whether the Solar Spots adheare to the disk of the Sun or not N B Continue to observe all the month of Aprile Let me desire you again to give every one of your little Childring 2 pence in my name and bid them bless god in their evening prayers that their Uncle is well and that he desire them to read their Bible to love and fear God –

I cannot conclude this letter without observing that the distance betuixt you and me is So great and the circumstances of our conditions of Such an kind that it is not very probable that we will Soon See one another let us then my Dr Brother meet duly at the throne of grace praying for one another that we may be enabled both to do and Suffer what ever is agreable to the

---

[108] This part of the line pasted over with a strip of paper and sealed with wax.

divine will and daily to Send Spiritual Complements by the hand of our great Redeemer – I hope that you will be dilligent and faithfull in the discharg of your duty as an Elder living above men and fearing non but God beliving that a youseful life is a happy life – The lord hath brought me thro a Straing Course of providences and Supplied me I hope with Some youse full experiences for future life many times have I ben neare to death from outward accidents yet always preserved many times near to distruction from my oun conduct yet always prevented – He hath Sewed me that there is no hope but in god and that there is help in him – Last Sunday but one was our communion Saboth there ye were all remembered may the lord grant all my desires and foll all my requests – And now my Dr Brother may the good [w . . .] of him who dwell in the Bush the blessing of him in whom all the faimilies of the earth Shall be blessed be with you yowr wife and little family and may the portion of Jacob be their portion

> From your loving brothe at present in good health
> Cheerful in his temper and in Some measure loving and
> fearing God thro Christ – Saturday night

> Hugh Simm

Saturday night at 9 of the clock

I forgot to inform y that a few days ago I recived a call from the City of Albany offering 130 pounds per anum to go and teach a grammar School there which I did not then accept of as I could not go befor the Spring at which time they propos to give me a Second invitation but I am uncertain whither I will go or not as my Situation at present is very agreable and my wages near to 150 pounds if I do go I will inform yo by the post – You have no doubt heard of the great Storm in the west indies[109] we felt nothing of it here tho I have Seen one Since I cam to America much more terrible then any I have ever Seen in Scotland overturning the most Statly oaks in Such a maner as to make the woods look lik a field of battel – Mr Galdbreath goes away on munday morning it Stricks 10 farewell

> H Simm

---

[109] The "great Storm" was a violent hurricane that passed through the West Indies in late August 1772. In November, the *Scots Magazine* devoted four columns to news about the devastation. Dramatic reports of near total destruction came from Antigua, St. Christopher's, St. Eustatia, Dominica, St. Croix, St. Martin's, St. Kitt's, and other islands. Damage estimates ranged from £30,000 (Tortola) to £500,000 (St. Christopher's). *Scots Magazine*, 34 (November 1772), 629–630.

Hugh Simm to Andrew Simm, New York, January 9, 1773[110]

N-york Ja[nua]ry the 9 *1773*

My Dear Brother

I have nothing material to write Since my last with Mr Galbreath but having this oportunity to Send this letter with the Shipe Buchanan I think proper to observe these few things − 1 Tha[t] I received your letter dated the 8 of October the midle of last month with the news a welcom compliment for wich I return you Sincere thanks I am glad and bless god to hear that you are well 2ly I hope you will be carefull to observe the Spots on the Sun as I directed you in my formar letter marking them with a pen on a circle one inch in diameter as near to their Size and Situation as possible beginning on the first of Apirile and continuing all that month making your observations at 1 in the afternoon whilst I do the Same here at 9 in the morning − 3 I have refused to go to Albany − 4 I think it probale that I will be [   ]¹¹¹ in a few weeks in a very agreeable [   ]¹¹² but of this [more afterwords]¹¹³ − 5 I have Just now retur from widow young She Seems to be a very agreeable and generous woman She proposeth to Settel a Sallary on her Brother yearly to be payed by the Buchannans in glasgow and is much pleased with Robert's comming over at present She Sends a box with Several compliments − Remmember me again to William Sclater and James Tannihill I expect a letter from each of them with Robert Knox − In a latter directed to Mr Galbreath I See an account of the badness of trade in pasley that 600 Weavers are turned off¹¹⁴ which I am very Sorry for and hope that affairs will Soon take a better turn − This is Saturday afternoon near three of the clock and I am Just going doun to the Ship to deliver this letter which is to Saill tomarrow − I recomend you and all

---

¹¹⁰ Letter addressed to Andrew Simm, "weaver in town head of Paisley N-Britain With the Ship Buchannan."

¹¹¹ Erased.

¹¹² Erased.

¹¹³ Erased.

¹¹⁴ Simm had a personal interest in the plight of the weavers; his father John as well as his brother Andrew were weavers. The *Scots Magazine* reported for February 1774 that Paisley could not "support those ingenious mechanics . . . but they are forced to abandon their friends and country, and seek that subsistence in a distant clime, which they cannot obtain in their own." Indenture of Andrew Symm, Simm Papers; *Scots Magazine*, 36(February

your little family to the grace of god and Shall ever remain your tender and affectinate brother

Hugh Simm

Hugh Simm to Andrew Simm, New York, April 1, 1773[115]

N york April the 1 *1773*
at [   ] the morning

My Dr Brother

Sometimes I have wrote to you formaly when labouring with Some pressing difficulty at other times when in more agreable circumstances but never when So many oposite passions contended in my mind as at present – Such is the nature of temporal happiness [that?] whilst bestows a favour with one hand She often Snatches away Somthin as valouable with the other that we are Seldom permited to rejoice to excess and have alwise reason to mix trembling with our mirth – That you may understand the meaning of this I am to inform you that this day I am to be married this maks me glad but as that Situation of life may possibly deprive me of ever having an oportunity of ever Seeing you again this reflection makes me very Sad whilst I lift up my hand to heaven and bless god for the favour I am presently to be put in possession of I cannot but hang doun my head and drop the bitter tear Saying alas my brother Shall I never See you more but Stope I will not take an everlasting farewell I hope yet to See you and if I may Speak my mind freely it is this that I Suppose at the end of two or three years I will either be tired of teaching or my health will obledge me to quite it in which case it is my desine to return to Scotland but I must not forget that tho many purposes are in man's heart yet the counsel of the Lord that Shall Stand

You will not doubt expect that I Should give you Some account of the young woman now about to be the future companion of my life what follows may be Sufficient – her name is Mary Boyd about 26 years of age originally from Ireland not tall in her Stature agreable in her person and cheerful in

1774), 64. See also report on present state of linen manufacture in Scotland in *British Chronicle* for 1774, February 28–March 2, p. 207.

[115] Letter addressed to Andrew Simm "in town head Paisley North Britain – by favour of Mr Duncan."

her behavour her Father is a respectable planter on hudsons river 60 miles above N-york –

I think I my now Say that at last I have arrived at the meridien of life at present in good health both of mind and boday yet am possibly much more then half way from the cradle to the grave and as I have Seen the rising So must I now See the Setting Sun gladly will I turn my face that way if possible that I may finish my course with Joy and lay hold on eternal life – I cannot but Look back with wonder and [asso . . . ent] when I [review?] the Strainge path of life thro which [I] have gon fenced in with thorns on every Syde and urged forward and tho I have Stumbled much yet I have not falen at least falen over a rock but as yet my natural and Spiritual life is preserved tho both have often ben in great dainger blessed be god who hath hitherto helped me and who hath promised that he will be our guide even unto death –

I have often with much pleasure in Scotland read the 107 psalm and have now Seen it almost all fullfilled [in?] I have Seen the daingers of the Sea and experienced the inconveniences of a wilderness my Soul fainted within me with Sorrow and grief I cried unto the Lord and delivered me he hath brought me to a city hath given me a convenient dwelling and is now about to build me up into a family I wish that the duty there appointed may be well performed by me that I may praise him with gladness having experieced much of his goodness and I hope that his mercy will continwe forever but le not you and me forget My Dr Brother that here we have no continwing City let us therefor Seek diligently for that city which is to come which hath foundations whose builder and maker is god –

What a great addition would it be to my happiness this day the day of my espousals and the day of gladness of my heart if I could Say with Mr Perkings that on my marriage day I have received the assurance of that inheritance which Shall never be taken away which is reserved in heaven above tho I will not go So fare yet I will Say with Luther (who when he received a great compliment from one of the Germon princes threw it down and lifting up his hands to heaven Saying) I protest that I will not tak this world and all its glory for my Portion –

This is the 1 of Aprile but I have not ben able to mak any observations on the Sun it is So cloudy which is not usual at this time of the year – 4 of the clock in the afternoon is Just now Struck and I am now going to dress and will be married about 7 in the evening how glad would I be to have your company and my Sister in law's this evening yet alas what I often wished for is denied me which was to live and die with my friends in my oun cuntry –

I am in [great?] hopes that Some discovery will be made on the [   ] Spots by observing [them] in Scotland and America at the Same [time] at least that it will apear probable whither they adhear to the disc of the Sun or not which will be no immaterial point I will expect to receive your observations before [this?] letter comes to hand – I am informed that Dr WitherSpoon is much blamed in Paisley for treating the Boys ill whom he brought over here I cannot Say that he deserves it they behaved very ill and I Suppose that he hath had more loss then profite by them – I return you thanks for the News papers you Sent over I have Just now finished the reading of them I See the canal is going on and would be glad to See it[116] – Please to remmember me to my Step-mother and Brother to James Tanahill William Sclatter and John Barr – I Shall concloud this letter with the following litle Hymn which if you think proper you may make yoar little childring learn by heart perhaps it will recomend it to them when they know that it was Sent to them by their Uncle from America – Your loving brother

Hugh Simm

What tho wholl mines of yellow oar
What tho the vast unbounded Sea
Showld gather all their yellow Store
And pour out all their wealth on me

Tho I in royal pomp could Shine
And dim the bright meridien hour
Seem to the gazing croud divine
And Shake the Septer of my power

Tho wisdom from her Secret Springs
Did me with Such vast Skill inspire
That I could Speak of heavenly things
Till Angels wonder and admire

Yet am I Still but mean and base
Unewise and foolish would I be
O God without they Sovreign grace
And care for my own Soul and thee

---

[116] The Forth and Clyde Canal was begun in 1768, the year Simm left for America, and was finished in 1790. T. C. Smout, *A History of the Scottish People, 1560–1830* (Glasgow, 1969), 246.

Lord without thy clestial light
To point the path that I Should run
I would but dwell in endless night
Lodg'd in the center of the Sun

Hugh Simm to Andrew Simm, Albany, New York, September 27, 1774[117]

Albany September the 27 *1774*

My Dr Br

It is with no Small degree of gladness that after So long a delay I again find it Convenient to write to you – In my last dated the 8th of June 1774[118] I promised to give you a discription of Hudson's River but the many things Concerning which I have at present to write constrain me in this as well as in many other things to be very Short – The breadth of it is about 1/4 of a mile I Sounded often and found it either 8 or 10 fathoms – This River abounds with fishes particulary a kind Called Sturgeon which are frequently to be Seen leaping above the water the noise of which when falling back into the water may be heard at a prety great distance – The agreeable view of the woods on each Side of the rever interspersed with plantations in different places recals to the mind the discrip which Rauling gives of the River Niel in Egypt[119] – The distance betwen N-york and Albany is about 150 miles where we arrived on the 3d day after our departure which was the Sabath day

Albany is Situated on the west Side of the River it Contains about 100 houses and 300 inhabitants[120] mostly dutch which Speak their own language and have a dutch minister – There are Still many remains of the war[121] to be Seen in and about the place part of the wooden wall remains a fort but not in repaire a large barracks [and] hospital which are Still very yousefull

---

[117] Letter addressed to Andrew Simm, "Weaver in Paisley N-Britain Postpaid to London pr. packet."

[118] This letter is missing.

[119] Mr. [Charles] Rollin, *The Ancient History of the Egyptians, Carthaginians, Assyrians, Babylonians, Medes and Persians, Macedonians and Grecians . . .* , translated from the French, 10 vols. (London, 1734–1736). See vol. 1, pp. 13–21.

[120] See p. 93, n. 13, this volume.

[121] The French and Indian War (1755–1763).

for Straingers to lodge in – There are 5 Churches in it 1 of the church of
england 2 Germon and 1 of the low dutch also a presbyterian but at present
without a minister – The School here is pretty large there are two masters
belonging to it one for the english and one for the latin – In the english we
teach Navigation Surveying Book-keeping and Algebra besidest reading
writing and Arithmetick – I teach in the Grammar School latin Greek french
and Geography I am also provided with an air pump two [Globes?] and
intend in Some Short time to Attempt to make an Orrery – I receive £200
from which I pay £80 to the english teacher – I have Spent much time Since
I came to Albany in learning these Subjects which are taught in the english
School with which I was not Sufficiently aquainted before – But my greatest
labour hath ben [since] I came to Albany in learning the dutch I informed
you before that the dutch is the Common language in this place and that
there was no minister in the presbetyrien church it was necessary then that
I must learn dutch or be deprived of public ordinances altogether – I therefor
applied to it with diligence and Care and am now able to understand their
books and Sermons pretty will and go Constantly to the dutch Church and
Speak it often with my wife in the faimily – There is a great agreement
betwixt the old dutch and the old Scotch which not only makes it more easy
to learn but also enables me to undersand many old Scotch words mutch
better then I could do before Such as the word dale hutt the 1th Signifies a
plain Cuntry the Second the place where the Generals tent Stands in an
encampment – My wife is in good health at present She Sendeth her kindest
Complements to her Brother and particularly to her Sister in law and returns
her the mors obleging thanks for the prests Sent over desireth very much to
See her in America and wisheth her all Happiness – It hath pleased the
divine providence not yet to bless us with any Childring tho there is Some
probability of it – I find my Self very agreeab[ly] Situated in the married life and enjoy all the Comfort and happiness which that relation Can
afford –

I am very Sensible My Brother how much both of esteem and otherwise
I am owing to you I hope Soon especially if you Come to America to have
a proper oportunity to repay both but of this more hereafter

I was not a little pleased [that] [   ] [to be] So many with whom I was
forma[rly] aquainted comming over to America especially that they have
Setteled at no further distance then 24 miles more to the west which place
they have namd New Paisley – John Burns was here a few days ago and Sais
that they are all in good health they love the place and he hopes that they
will do pretty well – I intend as soon as it is Convenient to go to See them

[and?] Since I may never See the old to wish them good Success in Laying the founda[tion] of New Paisley – I have also Seen Thomas Stark one ha-mal[ton] and Stievens who are Sett'led about 40 miles to the north of this place in a part called New pearth[122] and one McClean with his wife are about 50 miles

I dwell in an upper room tho I possess also the lower part which Serves as a kitching and bed-room for this with a Small garden I pay £6 of rent in N-york I paid £10 for one much the Same – My family Consists of myself and my wife the teacher of the english School a dog named paisley and a Cat named derry – My Chief recreations are either fishing or Shooting in the formar of which I am Some times pretty Sucessfull a few nights ago in the evening I took [   ] good in about the Space of 2 houer John Burns was in my house that nig[ht] and told me that there is good fishing and fowling at New paislay – The air of this place is very healthy tho pretty Cold in the winter – There is a public Library in the town I read the news but can get neither the english nor Scotch Magazines

I am Sorry that our obsavations on the Sun have not Succeeded So well as might have ben expected those 4 [which] you Sent taken in the month of Aprile when Compared with the 4 taken by me on the Same days Seem all to differ but without a Sufficient number of obsarvations no Certain rule Can be determined – I would be glad to make another trial – The Subject deserves it

I am well informed by the news as well as by privat information of the low State of trade in paisley and how much the Spirit of transportation to America prevails I observe also in your own letters Some hints that possibly yourself may be under a nesscessity of providing for your Self and family in America as well as othethers and therefor it may be reasonably expected that I who have ben So long in America may be able to give you Some proper information with respect to Such an important undertaking which I Shall endeavour to do in the following directions but 1th let me observe that I will Suppose that your desire is not to improve land but that you intend Still to continue at your employment to which I also would advise you lete me Suppose also that your are Skilled in working any kind of cuntry work Such as table Cloaths hand Cloathes and the like and Can bring £50 with you ashoare I would advise you

---

[122] For New Perth, see James Whitelaw to William Whitelaw, July 15, 1773, p. 94, n. 17, this volume.

1st endeavour to aquire Some Small Skill in Dying especially what they Call the Cold fat this will be of Considerable advantage

2ly bring with you 2 looms which for Convenincy may be taken to pices reeds from an 400th to a 900th with a quantity of twine Suitable to the reeds

3ly it will be best to Sail as soon in the Spring as Can be conveniently dun in a Ship bound for New-york the fewer the passengers are is So much the better

4ly when arrived at New-york hire a room for your own family and be careful that too many do not lodge together in the Same room this will prevent Sickness

5ly I would then advise you to leave your faimily there and go over to long island which is no more from york then the distance of 1 mile and endeavour to find a house there with 1 or 2 acres of land within 10 or 15 miles of N-york this is the most pleasant and healthfull place of all this part of Ameria and as it is well inhabit[e]d it will be the more Convenient for your employment – After you have Set in order your house and planted your land it will then be proper to publish in the News the different kinds of work you are Skilled in and I make no doubt but that in a Short time you will have a Sufficientcy of employment – If you find it reasoable to leave Scotland and that you Cannot Support your family in [   ] maner I think it very probable that by observing my Advice you will Succeed as well as can reasonably be expected and [tho?] not at first yet afterwords I hope you will approve of your Conduct in Comming to America – Let me also advise my Sister in law that if She finds it reasable to Come over to America not to fear too much the difficulties that are in the way these appear greater at a distance then they [   ] reality and that her Small family Can more eas'ly be provided for when [   ] America when young and Can more easyly proveid for themselves when groun [   ] in Scotland – If you intend [to] Settle at N-paisley you may expect to be [   ] [. . . ly] received by me at Albany and if to long island I will See you as soon as [   ] as possible – I wish you would write with the post to let me know your desing

I think it very improper for families to indent but approve of parents [inde]nting their Childring if they are below 20 years of age[123] – [   ][124]

---

[123] In the three years before the Revolution, about 104 heads of family households indented (17.6% of all heads of households in this pre-Revolutionary migration). About half of these were heads of families that contained children. Almost 54% were Scottish, and the rest were English. See Bailyn, *Voyagers to the West*, 184–185.

[124] Whole line illegible but has to do with people Simm knows in Paisley.

and T. Tanahill and inform them that I received their letters and hop that this will in part Serve as an answer till I have Some further oportunity and that I will be very glad to See them at Albany if they Com to Continue at their employmens I recomend long islang or the Jerseys if to improve land I know of no place better the N-paisley or N-pearth – in the first of which there is a presbyterian and in the Second a Seceding minister – please to remember my Complements to Baily Willison Mr Ellies my Stepmother and John Barr inform them that I am well and wish them all happiness –

And nou my Dr Brother I earnestly recomend you the of him who is made unto us wisdom and prudence as well as Compleat Redemption

Hugh Simm –

Hugh Simm to Andrew Simm, Newtown, New York, October 2, 1778[125]

Newtown on Long Island October the 2d *1778*

Dear Brother

In my former Letter to you dated from New York in January 1778 I there informed you of my arrival at that place, and that I was well, but ommited to Say any thing of my Situation at that time or how I have escaped the Danger with which I have ben often threatened I hope it will therefor be proper to informe you of the following particular Circumstances beginning from Albany.

The unhappy situation of the Friends of Government in the midst of the Subversion of Civil and Religous order is too difficult for me to describe. Every Word and action of theirs was [   ] well known [   ] and misinformation was approved, and often [conjectures?] substituted in the place of [certainties?] find Some [pretense] or other for seizing their Persons, or plundering their Houses, and destroying their Property Except the Fear of [exp . . .] what [State we are?] daily Suffering, I received no material injury from the Committee [   ] time when General Carlton[126] Came first over the Lake Champlain to reconoiter the Situation of Ticonderoga for refusing

---

[125] Letter addressed to Andrew Simm, "Weaver in Paisley North Britian." Andrew Simm received the letter "at paisley June 5 1779."

[126] General Sir Guy Carleton was a British general and served as governor of Canada. In 1776 he failed in his attempt to push down from Canada to Lake Champlain where he was supposed to meet Howe's force coming up the Hudson River.

to go with the Militia at that time I was fined in ten Pounds, and for not going against General Burgoyne[127] I was fined in thirty Pounds.

My Wife was far advanced in her Pregnancy at the time when General Burgoyne was approaching neare to Albany, and at the time of the Battl[128] She was in Childbed The Noise of the Cannon her Fear for her presant Situation but especially information [   ] was Sent her from one of the Committe men (with Desire to distress her) that tomorrow I would be put in Prison gave Such an impulse to the Sorrows of her presen Condition, as not only exposed her own Life to the greatest Danger, but Seemed to occasion the Death of our little Son and to add to our Grief out first-born. After Burgoyne's fatal Defeat at Saratoga the Inhabitants flying from the City, my School was broken up, and in a Short time finding a happy oportunity, I Came to N. york on the fourteenth of December 1777 with my Wife and all my Furniture

I found this City in a Condition very different from that in which I had left it a few years ago. It was then full of inhabitants abounding with Plenty and Wealth. But now it was Lying in Ruings, the Inhabitants poor and despireted. my Condition in this place for the Space of Six months was extremely distressing. House Rents were dear, Provisions exorbitant, nor was it in my Power for a long time to find any Employment. Often in that time have I Seen the last Stick on the fire and the last handful of meal baked: even Water began to fail, for that Comodity is also Sold here for money. And nothing was more probable then that we would both perish in a Short time for want. At last when all human Help Seemed to fail and total Ruin unavoidable, the Angel Who had fed me all my Life long to this Day pointed out a new and very unexpected Source of Support Which was this.

In the Beginning of this year a new Regiment was to be raised in N. york and the Command of it was given to one Collonel Ritzina[129] with whom I

---

[127] In 1777 General John Burgoyne led an army of 8000 British troops south from Canada to recapture Fort Ticonderoga, which fell to the British in July, forcing the retreat of the American forces.

[128] After his victory at Ticonderoga, Burgoyne continued to push south toward Albany and met the American army under General Horatio Gates at Bemis Heights. The ensuing battle, which began what was called the Battle of Saratoga, ended in a draw, but the British suffered heavy losses, which they could not replace. On October 7, Gates's army, more than twice the size of Burgoyne's, attacked the British and, by the end of the day, had pushed the British army back to the heights around Saratoga, where Burgoyne surrendered.

[129] Rudolf Ritzema was an American, educated at Kings College (later Columbia University) in New York City. He entered the war as a lieutenant colonel in the Continental army, and was later promoted to colonel and given the command of the 1st New York Regiment.

had Some Small aquiantance. He offered me a Commission to be Quartermaster of his Regiment which I accepted of: And Since the 14th of May I have been employed in that Service, which I love better then I expected.

My Wife is this day in Child-bed and I [fear in great?] Extremity My [   ] Shall if possible be dated from tomorrow, and in the mean time recomen [   ] the grace of God, I Shall Close this Letter with the presant State of New-York

The town Contains of Houses......... 2400
Burnt and in Ruins......................800
Number of inhabitants 10000
Number of Such as remained after the Taking of the City
only 1000
Ships in the Harbour....................500
Ships of war 16
Troops 25000

I remain your affectionate Brother at presant in good Health and Cheerfull [   ] temper

Hugh Simm

Hugh Simm to Andrew Simm, Newtown, New York, October 4, 1778[130]

New-town on Long island October the 4, *1778*

Dear Brother

In my Leter yesterday I informed you that my Wife was in Child-bed, and in a dangerous Situation I promised if possible to write again this Day, Hopin to give to you and my Sister in Law the Joyfull information that my Wife had again repaired our former Loss and Supplied us with another Son: but I must refrain from my transports and mingle tears with my relation whilst I inform you, that my Wife was indeed brought to Bed yesterday of

---

In November 1776 he turned coat and joined the British army. In 1778 he formed the Loyal American Regiment and asked Simm to be quartermaster. Hugh Simm to Andrew Simm, March 22, 1779, Simm Papers.

[130] Letter addressed to Andrew Simm, "Weaver in town Head of Paisley North Baitiain."

a Son, but that He also like his brother died at the time of Birth and that His Mother Scarcely escaped with her Life.

My Wife desires me Just now to inform her Sister in Law to the following Purpose. I am now much better then yesterday, and I hope, in a fair way of Recovery. And as I hope that you will lament with me that I have brought forth another Son for the Grave, So I also rejoice with you in being the Mother of So large a family, but must observe, that, tho this may be Supposed to be a great Blessing in Scotland, it would not be So here in America. The Calamities of War and public Distresses are at presant So great that we Women may truely Say blessed is the Womb that beareth not and the Papes which give no Suck.

I am now Sitting in my Room alon and no body presant with me but my dead Son one the one hand and my Sick Wife on the other and am about to Lay him in the Coffing and to Carry him to the Woods to burry him there for there is no Ground for that Purpose in this Place.

I have now returned from burying my little Son in the Faith of that Promise, that not onlly the Seas but also the Woods Shall give up the dead that are in them. I remember our Father used often to observe on Such Occasions that the grave was God's Coffer where He would Safely heap all his jewels till that Day. Till that Day when the Redeemer Shall be gloryfied in his Saints and admired in all them that Belive: then Shall these little jewels appear like polished jems in his Crown and in Some manner different from aged Persons illustrate the Wonder of redeeming Grace.[131]

Your Brother Hugh Simm

---

[131] The following year the Simms had a daughter whom they named Mary, "a fine healthy Child." Hugh Simm to Andrew Simm, October 29, 1780, Simm Papers.

CHESAPEAKE

John Campbell to William Sinclair, Bladensburg, Prince George's County, Maryland, July 26, 1772[1]

JOHN Campbell came to America as a storekeeper for the Glasgow merchant firm of Findlay, Hopkirks and Co. As such, he was not a typical emigrant; he did not have to find employment or a place to live when he arrived, and he probably planned to return to Scotland some day. However, he is typical of the kind of young man, many of them younger sons of gentry, who went to the Chesapeake as free emigrants in search of their fortunes. Glasgow tobacco firms set up stores in the Chesapeake and staffed them with storekeepers (factors), assistant storekeepers, apprentices, and other personnel. Factors like Campbell, who supervised the colonial operation, were crucial to their firm's business interests, and were therefore carefully chosen, generally from well-known families or families that were related to business associates. Campbell, for instance, was probably recommended to Findlay, Hopkirks and Co. through one or more of his Oswald relations, who were prominent merchants in Glasgow. In order to encourage loyalty, honesty, and trustworthiness, the partners often gave

---

[1] *Source:* Sinclair of Freswick Muniments, GD 136/416/1, Scottish Record Office, Edinburgh. *Courtesy:* The Rt. Hon. Viscount Thurso of Ulbster, J.P. The letter appears to be a recipient copy. Campbell's cousin, whom he addressed as "Dear Will," was probably William Sinclair of Lochend (1748–1838), who got his M.D. and later practiced in Thurso, Caithness, before inheriting the estate of Freswick, near Wick, Caithness. During the early 1770s, when he corresponds with Campbell, he was a student at the University of Edinburgh. Roland William Saint-Clair, *The Saint-Clairs of the Isles* (Auckland, New Zealand, 1898), 231–233; John Henderson, *Caithness Family History* (Edinburgh, 1884), 57.

company shares to their factors. Campbell received 4 shares out of a total of 42.[2]

As loyal representatives of their Scottish companies, storekeepers remained faithful to Britain when the Revolutionary war broke out, and perhaps for this reason Campbell wrote that Scottish factors were regarded as enemies to America. His business duties kept him in America longer than he would have liked. He was harassed and persecuted by the patriots, and only after "the utmost difficulty" got permission to return to Scotland on a ship bound for Lisbon in the summer of 1776.[3]

Campbell wrote this letter to his cousin William Sinclair, a medical student in Edinburgh.[4] The first part of the letter concerns a private legal matter in which his cousin was involved. It has no relevance to Campbell's experience in America, but it reveals that Sinclair was unhappy in Scotland and had evidently asked Campbell about opportunities in America, to which Campbell wrote an encouraging reply about the practice of Physic. These early pages also establish that Sinclair was a close and trusted confidant, and therefore someone to whom Campbell would be open and honest about other matters, like his views on emigration to America, which fill the last half of the letter.

Dr. Will   Maryld. Bladensburgh, July 26, 1772

I only received yours of the 28th. December past, yesterday by a Vessell just arrived from Glasgow, & take this early opportunity of assuring you my long silence has not been so much my fault, as you might naturally imagine, & can fully acquit myself, of your charge of forgetfulness, when I solemnly aver that since my writing you from [Boardeaux?], I have not heard a Syllabble, of or from you, untill my brother came in, whose Information was but little, & since that time it has been [a] matter of doubt with me, whether you were in the frozen Regions of the North, or in the burning climes of

[2] T. M. Devine, *The Tobacco Lords* (Edinburgh, 1975), 77, 188.

[3] Devine, *Tobacco Lords*, 84; John Campbell to William Sinclair, August 28, 1776, Sinclair of Freswick Muniments, GD 136/416/4.

[4] Campbell wrote three other letters to Sinclair: January 11, 1774, October 16, 1775, and August 28, 1776. These letters consist almost entirely of political matters regarding the conflict between America and Britain. Sinclair of Freswick Muniments, GD 136/416/2–4.

the East – I cannot account for the miscarriage of your Letters, as I am pretty confident, if they got to Glasgow, directed to the care of Mr. Oswald,[5] it would be next to an impossibility their not getting safe to hand – but this is a mystery wrote in the great Book, of Fate, & not to be resolved by us purblind [ ] – My brother has not disapointed me, in [ ] [. . . tions] of him, & it gives me a very pleasing and [innate satisfaction?], to observe in him the dawn of abilities which will, in a future day, make him conspicous in his Station of Life, & compleat the warmest wishes of all his real friends – In his disposition he has not that pliability I could wish, but doubt not that, time, acquaintance with the world, & my constant endeavour, will have their wished for effect of curing him of his present too great opiniatreté – I have not had a Scrape of a pen from Oswald,[6] since I saw him in Glasgow – By what Judgement I then formed of him do not think he is deficient in natural affection, tho rather phlegmatic, & his Silence to us both, impute more to a remiss careless habit, we are too liable to contract & wh[i]ch often gains such an asscendancy, as to render it impossible to call home our scattered & volatile Ideas, even for so long a time as to pen a Letter – I have just recd a Letter from my mother, acquainting of his being in the army, but in what Station, regiment, or quarter of the Globe, am quite ignorant – Your old friend John Bowie,[7] am well acquainted with as also his lady – they are a very amiable couple & seem to enjoy the matrimonial Sweets in high perfection – he was some time parson of our parish, but those good qualities you observe his being possessed of soon gained him such a reputation, that a vacancy happening on our Eastern Shore by the [Inter . . .] Governor he got the berth, which is of much more [ ], than what he formerly enjoyed – I have seen him since & he informs me, both himself & Mrs. Bowie, are well satisfied with the Change – all his relations live in this Neighbourhood Shall soon see him, & remember you to him – What I

---

5 Probably George Oswald, a merchant in Glasgow. I would like to thank David Hancock for sorting out the various Oswalds in this letter.

6 Probably Oswald Campbell, first cousin of William Sinclair, Jr., John Campbell's correspondent.

7 The Rev. John Bowie (1746–1801), son of John Bowie, Jr., and Elizabeth Pottinger, was born in Prince George's County, Maryland. He went to Scotland in 1765 to study at the University of Edinburgh and at King's College, Aberdeen, and it was probably in Edinburgh where he met William Sinclair. He married Margaret Dallas, daughter of the chief of the Dallas clan and Laird of Cantray, and after his ordination in July 1771, they sailed to Maryland, where he received a curacy in Prince George's County. About a year later Governor Eden appointed him to St. Martin's Church in Worcester County on the Eastern Shore. Effie Gwynn Bowie, *Across the Years in Prince George's County* (Baltimore, 1975), 668–671.

mean by the Eastern Shore, is that part of our province lying in the E side, of Chesapeak Bay –

Your Strictures on the Cathuisians,[8] are very severe tho I dare say just – [   ] being capable of reflection have been of opinion, that the principles of true Justice & equity, were rarely to be found amongst our Countrymen & that all liberal & noble passions of the Soul were generally absorbed in the fiend like attribute of Pride – I have often observed that good actions, sometimes take their spring from evil principles, which made me think that even this last amiable quality, would have spurred them on to pay their debts, to save them from the Ignominy, generally attending a Law suit, but when the Soul is once in a manner [   ] hardened against all that's good and generous, it never feels the Stings of Shame or Remorse – Your Situation I heartily pity, whilst amongst a Set of beings, you so cordially despise & think [yo . . .] [   ] fall upon the most speedy method of getting [yo . . .]] [   ] settled, so that you may with convenience [carry?] yourself to some more propitious Shore – it is amazing to me you did not sooner discover the true principles of those you had to do with, but it pleases me you have at length drawn aside the veil, & that there is a probability of seeing one another in this Western Hemisphere – Your younger Sister Jeanie I heartily sympathize with – She will be the only & chief Sufferer, by your leaving the Country – a Country! where the most perfect Innocence is not free from the rancorous tongue of Envy and Detraction – but let us trust that the great Disposer of all events, who hath been pleased to deprive her of her best friends, will himself supply their place, & guide her steps, whilst on the Stage of Life – You desire my Sentiments on the practice of Physic in this part of the world – You shall have it, & that of those I have conversed wt on the Subject – there is not any business followed on this Continent, which in the end would prove more advantageous, than the practice of Physic & Surgery,[9] but you must take this along with you that like all other Employmts, it must be attended with the utmost, care diligence & attention – A regular Education is necessary so as to be master of the Theoretical [   ] this you are already possessed off – In this pro[vince &?] the Neighbouring Colony of Virginia, it will amaze you how few of those who pretend to the practice of Physic, and are dignified, with the name of Doctor deserve the appellation – mere Smatterers, who found their Skill wholly, on spending about 2 years in the Philadelphia or Jersey College, where perhaps they may

[8] The Carthusian Roman Catholic religious order was founded in 1084 by Saint Bruno.
[9] See David Duff to James Grant, January 5, 1774, this volume, for other remarks on the study of medicine in America.

learnt enough of cramp technical terms, to give the ignorant a great opinion
of their Knowl[e]dge, & themselves the power of making out an unintelli-
gible & enormous high charged Bill – Of such as I have now described
consist by far the greatest part of our Sons of Asculapius[10] which when you
read, the credulity of the people entrusting their lives in their hands, will
naturally strike you but such is the case – You must at once see the advantage, one who has enjoyed a liberal Education must have over this class,
especially when attended with abilities attention, & an engaging, insinuating
behavior – It is both true & certain that this business here, as well as elsewhere, is somewhat precarious – a great [Run?] of practice and a celebrated
Character, often I believe depends on some lucky [hits?], at the first outset,
more than on real [   ] – The W Indies, have understood to be a [   ]
favorable clime, to your profession, tho in [   ] your own health and Constitution you run a greater Risk – I have it not in my power to point out to
you at present, any particular place, in this or the neighbouring provinces,
as most proper for pitching your Camp in, provided you crossed the Atlantick, but shall make enquiry, & I cant say should be sorry to see here, before
any advice by Letter could reach & of giving you what Information I may
glean on this matter in *propria persona* – for DW,[11] I cordially wish you out
of that nook of Terra Firma, you at present reside in, where the prince of
Darkness, hath sown such deadly feuds & animosities, between the landed
Gentln. that it is impossible, for a man of Candor, openness & warmth of
temper, to live amongst them, without often bringing himself into disagreeable Scraps – Such unrest that be at present subsisting between you &
Wester – Youll always be the Sufferer, in hav[in]g any disputes with men
of their tune – dead to every noble & worthy Sentiment, they are wholly
swayed by the dictates of Revenge & party, to gratify which there are no
obstacles, however mean, but what will be overleaped, what chance does a
man of a bold intrepid mind, who dares to speak the true Sentiments of
[   ] [& hold?] in abhorrence, every thing base and [   ], stand with
men of such a Stamp – however conscious he may be in his own mind, of
the rectitude of his proceeding yet often the opposite party, have [   ]
enough, to prejudice the world in their behalf, which for the most part, is
too dim sighted, to examine clearly the merits or demerit of any action, &
certainly tho the applause of the multitude is not to be sought after, or even
regarded when in competition with what is great and honourable, yet in our
conduct in this world, regard as far as possible shd be had, to the public

[10] In Greek mythology, Asclepius was the god of healing.
[11] Dear Will.

opinion – I am not yet so hackneyed in the ways of the world, as to be able to disguise my real Sentiments on any matter, & when I write a friend, will do it with freedom, must therefore confess that I even have some doubts, that you have yourself been hurried in some measure into this quarrell, by party & passion, both which are unworthy to be owned as the motives of our actions – I again repeat my former wish of your being out, of your present place abode; it appears to me impossible for the most disinterested cool and dispassionate, to conduct themselves in ye [Country so?] as not to draw upon themselves, the envy & [   ] one party or another – & do think it, as [   ] as the strongest mathematical proof that you never can exist there to your thorough Satisfaction The cordial and inveterate hatred of one party against another is now too deeply rooted, ever to be eradicated, & if it seems to be a point, to hand down to their Posterity, along with their parchment Scrolls, all their little [   ] private quarrells – Think seriously of this matter, – I hope before receipt of this, you have got clear of the present troublesome affair – As to the Decision, I am prepared to hear the worst, & knowing whom you have to deal with am well convinced, that as far as the utmost stretch of rigid Laws will allow, your punishment will be Severe – What sweet enjoyment would it give them, if they cd. only bring about their wished for point, of expulsion, but from your state of the matter, do not fear such a Conclusion & can only supposed your being [immerced?] in some pecuniary [mulch?] – If B. [S.?] of C—der, has acted the part suspected in yours, he deserves to be stigmatized with eternal infamy, dispised by all men of Spirit, & held up to the world as a poltroon, but hope & earnestly it may not have been so – however desire, youll favr. me on Rect. of this, (if not before done) with a full and circumstantial account of [   ] proceeding – You desire m[y sen]timents on Emigration to the Colonies – it is a subject I have not seriously thought off, but any rate I look upon this Province, to be an improper place, for those I suppose you mean to come out to – I imagine by Emigrants you mean people possessed of some property at home, but rather discontented with their Situation, who would wish to convert what little they have into some of the fruitful acres of the West – this they will not find it so easy to do at this time – what part of this province lying contiguous to trade & Navigation, being already well peopled, & consequently the value of Lands, pretty high – & as for the back unsettld Country, those who have already gone out, are now driving in again as fast as possible from the dread they are under of the Indians – who it is said have come to an open declaration of war – these poor Savages, have been hardly dealt with, by us – not content, with dispossessing of their most valuable property which they held by the great Laws of nature, this

present disturbance, has arisen from the avariciousness of some of our back
Settlers, who looked with a greedy eye on some of the fine Lands, on the
W. Side Ohio, (the [   ] by the articles of last peace) its being on a wicked
[   ] and deliberately murdered some of these poor Wretches; who were
thus obliged to take up arms in self defence; & I make no doubt of there
being a great deal of bloodshed, before matters are accomodated – It is true,
they were too much reduced last Campaign, to be able to make a long
resistance, yet it is my opinion, this War, will be of longer duration than is
generally imagined; & that when they consider the insatiableness of our
desires, with the little regard paid to treaties, & see that they have no [oyr?]
resource left, but totally relinquishing their possessions or taking up the
hatchet – preferring the last, they will sollicit, the assistance of many nations
hitherto unheard of, who no doubt will readily join the good Cause of re-
pelling a common foe – Their method of fighting will likewise serve to
prolong, for they never if possible come to a pitched & open engagement,
but go about in small party's skulk[in]g in the woods, watching [thr.?] opportunity of falling upon the Enemy at unawares; & their great act of War
is to cut off, as many of their enemies as possible, with[ou]t endangering
the Loss of their own men – but our back Settlers must in the end prevail,
as they are now well acquainted with Bush fighting, and excellent marksmen
this is a long digression, but Humanity [&?] Mankind in general led me
into it – to return to [   ] Subject of Emigration – it is beyond a doubt,
but that this Continent for the fertility of its soil, & cheapness of Land
when put in competition with your barren Acres of the [   ], is greatly to
be preferred, as it will always, render unto the Industrious and careful, a
suitable return of their labour, but it is not to be imagined, the general curse
upon mankind, does not prevail here, of reaping the fruits of the Earth, by
the Sweat of their Brow tho it may in a less degree, than in many other
parts – a man of a slender fortune can live here much more easy and to his
Satisfaction, than he can in Britain – there are no sett of people in the world
who I think might live more at their ease and independent, provided they
were only, frugal & industrious; but in general there is such a turn for levity
& dissipation, prevails (always remarked in warm Climes) that prevents them
enjoying the benefits & advantages, conferred on them by nature – What I
chiefly speak of are the Tobo. Colonies with whom am best acquainted –
to give you a more clear and explicit idea of their method of life [I] shall
just state you a Case – A man, his wife and their Children able to assist
him in labour, rents from 150 to 200 acres land, 50 of which may be cleared
& fit for Culture; for this he may pay an annuall rent, of 1000 wt. tob[acc]o,
equal on an average to abt £10 Currency – from 2. to 3000 wt. tob[acc]o a

hand is often made on good Lands, but not to exaggerate in any degree, we shall suppose him, to make 5000 wt. (exclusive of rent); besides raising Corn, maize, Wheat, & other grains sufficient to support his family in great plenty & even to dispose off – his tobo. brings him £50. Curcy. & oftener more than under, if he is a good Aconomist he will raise many family Necessaries within himself but we shall suppose, he lays out for british Manufactures £20 – the bala. £30 he annually lays up to be converted into Land or Negroes, when opportunity offers, & as it may best suit him—as for the necessaries of Life – he has them in abundance – Bacon, (the Staff of Life in this Country) Beef, & Poultry, he can raise almost without any expence – the Hogs running loose through the woods almost the whole year supporting themselves on Acorns & the [   ] of the trees – all manner of Vegetables, are likewise produced with very little trouble – This is a happy Country, to those who can make use of its advantage, but as I before observed, the natives in general are too lazy & indolent, & consequently for the most part are greatly indebted to british Merchts – I have often remarked that our Countrymen do well – Many who left their Country in the year 1715[12] being now in a very thriving and prosperous way – As to that Species of Emigration, when many poor Tenants, whose rents are screwed up by their hardhearted & avaritious Landlords, to such a pitch, that they can scarce hardly exist, chuse rather to transport themselves, in hopes of a better fortune and a more propitious Clime, even at the Expence of 4 or five years servitude[13] – for this all those who cannot pay their passages must submit to, if they are only urged thereto, in behalf of their posterity, they certainly act for the best – but as to themselves, especially when in advanced years, the change of Climate, hardships they often undergo, during their Servitude, under tyrannical masters, with the pressure upon their minds on being rank'd & deemed as Slaves, are such, that they seldom surmount – As to the younger Class, it is otherwise, for they become more easily habituated to the Clime, are better able to undergo, any hardships, & their Servitude for a few years, is in my opinion of service to them & may be looked on only as an aprenticeship, in which they become acquainted with the manners, Customs of the Country,

[12] The rebellion of 1715 was one of two Jacobite uprisings; the other was in 1745. The center of Scottish sympathy for the Stuarts was in the Highlands, where resistance was the strongest. After their defeat, some of the Jacobite prisoners were shipped to the British colonies. William R. Brock and Helen C. Brock, *Scotus Americanus* (Edinburgh, 1982), 14, 68.

[13] Campbell is referring to indentured servitude, the practice of selling one's labor for four to seven years in exchange for transportation to the colonies, room, board, and clothing, and in some cases a small salary.

Culture of its different produce, & by ye means, on its Expiration, are more able to do for themselves I have of late seen many families of highlanders, chiefly from Sutherland & even some from Caithness – they in general are much disapointed in their expectations, not having had a clear idea of what their Situation would be on their first arrival here, & also owing to wrong representations, as is often the Case, from distant Countries – I have thus in a hurry, thrown together, with[ou]t much Connection what occurs to me on this Subject – Shall conclude with citing the value of Commoditys & Labr &c – Land contiguous to Navigation, or even on the heads of rivers so as to have a Water Carriage for the produce, generally if of a good quality, sells from 40/.Stg to £3. an acre – there are lands, 80 or 90 miles, back from this place, for which £3 Stg has been refused; but of an extraordinary soil – The unsettled tracts on the Ohio, & down the great Kanhawa, sell as yet low, tho very rich – Warrants to Officers, agreeable to the Kings Proclamation,[14] & that of the Colony of Virginia, for their Service in last War, may be purchased very cheap – 2000 Acres, for £200, to £300, & in Currency – Many are now speculating, in buying these Lands, & for a man well stocked with Cash, & wishes to provide for his posterity, think the Speculation well grounded, & that it will fully answer his most sanguine expectations for these Lands, of a certainty, will in a future day be very valuable, tho not probably in your days or mine – in Virginia, this Article is upon the whole cheaper, than in this Province – Labour is high from 2/6. to 3./ P day for common labourers – Tradesmen have generally from 5./ to 6./ P dim; & when work is done by the piece, it is proportionably high – The most necessary, are Weavers, Taylors, House Carpenters or Joiners Blacksmiths, Shoemakers, Spinsters of flax & Wool, in short every branch of Manufactures, (considering the present disputes, betwixt the mother Country & her Colonies) that will have the most speedy effect of rendering them independent, will meet with good encouragement – healthy stout fellows, used to country work, particularly, ploughing, thrashing mowing, reaping, ditching &c. would do very well few in this Country, being expert at these employments – do not think, Seasons are much to be regarded, the Autumn, is the worst being most sickly – Wheat is the principal Grain raised here, which

---

[14] The Proclamation of 1763 set up a boundary line in order to keep the European settlers from migrating beyond the Appalachian Mountains and to reserve lands west of this line for the Indians. The proclamation also rewarded soldiers and officers who had fought in the French and Indian War with land grants in varying amounts from 50 to 5000 acres according to rank. For the text of the proclamation, see Merrill Jensen, ed., *American Colonial Documents to 1776* (London, 1955), 640–643.

generally sells from 5/. to 6/. P the Winchester Bushell, great quantities of which are annually exported to Spain & Portugal or when manufactured into flour, to the W Indies, who for their support, principally depend on this Continent Indian Corn, is likewise much cultivated & principally used by the lower Class as bread, being very wholesome & much fitter than any other grain, for Labourers – there is likewise of this a very large annual Exportation All the oyr. various species of grain, are raised here tho not in any quantity, the soil & Climate being peculiarly adapted, to the Culture of the two first mentioned & tob[acc]o of which have noted the average value before – I have wrote so much that I must draw to a Conclusion, & from the length of the epistle, [   ] there being a deal of Stuff, in it, however like the matrimonial State you must take it for better, for worse – for apologies to a friend are unnecessary, & too Ceremonious – Remember me to all those you may deem my true friends in which Commission think youll have but little trouble & with Compts. in which Rose joins me to ye sister Jeanie am truly D Will Yr afft Cousin & [hb Sert?]

John Campbell

Letters of David Duff, Maryland, 1772, 1774, and 1780[15]

COLONIAL education was often badly understaffed, and as a result, schoolteachers, unemployed clerics, and former university students could usually find teaching jobs in the colonies, if not in schools then as private tutors. David Duff was typical of the educated young man,[16] perhaps a younger son and therefore not likely to inherit property or position at home, who migrated to America in search of a career. He had originally hoped for a preferment to a Maryland parish, but was disappointed, even though he found other employment

---

[15] *Source*: Seafield Muniments, EXGD 248/349/3, GD 245/228/1/94, Scottish Record Office, Edinburgh. *Courtesy*: Lord Seafield. The letters were addressed to James Grant of Grant Esqr. at Castle Grant, N. Britain, and they are recipient copies.

[16] This may be the David Duff from the county of Moray, who matriculated at the University in Aberdeen from 1766–1770, and received a Masters of Arts. Peter John Anderson, ed., *Roll of Alumni in Arts of the University and King's College of Aberdeen, 1596–1860* (Aberdeen, 1900), 86.

almost immediately, and after only two years moved on to a better job teaching at the Eden School in Somerset County.

Prior to the Revolution, education in Maryland suffered in comparison to that in some of the other colonies, and certainly to that in England. Maryland had no college, and only one school with an adequate endowment, King William's School. Schoolteachers were often selected from newly arrived indentured servants and convicts. As Jonathan Boucher expressed in 1773: "at least two thirds of the little education we receive are derived from instructors, who are either INDENTED SERVANTS, or TRANSPORTED FELONS. Not a ship arrives either with redemptioners or convicts, in which schoolmasters are not as regularly advertised for sale, as weavers, tailors, or any other trade." Duff fell into the other third – "aliens, and in very few instances members of the Established Church."[17]

Part of the reason for the lack of proper education was that salaries for masters did not provide "sufficient encouragement." For this reason, the Somerset and Worcester counties' schools consolidated their funds in 1770 in order to set up a boarding school to be run by a Board of Visitors selected from each county and to be financed in part by private subscriptions. This school, called the Eden School after the governor of Maryland, Robert Eden, was located at the headwaters of Wicomico Creek, about five miles from Princess Anne. It was here that Duff finally settled as master of local children. This small school was not, however, the only boarding school in the area. About five miles away was the School at Back Creek, or Somerset Academy (later incorporated as Washington Academy), which was founded by Presbyterians in 1767. By the time Duff had taken his position at Eden School, the Back Creek School had an enrollment of 70 scholars who came from all over Maryland and Virginia. Their masters were three prominent Princetonians: Luther Martin, Hugh Henry Brackenridge, and Philip Freneau.[18]

17 Bernard C. Steiner, *History of Education in Maryland* (Washington, D.C., 1894), 38. Jonathan Boucher, *A View of the Causes and Consequences of the American Revolution; in Thirteen Discourses . . .* (1797, reprint New York, 1967), 183–184, 189. And see also Edward Kimber's remarks, "Observations in Several Voyages and Travels in America," *William and Mary Quarterly*, 15(1907), 15–16 [157–158]. John Harrower was an indentured servant who was hired by Colonel William Daingerfield of Belvidera plantation near Fredericksburg, Virginia, to teach his children. For Harrower's account of his service to the Daingerfields, see *The Journal of John Harrower: An Indentured Servant in the Colony of Virginia, 1773–1776*, ed. Edward M. Riley (Williamsburg, VA, 1963).

18 Steiner, *History of Education in Maryland*, 37, 39n; Reginald V. Truitt and Millard G. Les

Duff stayed where he was at the Eden School, remaining its only master during the latter part of the Revolutionary War. When he wrote to his benefactor James Grant in 1780, he was a well-established schoolteacher and farmer. Although he had plans to move to South Carolina, he no longer felt the dissatisfaction and restlessness that characterized his first few years in America.

David Duff to James Grant of Grant, Talbot County, Maryland, 1772[19]

Dear Sir

From Castle Grant[20] I went for Aberdeen, but by means of bad weather, was detained there some time, at last I got a very favourable passage by water from Abdn. to Lieth, and went by land from that to Glasgow; when I came there I was informed there was only one ship to sail for Maryland for some time, which I [unfortunately?] missed by four hours; my only resource then [   ] passage in the first ship for Virginia, which [sailed?] [   ] of April, and in less than five weeks landed me at Norfolk, from whence I went by water to Port Tobacco,[21] where as soon as I arrived I was offered 30£ sterling P. annum, with bed, board and washing, which I rejected, being prepossessed by a Countryman of mine, with a notion of getting the free-school[22] in that place, which was then vacant, and which he made me believe

Callette, *Worcester County: Maryland's Arcadia* (Snow Hill, MD, 1977), 314–315; Paul Baker Touart, *Somerset: An Architectural History* (Annapolis, MD, 1990), 67, 36; Leo J. McCormick, *Church–State Relationships in Education in Maryland* (Washington, D.C., 1942), 84.

[19] Sir James Grant of Grant (1738–1811) married Jean Duff, the only daughter and heiress of Alexander Duff of Hattan and Lady Anne Duff. Therefore, David Duff was probably related to James Grant by marriage. Lewis Namier and John Brooke, *The House of Commons, 1754–1790* (London, 1964), II: 531–532. The letter was undated, but the docket on the address leaf gives the year as 1772.

[20] Castle Grant, near Grantown in Elginshire, was the main residence of James Grant after his marriage in 1763. Earl of Cassillis, *The Rulers of Strathspey: A History of the Lairds of Grant and Earls of Seafield* (Inverness, Scotland, 1911), 147.

[21] Port Tobacco, Maryland, was on the Potomac River.

[22] Free schools were funded by taxation and charitable contributions for the purpose of sub-sidizing the education of poor children. Those who could afford to do so, paid tuition. A

I would not have the least difficulty in procuring; but after waiting for it some time without any appearance of its being soon settled, I was advised to cross the bay[23] in quest of another School, but by being a few days too late, was disappointed there too. Immediately after I was sent by a Gentleman to a Parson to be examined, and upon his giving a favourable recommendation of me he allows me for the education of his children 16£ sterling with bed board and washing, and as many Scholars besides as I can get; I hope to clear by my place 40 or 50 £ ster. P. annum which is here reckoned very handsome. If you have any desire to see any of the curiosities of whatever kind which this part of America can produce, I shall do all that lies in my power to have them transported to you; I shall be exceedingly to have an opportunity of expressing my gratitude for the many and singular instances of the unmerited goodness and favour of my most generous and Benevolent Benefactor – I am with respect yours &c &c

David Duff

P.S. I intended to have wrote you something concerning this Country, but I shall not fail for the future to write you every thing that I think worth notice. I should be very glad to hear from you, if convenient.

Direct For Me to the care of James Lloyd Chamberlaine Talbot County Maryland.[24]

To be put on board any of Speirs and French's ships for Oxford which is within eight or ten miles of Mr. Chamberlaine's house where I live.

David Duff to James Grant of Grant, Somerset County, Maryland, Jan. 5, 1774

Sir

Last year I wrote you of my situation but have not had the pleasure to receive any answer. I am heartily sorry for neglecting so long to write you,

---

1723 Maryland law stipulated that each county set aside 100 acres for a free school. Truitt and Les Callette, *Worcester County*, 314.

[23] He crossed the Chesapeake Bay to the Eastern Shore of Maryland.

[24] James Lloyd Chamberlaine (1732–1783) was a wealthy merchant, politician, landowner (of c. 4000 acres), and local official. He and his wife, Henrietta Maria (Robins), had four children. Edward C. Papenfuse, *A Biographical Dictionary of the Maryland Legislature, 1635–1789* (Baltimore, 1979), 206–207.

but when I was about to do it, I was obliged to shift my station, and have removed to a public school, lately erected, built wholly of wood, and the front is 120 feet in length; the bulk of the scholars, as also the masters are boarded in the house.[25] I live much more comfortably, and can save more money, than in my former situation, which did not answer my most moderate expectations, but find myself greatly at a loss, what to pitch upon for the business of life. My ambition alone forced me to Maryland in secret hope sometime to obtain one of those lucrative parishes, but they are entirely at the Governor's disposal, and their value induces so many of the natives to make their sons clergymen, whom the Governor is obliged in duty to provide for,[26] in preference to strangers and foreigners that I cannot help thinking it vain to entertain any such notion, and the more so, as I cannot speak even nonsense fluently, and the people in this part of the country, in my opinion, prefer the pleasing the ear to the mending the heart. I have some thoughts of applying to the study of Physic, and should be anxious if possible to excel, but should be glad in the first place to hear your opinion concerning that matter.

The Physicians in this country never have more than about 7s.6d. sterling for each visit, and often not so much, but if they be well employed, and are industrious, they seldom fail of making money.

We have had here a very great noise about the payment of the Clergy's 40 P. poll, that is 40 lb of tobacco a year from every white man whether poor or rich, and the same for every negro he has whether male or female, above sixteen years of age, so that the clergy's income always increases in proportion to the number of taxibles. The laity denied that there was any such law, and exclaimed that it was iniquitous and unjust, the clergy affirmed that the law was in force; our papers were for a long time filled with little else than the disputes of the opposite parties, and how soon they are reprinted I shall send you a copy of them, it is however decided in favour of the people.[27] If you are desirous to peruse our Maryland body of laws I shall

---

[25] This was the Eden School.

[26] At this time the Anglican Church in Maryland was oversupplied with ministers; therefore those candidates recommended by the proprietor had the advantage. Carol van Voorst, *The Anglican Clergy in Maryland, 1692–1776* (New York, 1989), 145; and see also p. 151, this volume.

[27] The Inspection Act of 1747, which required £30 of tobacco per taxable person as a clergy poll tax, expired in 1770. The clergy claimed that £40 was appropriate according to the old law of 1702. A political controversy ensued, but in November 1773 the Assembly set the poll tax for clergy at £30 in accordance with the rate of 1747. Aubrey C. Land, *Colonial Maryland: A History* (Millwood, NJ, 1981), 293–295. For a full explanation of the controversy, see Jean H. Vivian, "The Poll Tax Controversy in Maryland, 1770–76: A Case of Taxation *with*

send them to you. My heart glows with gratitude upon the recollection of your unmerited favours, and should be glad of any opportunity of testifying my obedience to my best friend and Benefactor

I should be glad to hear from [y . . .] [   ] convenient. Please direct for me at Eden-school Somerset county Maryland and [   ] it to my father. I am with respect and regard your most obliged humble Servant

January 5th 1774   David Duff

David Duff to James Grant of Grant, Dorset County, Maryland, May 20, 1780

Hond. Sir

At this time when an opportunity to Scotland is so very rare, I should have been wanting in my duty if I had omitted writing to my best friend and Benefactor. I am yet unmarried and in good health, and have done the best I could to keep myself above board. I still continue at Eden school, and have been the only master there for the three years last past. For the two first years of which I rented out the Plantation belonging to the School for one third of the produce annually, but last year I altered my plan by purchasing another horse and hiring a negroe-man to make me a crop. I had the pleasure to find, notwithstanding the difficulties I laboured under, that my scheme succeeded beyond my expectation, and this year I am [pur]suing the same plan a little more extended. I am in hopes [   ] to make Indian-corn, Indian pease Turnips Oats Flax, [C . . .], Cyder and Brandy. My wheat as well as almost every one's else in this part of the country is blasted by reason of the uncommon severity of the frosts last winter. Besides the privileges arising from the plantation, I had the first year after the school was new modelled 4£ paper Curry. as usual, the next 6£, the next 12£ a year P scholar This year I asked 100£ a year P scholar, my proposal was treated with ridicule, but I agreed for as much of this country produce as greatly exceeds that sum. I ardently long to see the times settled which if I should be happy enough to see I intend to remove to Charles town, South Carolina to teach school on my own footing, if you approve of such a scheme. It would give me the greatest pleasure to hear from you. Andrew Ragg Esqr.

Representation," *Maryland Historical Magazine*, 71(1976), 151–176. The controversy raged in the *Maryland Gazette* throughout the summer and autumn of 1772.

who promises if possible to wait on you at Castle-Grant will inform you how it may conveyed with the greatest convenience.

I am Hond Sir with the greatest esteem and regard

Your's and Mrs. Grant's very much obliged humble Servant

Dorset County, Maryland   David Duff
May 20th. 1780

Rev. Thomas Feilde to Dr. Mackenzie, Kingston Parish, Gloucester County, Virginia, February 16, 1771[28]

THE Reverend Thomas Feilde was licensed on August 2, 1770, by the Church of England to serve in America. He arrived in Virginia in the autumn of 1770, and by December was offered a job in Kingston Parish, Gloucester (now Mathews) County. Once he had a place to settle, his wife, Elizabeth, and three children joined him the next year. He seemed to be pleased with his new situation. The rector's house was situated on 500 acres of glebe land overlooking a river in a well-populated parish. His annual salary started at 13,055 pounds of tobacco, but the next year was raised to 16,000 pounds, equal to about £160 plus about £40 in fees. This was customary, but also quite sufficient. Anglican ministers seemed to do well in Virginia at this time. The Rev. Price Davies, for example, came to America in 1763 and was quickly offered the rectorship of Blisland Parish with a salary of 16,000 pounds of tobacco and a house with 200 acres of glebe land. Six months after his arrival he married Elizabeth Perry, who owned a comfortable fortune that Davies referred to as "a necessary ingredient in the matrimonial state." Davies remained as rector of Blisland parish until his death in 1793, at which time he owned 750 acres of land and 35–40 slaves.[29]

---

[28] *Source*: T[homas] Feilde to Dr. Mackenzie, A.L.S., BR Box 117 (1), Huntington Library, San Marino, California. *Courtesy:* Huntington Library. The letter is a recipient copy, and endorsed, "Answerd by me 19th September 1771."

[29] G. MacLaren Brydon, "The Clergy of the Established Church in Virginia and the Revolution," *Virginia Magazine of History and Biography*, 41(1933), 138; Peter W. Coldham, ed.,

Feilde had an easy start in America, unlike most newcomers. He immediately found a position that "succeeded beyond [his] most sanguine Expectations," and reported to Mackenzie that he would probably be living in Virginia "for some time & perhaps for Life." He would have done very well as rector of Kingston Parish, but in 1777 he refused to take the oath of allegiance to the American cause, and was dismissed by the vestry in July. In early 1778 he and his family went to New York, where Feilde enlisted in the British army as chaplain to the Second Batallion under the command of Brigadier-General Oliver DeLancey. He died on Staten Island in February 1781.[30]

In his letter, written only a few months after his arrival, he does not say much about his experiences, but shares with Mackenzie his intense interest in gaining a "natural Knowledge" of America and of making "little Excursions into the Country" to look for curiosities. He had already learned something about the "shell strata" covering much of coastal Virginia, the soil, and how to plant Indian corn, and had collected specimens to send to Mackenzie. Feilde did not have much to offer, other than fossil shells and "a few other trifles," but intended, nevertheless, to send a box of "everything" he could, even "common" Indian corn and Virginia coal, lest he neglect anything Mackenzie might want for his curiosity cabinet.[31]

American Loyalist Claims (Washington, D.C., 1980), 1: 152; Gregory Palmer, *Biographical Sketches of Loyalists of the American Revolution* (Westport, CT, 1984), 271; C. G. Chamberlayne, ed., *The Vestry Book of Kingston Parish, Mathews County, Virginia, 1679–1796* (Richmond, VA, 1929), 94, 99; Sir David Evans, ed., "Price Davies, Rector of Blisland Parish: Two Letters, 1763, 1765," *Virginia Magazine of History and Biography*, 79(1971), 158–160; and see also Otto Lohrenz, "Clergyman and Gentleman: Archibald Campbell of Westmoreland County, 1741–1774," *Northern Neck of Virginia Historical Magazine*, 39(1989), 4435, 4447–4449.

[30] Palmer, *Biographical Sketches...*, 271; George MacLaren Brydon, *Virginia's Mother Church and the Political Conditions Under Which It Grew* (Philadelphia, 1952), II: 424, n. 26.

[31] Dr. Andrew Scott was another eighteenth-century "supplier" of curiosities to collectors in England. His specimens finally ended up among the artifacts of Sir Hans Sloane, whose massive collection became the foundation of the British Museum. See pp. 11–12, this volume; and see George F. Frick, et al., "The Practice of Dr. Andrew Scott of Maryland and North Carolina," *Maryland Historical Magazine*, 82(1987), 123–124.

To Dr Mackenzie   Kingston Gloucester
     Dear Sr.   County Virginia –
                                          Feb 16 1771 –

You perhaps from my long Silence may conclude that amidst other Av-
ocations I have forgot my Promise to You of procuring some of the natural
Curiosities of this Country, but when You reflect that my first Concern
would be to procure a Settlement, You will not be surprised that I found
but little leisure to look after Curiosities. Yet in that respect I was not totally
inactive for whilst I continued at Williamsburg, I made a collection of several
fossile Shells which along with a few other trifles I propose sending to You,
which although they may not be capital Articles in Your Collection may yet
serve as a proof of my readiness to serve you, as far as his in my Power, &
an earnest of a Present more worthy of your Acceptance, when a further
Acquaintance with this Country shall enable me to do. The Insect Tribe
You will naturally imagine are in a dormant State at present but as the Spring
comes on I shall have Business enough upon my Hands for I believe their
Genera are very numerous here. I doubt not but it will give You Pleasure to
hear that I have succeeded beyond my most sanguine Expectations In the
eleventh Week from my landing in Virginia I was chosen Rector of this
Parish,[32] one of the best in the Colony worth I may venture to say 200 [   ]
pr Ann I am now writing in my own House, adjoining to which I have a
Plantation of 500 Acres of Land upon a beautiful River & not far from the
great Bay of Chesapeak which is indeed the Boundary of my Parish on one
Side. The Country herebout is the most Populous in Virginia there being
considerably above 2000 Souls in this Parish. As it thus pleased Providence
to provide for me so speedily & so amply, I shall employ a considerable part
of my leisure Hours in the pursuit of natural Knowledge & in collecting
such Objects of it as this Country affords. It will give me great Pleasure to
hear Yours & Mr. DaCosta's remarks upon such things as I shall send You
if it be not too much trouble to You & I shall at any time be glad to send
fresh Specimens of any Article that You wish as well as such additional ones
as shall come within my Power. You will imagine that now I have got an
Habitation I can with more Pleasure make little Excursions into the Country
& shall not fail of cultivating an Acquaintance with such Gentlemen as may
be useful to me in making this Collection. Tell my good Friend Mr. Da

---

[32] Feilde was one of four applicants, one of whom, Rev. Thomas Baker, was the interim
    minister. Feilde was elected at the December 19, 1770, vestry meeting, but he was not
    installed as rector until January 5, 1771. This would make his arrival in America about the
    beginning of October. Chamberlayne, *Vestry Book*, viii, 91, 94.

Costa that I intend to take a Journey into the Mountains & I hope to do it the next Autumn & though it is not to be imagined that the Bowels of the Earth will be so easily searched into as in those Countries where they have be opened purposely in search of Minerals Yet I doubt not but the Gullies which are large & numerous in this Country not only owing to the Heavy Rains but to the looseness of the Soil, will afford something worth picking Up. In the Catalogue on the other Page I have Numbered the several Articles of which I keep an Account by me, that if at any Time You should wish for a second parcel of any Sort, or any observation you shall be pleased to afford me will be more useful when I know the Subject You are treating upon. I shall be much obliged to You to send the small parcel inclosed as directed to my Daughter. I beg my best Compliments to Mr. DaCosta & any thing I can perform here in the way of natural History for him or You I shall do it with pleasure & as I am likely to be stationed here for some time & perhaps for Life, I may be able to do more within my Sphere than a Person who makes but a short stay. There are many Articles in View of the insect & other Tribes which I shall diligently pursue the fruits of which you shall reap as fast as they are produced, excuse me if any thing trifling should drop from my pen, or be included in my collections, my plan is to send you every thing Yours must be to make choice of what is worth preserving I remain Dear Sr. Yours most sincerely

T. Feilde

Direct to me Rector of
Kingston Parish Gloucester
County Virginia

P.S. If you should have any opportunity in the season of procuring me a few of a new sort of Potatoes I know not by what name to call them but it is remarkable for its extra ordinary produce & growing in large Clusters a Pound of Lucerne Seed & little of the Turnip Cabbage Seed & Turnip Rooted Cabbage Seed I should be much obliged to You, for as I have a large tract of Land I propose to make some Experiments as the Country seems capable of producing any thing.

Catalogue of Articles in the Box

No. 1 One of the Vertebrae of a large fish
x   No. 2 Coralloid *fine Corallium Stellatum*[33]
x   3 Escallop Shell *fine*

---

[33] Words in italics and "x" 's were added by Dr. Mackenzie.

x   4   A Bone

x   5   Escallop with Pholades upon it

x   6   A Cockle *fine*

x   7   Another Sort. *fothergills kind* – N: this sort
       is found here recent & is the common cockle of
       this Country –

x   8   An oblong Do.[34] *cuneiform fine*

x   9   Oyster with Scallop Edges. N. this sort is here recent

x   10   A fluted Cockle Shell *Momboidal Multarticulate Cockle*

x   11   A Spiral Shell *Cockled Clavicule production*

x   12   – *Vermiculi*

x   13   A Mass of the Bed in which these Shells lie

x   14   & x15 Shells *Ostreoida*

The above are all fossile, collected by myself, all or most of them out of the Governors Park in Williamsburg; this Stratum of Shells seems to extend over a great part of this Country at least in the low lands, covered by a bed of sand & sandy loam of different thickness; as gravel & Marle is found in England the thickness of this Stratum I have not been able to discover, as it appears only in small openings made by the washing of the Rain water, or on the banks of little Rivulets, only in the Governors Park a Pit is opened purposely for getting this matter which is used for making Walks instead of Gravel, but I am much mistaken if it would not be a rich manure for the Land especially if burnt it was out of this Pit that No. 13 was taken & which seems no other than fragments of Shells, this opening is made in the manner of a gravel Pit, & they have dug to depth of 7 eight or more feet in the Stratum but how much deeper it lies I know not. These Shells do not always lie in a Stratum of this sort, I mean so free from other mixtures, for in the same piece of ground I found them in amazing plenty amongst the Sand & Loam. That several of the Shells above are found recent you know very well, I have mentioned two that are found here & in all Probability I may find more, but of the recent Shells I propose making a Collection for You which though we boast of few beauties Yet they may be varieties & so have an equal Right to a place in the Cabinet.

x   No. 16   the Head of an Indian Arrow

     17   Galls from the Oak – qu. whether these be of any use or equal
        to the Aleppo Galls

     18   A Black Sand found on the Shores of my Plantation *Iron Sand*

[34] Ditto.

x 19 The Nidus of the Mason or Dirt dawber – This is an Insect of
the Wasp kind according to the information I have received for
I am not certain that I have seen it as Yet. it builds these little
Nests, in our houses in every cell of Which she lays an Egg &
fills it full of Spiders for the Sustenance as is supposed of the
young Insect, the progress of this little Creature I hope to observe this Summer therefore say no more of it till I can speak
from my own Knowledge

No. 20 The nidi of some Insects whether the same or different Sorts
I know not, these are suspended in a Leaf & that Leaf is fastend
to the bough by the Insect which prevents it falling off from the
Tree with the rest of the leaves in Autumn. This is a remarkable
case of the instinct which nature has given to every Creature for
the Preservation of the Species what else could inform her that
unless she fastened not only her nest to the leaf but the leaf also
to the branch, her Offspring would be destroyed by the falling
of the leaf on which it hung.

No 21 An Ear of the true early Ripe Indian Corn
This is so common in the seed Shops that it might seem
useless to trouble You with it, but I had rather send some trifles
than omit any thing that might be agreable Perhaps You may
have some friend that would chuse to sow some of it in England,
this being the early sort is the most proper for the Climate & I
doubt not would ripen very well if properly managed, the Culture in a few words as follows. Plant it at the time You sow
Kidney beans that is as soon as the frosts are over & as it ad-
vances in height draw the earth to the Stem till there is a hill
of Earth raised about it near one foot in heighth, keep it perfectly clean from weeds, the Plants should be six foot asunder
& a Number of them together or the Fruit comes to little Perfection even here, the reason I need not mention to a Botanist.

No. 22 Virginian Coal – *light & like jet*

No. 23 A few Specimens of Oars what sort I know not they were
given me by a Neighbour as Oars of this Country but from what
part of it I could not learn. I hope hereafter to be more particular
on this kind of Substances –

NORTH CAROLINA

Letters of Alexander McAllister,
North Carolina, 1770–1775[1]

A LEXANDER McAllister [? – 1797] was descended from the family of McAllister of Loup, which originated with Alastair Mor, a younger son of Donald of Islay, Lord of the Isles, who died in 1299. The estate of Loup was the seat of the main branch of the Kintyre McAllisters to which Alexander belonged and was situated on West Loch Tarbert, Kintyre, Argyleshire, two miles north of Clachan. One of the letters in the McAllister papers was from Angus McAllister, 11th of Loup, the chief of the clan. Other McAllister estates not far from Clachan were Ballinakill, Alexander's home and the residence of his cousin John Boyd, and Ronachan, where James McAllister, one of Alexander's correspondents, lived.[2]

In the late 1730s, a group of Highlanders, among whom was Alexander's father, Coll McAllister, decided to emigrate to North Carolina with their families, hoping to find a better life than the one that post-Union Scotland had offered them.[3] Most of the families, if not all, were related to each other in one way or another, and most had substantial assets in property. Coll McAllister was the fiar of Balli-

---

[1] *Source*: Papers of Colonel Alexander McAllister, North Carolina Department of Archives and History, Raleigh, North Carolina. *Courtesy*: North Carolina State Archives. All references, unless otherwise stated, are to the McAllister Papers. The letters are all retained copies.

[2] Nigel Tranter, *Argyll and Bute* (London, 1977), 165; Angus Martin, *Kintyre: The Hidden Past* (Edinburgh, 1984), 94; Andrew Mckerral, *Kintyre in the Seventeenth Century* (London, 1948); H. Pirie-Gordon, ed., *Burke's Landed Gentry* (London, 1937), 1448; A. I. B. Stewart, "The North Carolina Settlement of 1739," *The Scottish Genealogist*, 32(1985), 8; Angus McAllister to Alexander McAllister, n.d.

[3] Scotland and England were united by the Act of Union in 1707.

nakill, which had been in the family since 1717. He sold his lands to pay for his emigration and that of his wife, Janet McNeill (a sister of another of the emigrators, Dugald McNeill of Losset), and his children, Hector, Alexander, Mary, Grisella, and Isabella. One daughter, Ann, remained in Scotland. Neil McNeill of Ardelay (Alexander Campbell of Balole's uncle), also sold his lands in Gigha in 1738 so that he could move his wife, Grizel Campbell, and family to Carolina. The McNeills' daughter, Florence, later married Alexander McAllister. In all, about 350 people sailed on the *Thistle* to North Carolina. During the summer of 1739, the ship picked up some passengers at Campbelton, on the lower tip of the Kintyre peninsula, and then sailed to the small island of Gigha to collect the remainder, including the McAllisters.[4]

This early group of emigrants to the backcountry of Carolina prospered. In the summer of 1740, the General Assembly of North Carolina issued land grants to Coll McAllister and about 20 other heads of households. These lands were located about 100 miles from Wilmington on the northwest branch of the Cape Fear River, a few miles north of what in 1762 became Campbelton (now Fayetteville), in an area that Governor Gabriel Johnston referred to as "the fag end of the provin[ce]." Coll McAllister became one of the early magistrates of Bladen County (known as Cumberland County after 1754), but lived only a few years after his arrival. He had died by 1745. Hector, his older son, returned to Scotland with the intention of coming back, but he never did. Alexander stayed in Cape Fear and married Florence McNeill, with whom he had four children, and later married Jane Colvin, with whom he had eleven more children. By 1787, he owned 2,599 acres and about 40 slaves. He had been a representative of Cumberland County at Hillsboro in 1776, and became a state senator from 1787 to 1790.[5]

The letters and documents of Alexander McAllister, dating from about 1751 to 1795, do not contain any accounts of his first impres-

---

[4] Stewart, "North Carolina Settlement of 1739," 7–8, 10, 12.

[5] Stewart, "North Carolina Settlement of 1739," 7–8, 10–11; Gabriel Johnston to [?], Brompton on Cape Fear River, February 10, 1736/7, South Carolina Historical Society, Charleston, South Carolina; William C. Pool, "An Economic Interpretation of the Ratification of the Federal Constitution in North Carolina, Part II . . . ," *North Carolina Historical Review*, 27 (1950), 293; John H. Wheeler, *Historical Sketches of North Carolina, From 1584 to 1851 . . .* (Philadelphia, 1851), II: 124–125, 131.

sions of North Carolina after his arrival in the late 1730s. We do not know how he cleared his land, or what difficulties he faced settling in so remote an area. But throughout the following decades, McAllister not only established his home in the backcountry of Carolina, where he did very well, but he also retained an intense interest in friends and family who wanted to come to America, and he wrote many letters to these people, begging them to emigrate to Carolina. These seven letters, a selection from the entire McAllister correspondence, are included here because they are rich in the details they provide of everyday life in Carolina and in the instructions they give to prospective emigrants, and they offer insight into the friendship and kinship networks that were essential to the emigrant experience in all the colonies.

Alexander McAllister to Angus McCuaig, North Carolina, November 29, 1770[6]

Der Cusin   Barimore[7] November 29th 1770

I Recived yours which gives me great pleasure to heare of you and famile welfer, Mr Campbel & my Self is greatly obliged to our frind Balole[8] for his good oppinon of us I had Such oppinion of our frind Balole that I was Shure he would not Say any thing but what he Could Stand by you might know by what I write you what the Country is as for my peart I will not go to particulars but was I in that Country I would not Stay one day longer in it for you may Stay ther all your Life time & not geat one farthing a head morover what you have now in possesion your land lord will Sure be master of and then you and others wil wish you had com when it was in your power you or now man can Expect to be So wel Settled the first or Second yeare as you may be at present but if god Spers you in this Cuntrie but a few years you will blis the day you left that Country wher the face of the poor is keep to the grinding stone if you Stay ther what can you expect for your children morover if you cam hear if god Speres you and them they may be

---

[6] Angus McCuaig, whom McAllister addressed as "Der Cusin," wanted to emigrate to North Carolina from Scotland, but his wife was afraid that the first year in a strange place would be difficult for their children. Angus McCuaig to Alexander McAllister, August 22, 1771.

[7] Barmore (the home of the McAllisters of Tarbert) was the name Alexander gave to his estate in North Carolina. Stewart, "North Carolina Settlement of 1739," 11.

[8] Alexander Campbell of Balole.

of great Servise to you & you may [leave?] to each of them apice of land which is mor then they can expect where they are this is the best poor mans Country I have heard in this age ther is land to be taken up but the best is taken up many years ago as to purches any land for you I think it is not the thing for what would please me would not perhaps pleas you I have no more to add but that all frinds hear is wel Mr Farquard Campbel[9] & his famile is in good health my Sister Grise[10] leaves with hir Sister Mist Campbel my Sister Mist McNeall[11] & femile is wel I & my famile Joines me in our best wises to you & famile and al other frinds

PS if you dont Com pray let me know in your Next what is becom of your Granuncel Daughter Mist Gilcreast[12] that lived in Glenedgil and what Sircomstance She & famile is in

Alexander McAllister to Hector McAllister, North Carolina, Nov. 29, 1770 and Dec. 6, 1770[13]

Dr. Brother   Barmore Novembr 29th 1770

I had the pleasure of you three letters which gave me Great Satisfaction to hear of you & famile wellfer, but notting to the pleasure I promised myself

---

[9] Farquard Campbell was Alexander's brother-in-law who was married to his sister Isabella.

[10] Alexander's unmarried sister, Grisella.

[11] Alexander's sister, Mary, married Hector McNeill.

[12] Angus wrote back that his granduncle's daughter Mrs. Gilchrist & family were well; "hir youngest Dayed Desember Last" he said "only Ronald and Beell is in Life." Angus McCuaig to Alexander McAllister, August 11, 1771.

[13] Hector was Alexander's brother, who came to North Carolina with the rest of his family. He bought 640 acres from Gabriel Wayne "on the N.E. side of the N.W. River above long pond" adjoining property that Alexander had bought. Hector returned to Scotland on what he thought was a temporary journey, and left his lands under the management of Alexander. While in Scotland, Hector married, and his new wife was opposed to their coming to North Carolina. Although he kept trying to leave, he never emigrated. Hector was a tacksman for the farms of Monnyquill and Glaster, owned by the 7th Duke of Hamilton, on the island of Arran, Buteshire. In 1772, his rent for both farms was raised from £22.14.5 to £60. Alexander McAllister, Jr., to Mary Shannon, October 18, 1802; John Burrels Arran Journal, RH 4/19, vol. 1, 178, 206, Scottish Record Office, Edinburgh; see also Margaret C. Storrie, "Landholdings and Population in Arran from the Late Eighteenth Century," *Scottish Studies*, 11(1967), 49–74.

The beginning of the letter is dated November 29, 1770, and the end of the letter is dated December 6.

in [Seeing?] & famile Safe arived in this place but Im out of hopes of ever haveing that pleasure as you have not given me any mor ashurance then you Did Eight and [twenty?] years ago You intinded to com you would [   ] a carpenter for to buld you a house & you would Desire me to rise a crope for you at your one¹⁴ place I would advise you to quit the thoughts of Ever pretending to Com or put one a resilution with god permison nothing but death would stope you for the Sunner you Com the better if you dly [delay] much longer you cannot expect to See your famile wel Settled you must be one the decline morover you are a great hindrance to many a poor man in your predending always to Com & never [comes?] as you have ben in this Country & must know more about it than those that is Strengers to the ways of it your good plantsion of no Benifite to you or famile, if you find your Self in a capacity [of] purchasing a few Sleves [it?] would be more to y[ou]r advantage than Servents¹⁵ if not Servants is [   ] when one can do no better wher ther is Sleaves one Carful hand would be very nesicry, as for redemptioners¹⁶ they must be a loss to any that will ingage in that way as mony is So very Scarse litle or none Sirculating Since our mother Country wanted to name the Stamp Duty acte unto the Colines, all Governers hase positve orders not to Streak any mony one peen of lusing ther Goverment & being uncapbel of bering any Commission under the Crown,¹⁷ as Concerning the back land of troy¹⁸ they have ben taken up many years ago you never let me know any thing concerning them till it was too leet I have three Hundered ackers ther¹⁹ my Self which is mostly Swamps the rest is taken up by other Nebours, the four veshels you mension is Safe arived in good health as for Duncan McAlester & Samuel McAlestr William Shaw I have not yeat Seen I Supose they are gon up black river to my father in law²⁰ —

---

¹⁴ Throughout his letters, Alexander McAllister uses "one" in place of "own" and "on," and often spells who as "woh."

¹⁵ Indentured servants.

¹⁶ A redemptioner had a certain amount of time (usually 14 days) after his or her arrival to find the funds necessary to reimburse the ship captain for passage. If no one "redeemed" him or her, the master of the ship could sell the redemptioner as an indentured servant. For the redemptionist system, see Abbot Emerson Smith, *Colonists in Bondage: White Servitude and Convict Labor in America, 1607–1776* (1947; reprint, New York, 1971), 20–22.

¹⁷ Two legislative acts are referred to here: the Stamp Act ("Stamp Duty acte") of 1765 and the Currency Act of 1764. The Currency Act prohibited the American colonies from issuing currency and the Stamp Act reduced the amount of cash in circulation by levying a tax on nearly every form of paper used in the colonies.

¹⁸ Troy, property owned by Alexander and Hector, was near Cross Creek (now Fayetteville).

¹⁹ This 300 acres is in addition to what Alexander owned at Troy.

²⁰ Alexander Colvin was the father of Alexander's wife, Jane, whom he married on July 14,

if ther is any way that you can procure what Ballance is coming to you from your Uncle Estate Safe your Self & luse no time for they have Dun all that lay in ther power to Disposes both you & me of port neal[21] but fortun have been more kind to me, the land was taken at the Sute of the [Kinge?] unknown to me or any other in the Setelment til about ten Days before our County Court I was at Campbelton where I met the Sherrif who asked me if [I] knew the land caled port neal I Did Im going to advertise it for Seel the Second Day of Courte I could not blive him til he Shewed me the advertisment acordingly I became purchaer payd the money & Got the Shirrif Deed for the Same, your Uncle Ceres Sent our Cusin Hector McNiell a power[22] over last yeare & and as Hector did weate on the [Captin?] Caried the power home with him I understand ther is another come to him or the Same[.] as for our Cusin Miss Jean McNiell I have not yeat Seen hir but hear She is with hir Cusin Mist Debuise & Mist McAlester in Wilmington I did imagen She would write to me if She intinded to com up the Cuntry god knowes how things will turn out but Girles without a porsion Stickes long on hand hou[e]ver this is a better Country for them then ther one Country I will not be backword in my good Ofices to hir or any one frind that is in want, as for Duncan Brown or his son in law I have not Seen as yeat we have no nuse heare that his worth releting our frind John Currie Dyed 12th of Jully last mist Cure & Child lives Stil at troy Im Stil of opepenion that you do not inten[d] to com if not I would [willing?] make a purches of troy if you are inclind to peart with it as it is So conventent for me Im in hops you will give me the preference, as for our Sister mist makNeall and famiel they are very well in health & is Clearing the [Estate?] as fast as they Can Im in hopes in a few yeares they will be in a good way our Brothe mr Campbel & family is in good healh I Supos he will write to you our Sister Grissel is wel & leaves with hir Sister mist Campbel, I think it was very unkind in you not to let me know what is become of our Sister Ann

  I & my famly & Joines in our best wishes to you & family no mor at

1763. D. S. McAllister, *Genealogical Record of the Descendants of Col. Alexander McAllister of Cumberland County, North Carolina* (Richmond, VA, 1900), 149. Black River, where Colvin lived, is a branch of the Northwest Cape Fear River.

[21] According to Hector, the balance due him from the plantation of Port Neill, which was apparently owned jointly by Alexander, Hector, and their uncle, was £686.2.7$^{1}/_{2}$ Carolina currency. The copy of his account concerning his share in Port Neill was dated September 17, 1745. Hector McAllister to Alexander McAllister, September 12, 1771.

[22] Power of attorney.

present but Im Der brother your very affect Humbel Servent
Decmbr 6th 1770   AMcA

Alexander McAllister to Alexander McAllister of Cour, North Carolina, late 1771–early 1772[23]

Dear Cussin

I recived your agreable favour of 1th octobr which gave me great Satisfaction to hear of you & famile wellfere I have had a long letter from my
Brother in which he Says he will never be Satisfyed till he is in cape feare
Surly there is nothing would give me more Satisfetion than to have the
pleasur of Seeing him & famile well Settled heare but Im Doutful that will
never be I had a letter from his wife wherein She ack[n]oledgs whithr it be
for good or harm She is the only Hindrance which makes me dispere of
that happines how ever I would rather never See him hear if it were not
agreable to all his famile, if ever he comes it is time he Should be making
ready for it will take him three or four years before he can be will Sattled I
woul[d] be glead you would talk with him Seriously abot the matter, the
orfand of John Currie was Drounded last Summer & the widow is maried
to one tomson John McCallum is overseer for my father in law Samuel
Mcalestr & Daniel Mcalester & Duncan Mcalester Leaves about Mr Colvin

[23] Alexander McAllister, whom McAllister addresses as "Dear Cussin," was from Cour, Kintyre. McAllister of Cour had written a short letter to Alexander on August 17, 1770, saying
that, though he had never met him, he had heard many things about him from their mutual
friend, John Currie, who had emigrated to North Carolina. He wrote about the oppression
of the landlords, which would "soon help to plant your colony." Alexander (of Loup) wrote
his cousin in return (late 1770–early 1771), to say that their mutual friend John Currie had
died on July 12, 1770, leaving a wife and young son. He also wrote that he had mixed feelings
about reports of oppression: "it Effetcs me two ways I am Sorry to hear of much opresion
and Glad to See So many f[l]ying from it." He reported that an "imense Number" of Scots
had arrived in Carolina and that Cape Fear would "Soon be a new Scotland." The following
letter is undated, but internal evidence in the McAllister papers indicates that it was written
between late 1771 and the summer of 1772. In this letter, McAllister refers to a letter he
received from his brother, which was written September 12, 1771. He could not have received
this before late October or early November. McAllister also mentions the death of John
Currie's son "last Summer." Young Currie died in the summer of 1771, which means this
letter was written before the summer of 1772.

and all the arren people[24] comes no further which is sixty miles below me that is towards the See Bord they will have little arran one Black river which is the Name of the place wher my father in law leaves I would write to my brother abo[ut] making a purchas of his land if I thought he would not Com I would be glead if you would take the truble to Speak Serrious to him concerning his coming and if you find he will not com if he would Send me a dead [deed] for troy I would remite him the value of it as it Joyns the reast of my lands it would inabel me to Settle my famile Joyning one another and let me know by every oportunity how you and famile and all other frinds is Mist McAlestr & young ons Joyns me in our beast wishes to you and famile & all other frinds I am with Sincerity Der Your Most Affectionat Cousis till Death

AMcA

Alexander McAllister to James McAllister, North Carolina, December 1771–January 1772[25]

Dear Sir

Im Very Sory for your & my Dissapointment, for I would be glead of Corrisponding with one of your Caracter and a Mc[26] besids and like wise to Continue it as oft as opertunity offers you Desire me in your letter to aquant you how the people is Setled that cam over last year[27] ther is not one of

[24] People from the island of Arran, Buteshire, Scotland, where Alexander's brother, Hector, lived.

[25] James McAllister was from Ronachan, near Clachen, Kintyre, Argyleshire (James McAllister to Alexander McAllister, October 1771). The following letter is undated, but Alexander must have written it around December 1771 or early January 1772. He is answering James McAllister's letter of October 1771, which he could not have received before the end of November. At the end of his letter, Alexander says that he has four children by his second wife. His fifth child was born January 11, 1772; hence the letter must have been written before then. McAllister, *Genealogical Record of . . . McAllister*, 101.

[26] His surname began with "Mc," as in McAllister.

[27] On March 21, 1771, Governor William Tryon sent Lord Hillsborough a list of the acts that had been passed in the last session of the Assembly, one of which read:

"'An Act to encourage the further settlement of this Province' Was enacted on behalf of several ship loads of Scotch families which have landed in this province within three years past from the Isles of Arran, Durah [Jura], Islay, and Gigah [Gigha] but chief of them from Argyle Shire and are mostly settled in Cumberland County. The numbers of these new

them that I know but is in a way of doing well they mad all plenty of Corn for them Selves & famile and seemes to be very well Satisfied but as you observe they are the poorest Sort that comes & no Dout meet with Some Deficouldy be fore they can fix them Selves the most of them is now leards [i.e., lairds] for I beleve too pearts of them have gote land of ther one I dont Dout but the land holders will put ther one Construitisions on ther letters but let them construe as they will if they will prissist in the augmenting ther rents[28] I belive in a few years Som of ther land m[a]y ly weast [waste] all I bleam the pople for is that they do not com to this Country be fore they geet So poor but never the less the Country is realy good or one half of the [so many?] poor people that com this four yeares would be abegging and instead of that ther is none but what is in a good way as for the report concerning Servant it is apsullutly fals[29] for they geet above Serving when they com to the Country any one that is under a nesiaty of hyrring must pay them such extravant wages that a planter cannot mak any thing of them, as for Cousin Hector alless he is no more he salled from this port to the west indes apriel last and no accounts of him Since he was married to a daughter of Daniel [tannish?] by whom he hase too Childer a girl & a boy I will Endavor to Settle a corispondance with the young Gentelmen your [sons,?][30] Alexr. & angush McAlester[,] the McIlerest & Mc[Higgon?], or, [   ] I k[n]ow and is in a good way, my one famele conssist of too B[oys]

settlers are computed at sixteen hundred, men, women, and children. The reason they alledged for coming to America was that the rents of their lands were so raised that they
could not live upon them, and those who were mechanics were particularly encouraged to
settle here by their countrymen who have been settled many years in this province." William
L. Saunders, ed., *Colonial Records of North Carolina*, 10 vols. (Raleigh, NC, 1886–1890), VIII:
526.

[28] Alexander's friends and relatives in Scotland complained repeatedly about the increase in
rents and oppression. For example, Hector wrote that "it is impossible to live any longer
here. the poor people had Scarce to pay their rent hitherto and now when three rents is
laid on every farm, how can they Stand." (Hector McAllister to Alexander McAllister,
March 15, 1769.) And cousin Alexander of Cour remarked: "our Lairds or Landlords oppression will Soon help to plant your Coloney." (Alexander McAllister of Cour to Alexander
McAllister, August 17, 1770.)

[29] James had heard rumors that "a Servant Man cannot gett Sarvise with one Master above a
month or Soe at a Tyme and may goe fourty or Eiven a Hunder Milles or [before] hee
gett another Master to take his hand and his wages hee most take in the prodous of the
Farm at hunder milles from markett." James McAllister to Alexander McAllister, October
1771.

[30] James's two sons were Archibald and Hector McAllister, who both went to Norfolk, Virginia, in the employ of Messrs. Donald and Co., tobacco merchants in Glasgow. James
McAllister to Alexander McAllister, October, 1771.

& too girles by my first wife & the Same Number[31] by my Seco[nd] Mistr
Mcalister & the little folk Joines me in our Sinceer wishes to you & famel[e]
Im Der Sir your very humbel Servat
AMcA

Alexander McAllister to John Boyd, North Carolina, c. April 1772[32]

Der Cusin

I recived your very kind favoir by our frind Mr Simson woh interteand
me very agrea[b]le in Rehea[r]sing the conversasion that past betwee[n] you
and him Im greatly oblidged to you for the kindness you Shewed him &
the [Spirit?] of your letter in being a frind to adventerers makes you more
Deare to me & your goodness in wishing the poor & opreast releaved from
the tyranni of ther oppreasores Shues a sprit of generosity & freadom which
is Sealdom to be found in the gentelmen of that Country, you Desire a more
particoular account of the Country & its produce as for the country it is a
very good one [a?] poor man that will incline to work may have the value
of his labour for ther is nothing that he puts in the ground but what yealds
be yount any Idea that a Strenger can conceive Indian corn is the cheaf
griane that we plant it is good food for man & Beast & if one plants too
Bushels of this greane he will have at least Six or Siven hundered Bushils
wheat growes very well & Barly rye & otes puttoses tobaco and every other
thing grose Extrem well in truth it is the Best poor mans Cuntry I Ever

[31] Alexander's four children by his first wife, Flora McNeill, were Coll, Grissella, Janet, and
Neill. The first four children by his second wife, Jane Colvin, were Margaret, Alexander,
Hector, and Flora. McAllister, *Genealogical Record of ... McAllister*, 23–24, 101.

[32] John Boyd was a cousin of Alexander's from Ballinakill, an estate near Clachan, Kintyre,
not far from Loup, the main seat of the Kintyre McAllisters. Tranter, *Argyll and Bute*, 165.
Alexander seems to be answering two of Boyd's letters, one written June 21, 1770, in which
Boyd asks Alexander to give him "a particular account ... of the Countrey" and another
letter dated November 15, 1771, in which he asks for Alexander's help in finding a place for
his friend, Dugald Campbell, from the Isle of Skye. Campbell was "a good Classicale scholar
writes a Good hand and understands figures." Boyd asked, "if your Interest can be of any
Service to get him in to Business, I desire the favour you use it for his Behoof." The letter
is undated; however, in the previous letter (Alexander McAllister to James McAllister, December 1771–January 1772), Alexander wrote that Cousin Hector sailed from North Carolina
"apriel last" (i.e., April 1771). At the end of the following letter, McAllister wrote that Cousin
Hector sailed 12 months ago, which would date this letter around April 1772.

heard of and I have had the opertunity of hearing from South & north we
mak tarr in great plenty & it is a good Climeat for indigo we have Several
other Comodites which is too tediu[s] to Be mencioned it is Sertin poor
people will meat with many Deficulys before they are any ways comodiously
Settled but once they are Settled it is for life if they do not Chuse to muve,
your frind Dougal Campbel is with a merchant at Campbeltown I belive the
lade will do very well his father[33] hease made a purches of apece of land
whor ther is a clear plantsion and torrolable good houses Mr: McMillun is
gone with his soon in law who is very well Settled on his one land, you
would Do well to advise all poor people whom you wish well to take currage
and Com to this Country it will be of Benefitt to ther riseing generation I
will mak it my busnes to Corrispon with Mr Mcalester in antego he may
be of great Servis to me & I to him in the way of tread but aless Cousin
Hector Mcalester is no more he Saled from this port twelve months agoe
& is never heard of Since Mist Mcalister & our young fry Joines me in best
wishes to you this is all from your frind to Serve you whilest Im

AMcA

Alexander McAllister to Hector McAllister,
North Carolina, Jan. 22, 1774

Der Brother   Barmore Janry 22th 1774

I am much Suprised at your negligence in not writting to me as ther was
Sum of yours neighbours com from that Iland altho my letters did not go Safe
you might be Shure I would not negect writting by Every oportunity I Send
this by Mr William Campbel who is one of our recedenters [residenters] in
this province these three years and one that can give you all the newes if you
have the opertunity of Seeing him, he will not make any long stay in that country he will be back again in Six months at furdest we are in a deplorabel way for
want of law at preset as our Governer and the house of asemly Do not agree in
opinons for the house will not acept of law as he offers them nor will he pass
the law as they propose we dont know how long we will be in this situation our
land office is shute upe at present[34] and ther is no knowing [when?] it will be

---

[33] Dugald Campbell came from Skye with his large family. His father was "bred a Surgeon."
John Boyd to Alexander McAllister, November 15, 1771.

[34] On April 7, 1773, the Privy Council ordered the prohibition of all land grants in the American
colonies as a preventive measure to stop the flow of emigration from Britain. See Bernard
Bailyn, *Voyagers to the West: A Passage in the Peopling of America on the Eve of the Revolution*
(New York, 1986), 55–57. However, this act did not stall emigration. On March 10, 1775,

opened or one what termes we are of opinnion that it will be atended with more Expences that the fees will be higher & the Quitrents will be augmented we cannot find out the reason unleas it be for to hinder the Emigrations to north america we have had com this year upwards of Seven hundered Soles from Skeye and the Neburing Iles[35] & a great many Expected nixt year,[36] your arren frinds are wel Daniel mcalester Deperted this life Septemer Last Mist Currie that was & hir son is both Dead tho She merried one tomson about too years before She Deperted this life our Sister Mist McNiell Lost hir Eldest Son last apriel who was aged twentyone years & very wel grown he was Respected by Every body that was acquanted with him I think She was more a weidow when She Lost him then when Ever as ther was a long famile of young helpeles Childer and all Daughters but one Boy Named John who is about Sixtin years of age my father in law Deperted this Life in Janry 1773 [M]other in law is stil in being tho very freal I have no more to ad but to Coclude Mist McNeal and famile Jonies me and my famlie in our Best wishes and respects to you & Mist McAlester and the reast of your famile remember me to our Sister Ann this from your affecionat Brother & very humbel Servat to Command
AMcA

Alexander McAllister to Hector McAllister, North Carolina, early 1775[37]

Der Brother

Your long [packet?] by angush mcalester is at last come Safe you may [be?] Shoure as you referd me to it for particou[le]rs [I?] thought [long?] til

Governor Martin reported to Dartmouth, secretary for the American Department, that even though the 700 recent arrivals from Scotland were not "able to obtain Lands as usual at a small expence by Grant from the Crown they will seat themselves upon the King's vacant Lands in spite of every effort to prevent them." Saunders, *Colonial Records of North Carolina*, IX: 1159.

35 In 1773, at least one emigrant ship arrival was reported in colonial newspapers: the ship *Margaret* from the Isle of Skye arrived in Wilmington, North Carolina, at the end of November with about 300 passengers. *The Virginia Gazette* (Rind), March 10, 1774.

36 The rumors were accurate: Governor Martin reported on the influx of Scots in a letter to Dartmouth dated March 10, 1775: "Not less than 700 Scotch People have been imported here within a few months." Saunders, *Colonial Records of North Carolina*, IX: 1159.

37 This letter was undated. McAllister is answering his brother's letter of May 31, 1774, which he says was late in arriving. McAllister refers here to the Coercive and Quebec acts passed "Last year" (1774); hence the letter was probably written in early 1775, before news of the battles of Lexington and Concord (April 1775) had reached him.

it Cam[e] to hand Mist Mcalester & I Simpathies with you your Sister and the rest of your famile for the Loss you have meate with in your Son[38] who I understand was lamented by Every one who hade the least aquantince of him it must be a great pleasure to you both that he was So [des]rving tho it ades to your greaf that he was So very good [   ] may the almight[y] Strenthen you both to ber his Chastising [   ] grief [by having?] one any of [   ] more hurtfull to the Constitusion then to Sink under grief, Mr Campbel of Ballole is Safe arived with his famile which Consistes of 3 Daughters & one Sister with [soom?] Servants & William Campbel with his Sisters Childer one girle & too boys one Mr McLean from Islay who Came to see the Coun[try] he is traveled a good Dell through the Country Since he [   ] but still he knows but litle of the Country by what [   ] he would know if he was to Stay to the fall, the Colines [   ] is much alermed one account of Sume acts of parliment [   ] that was past Last year[39] we did Expecte this new [   ] parliment would repeile those pernisious acts whi[ch] will bring america to mear Slevery if they Should be put in Execu[tio]n all the Colines is unanimusly agreed not to receive them one any terms they are fuly Determined to fight to the last before they will give upe ther most valuable privledg which is [their?] liberty I doute not if the [   ] [parlmen?] will prissist in [puting?] [their?] acts in fors they will have a very Sever battle I Dont kno[w] but america will be the Sett of ware for Som time our assemlie meet in March last but Did no maner of Busn[ess] his Excelencis Desolved them very abruptly so that I dont Expet ther will be any thing Doon till those [fires?] is Settld betwin the mother Country & hir Colines the land office is Still Shute & n[o] one knows when it will be opned ther is a tak that my Lord Granvel office[40] will be opined this Summer one wha[t] footing I know not that offic has not been opned this Eg[h]teen or twenty years

You may be Shure ther is nothing would give me great[er] Satisfacttion then once moor to See you & famile Safe arivd in North Carolina tho I am Doute full it is not so orded that we will ever meet but we will bod for the best if you Should Come you will bring Some tredsmen with you for thy will be of Servis to you Such as a wivers [weaver] a Blacksmith & Shumaker

---

[38] On May 31, 1774, Hector wrote Alexander that his only son had fallen overboard and drowned on his way from the island of Arran to Kintyre to see some friends there.

[39] The Coercive (or Intolerable) Acts against Boston and the Quebec Act were passed in 1774.

[40] In 1663, Charles II granted the land in what became North and South Carolina to eight lords proprietors. In 1729 George II purchased the land shares from all the proprietors except Lord Granville. McAllister is referring to the land office for the Granville tract.

Carpinter and indeed all Sorts of treedsmen is very Servisable for if you are not in want of them Every body is in want of Such or you may hire them out you will be pleast to bring [   ] can Spin & [   ] industrius young [   ] for my one youse & if Coupers is plenty bring me one for I have [one?] Negrow boy a Cooper & for want of one being with him he dose note do me half work Every thing is very Deed at present people Dos not know what to be ate ther is no price for any of our Comodites at present willmington is full of tarr and no Sheping to carry it of they have 7 other [   ] Barreles if Sheping Dont Com Soon they [   ] moust Loose very Considerable we understand ther is teen thousand troups Sent letly to boston & fiften thousand that was ther before which will mak 25 thousand too many to Send to a new Country that [is] Destitoude of amonission or Cannon what the [   ] will be the lord only knows but I fear the worst if they Should prevell we will be brought to abject Slevery this is all the Newes that is Sturring at present our Sister Mis McNeill & famie is in good health & Mr Campbel & his famile Likewise and all other frinds the[ir] affict[ionate] Complts: and best wishes of me and my famylie waits upon you mis McAlester Childern and all frinds woh am Dear Brother ver[y] affectionat brother till Death
A[M]cA

Alexander Campbell of Balole to Lachlan Mackinnon of Corrychatachan, 1772[41]

MUCH has already been said in the introduction to this volume about Alexander Campbell of Balole's significance in this migration. It is important to note, however, that the following letter

41 *Source*: GD 153/51/71/12, Scottish Record Office, Edinburgh, Scotland. *Courtesy*: The Keeper of the Records of Scotland, Scottish Record Office. I wish to thank Alexander Murdoch for bringing this letter to my attention, and for the help he gave me in sorting out some of the details. See his article, "A Scottish Document concerning Emigration to North Carolina in 1772," *North Carolina Historical Review*, 67(1990), 438–449. The letter was a copy of Balole's letter and therefore not in his hand. The letter has no date, but the docket at the end of the document reads: "Coppies Letters about N. Carolina March 1772."

For Campbell of Balole, see pp. 29–30, this volume.

Lachlan Mackinnon of Corrychatachan was the tacksman, or principal tenant, of the farm Corrychatachan, owned by Sir Alexander MacDonald of Sleat, Isle of Skye, and held

was written before Balole emigrated to North Carolina in 1775. He knew as much about Carolina as the new settlers did, perhaps more, since his uncle Neil MacNeill had come to North Carolina in 1739 with the McAllisters and other Highlanders. Balole gained his knowledge of Carolina from his various relatives and friends there, and from his frequent visits. His advice carried great weight, not only on his home island of Islay and the neighboring isles, but also on Skye, where this letter was copied and circulated.

Copy Campbell of Bellol To Corriechatuchan:

I recd yours of 20th of last Month & observe the difft. Contents, in regard to your Queries about North Carolina &ca, And in answer to all take as follows; Last Year I brot. some passengers to that Country, I went first ashoar in S. Carolina it is the richest place I ever saw Suppose I lived 12 years in Jamaica, their produce is Indigo Rice Silk and Cottan with sundry others, but by all Accots I could learn, it is far from being so healthy as N.C: the produce of this last is Tarr Turpentine Beef & pork & some Indigo Rice and Tobacco all Sort of timber, with various other Commodities; N.C: is but a new Settlemt. in Comparison to S.C.: I have seen the first Child was born to the English there & I do not believe he is above 45 years old An Uncle of mine Niell MacNiel of Ardulay[42] brot. over the first High-

in tack by Mackinnon. The principal tenants of estates were referred to by the names of their farms, hence Mackinnon was called Corrychatachan. Many of Sir Alexander MacDonald's tacksmen and subtenants emigrated to America because of the sharp increase in rents that MacDonald imposed; and their enthusiasm for America was infectious. When Samuel Johnson and James Boswell were touring the Western Isles in 1773, Boswell noted that Mrs. Mackinnon "talked as if her husband and family would emigrate, rather than be oppressed by their landlord." George Birkbeck Hill, and L. F. Powell, eds., *Boswell's Life of Johnson*, 2nd ed. (Oxford, 1964), 520, 156, 161.

42 Neil McNeill was one of the leaders of 350 emigrants from Argyllshire who arrived in North Carolina in September, 1739. This was the first large group of emigrants from the Highlands to arrive in North Carolina, among whom was Alexander McAllister (see introduction to McAllister letters). Twenty-two of these emigrant-settlers, including McNeill and McAllister, received grants of land along the Cape Fear River from Cross Creek to the Lower Little River in Bladen County. McNeill's grants totaled 1271 acres. Duane Meyer, *The Highland Scots of North Carolina, 1732–1776* (Chapel Hill, NC, 1961), 79, 81, 82.

landers that went there 30 years ago, he then settled under many dissadvantages 40 Miles in the midst of Woods distant from any other Settlemt., which hurt him and them greatly, but now the Case is quite altered, the town of Wilmington which is now the princl. one in the province, is a fine thriving pretty place, it had but 3 hutts in it, when my Uncle went over, it is 24 Miles fm the Sea on a river[43] larger than the Thames, and has a considerable trade with most parts of England; 100 Miles above this town lies Croscreeks[44] on the same River, a very thriving place, the Highlanders are mostly settled about this last, each has a plantation of his own on the river Side & live as happy as princes, they have liberty & property & no Excise, no dread of their being turned out of their lands by Tyrants, each has as good a Charter as a D. of Argyle,[45] or a Sir A Macdonald,[46] and only pay half a Crown a year for 100 Acres they possess, in Short I never saw a people seemed to me to be so really happy as our Countrymen there, As to health they have no more Complaints than those in the highlands; It is impossible within the small Bounds of a letter to give you an adequate Idea of this Country, but as I dont choose to conceall any part of the knowlede fm any of my Countrymen that want to go there take the following Sketch; = The Calculation made in that Country is this, that if a person take £500 Str with him and employ it in any rationall manner he may live equall to any Laird of £500 p Annum in any part of great Brittain, & so in proportion with any Sum one carries wt. him free there As for getting lands no person needs have the least doubt about that for I was well informed if all the people in Scotland & Ireland were to go there theyd have plenty of land in that province, for what is known of it already is much larger than Brittain & Ireland put together; It is already divided into 32 Countrys,[47] what is settled of it I do not doubt but Argyleshire has as many Soulls in it as N.C. this day,[48] when I went there I was invited by Gentlemen in different Counties to go & settle with each in his own County, for there is nothing they

---

[43] Cape Fear River.

[44] See pp. 32–33, this volume, for a description of Cross Creek.

[45] John Campbell, 5th Duke of Argyle.

[46] Sir Alexander MacDonald, 9th Baronet of Sleat (c. 1745–1795). See p. 183, n. 41, this volume.

[47] Counties. In 1769, North Carolina had 30 counties. In 1770, four new counties were added. H. Roy Merrens, *Colonial North Carolina in the Eighteenth Century: A Study in Historical Geography* (Chapel Hill, NC, 1964), 27–29.

[48] The population of Argyllshire at this time was between 70,000 (in 1755) and 86,000 (in the 1790s). The population of North Carolina in 1770 was about 175,000. Meyer, *Highland Scots*, 49; A. Roger Ekirch, *"Poor Carolina": Politics and Society in Colonial North Carolina, 1729–1776* (Chapel Hill, NC, 1981), 6.

want so much as people I referred making a Choice positively untill I re-
turned when I woud have more leisure to choose; I must own I have a strong
Attachmt. to be and settle with my own Countrymen in the County of
Cumberland where I have some lands Relations & friends; In this County
I could buy a settled plantation with a good house Out houses 80 Acres of
opened lands & 500 Acres of wood lands, & which woud return more than
any farm in Ilay or Sky,[49] I say I coud purchase such a place for £150 or £160
Str. & some of them are Sold for £60, all on the river Side where you send
produce to town & getts of Goods & money, I would therefore advise all
the Gentlemen that are going to that Country to referr making any purchass
till they go themselves & have their own choice, for they have no more
Occasion for Anxiety about lands when they come there than they woud
have about Water & Stones in the highlands; You ask if the trees are farr
fm oyr:[50] They are so much that you can gallop a horse thro all the Woods
I saw there without touching a tree, there are also some spots without trees
at all but are not reckoned good lands, Upon the whole if that Country was
as well known as the little knowledge I have of it there woud be few tents[51]
or farmers in Scotland or Ireland in 5 years; I add no more &ca. – P.S. I
forgot that there is flower & great Corn there in plenty I am Sir Your most
obt Sevt. Sic Subscribitur

Campbell of Bellole

[49] Islay or Skye.
[50] Another.
[51] Tenants.

SOUTH CAROLINA AND GEORGIA

Letters of Alexander Cumine and George Ogilvie, South Carolina, 1763–1774[1]

THE following six letters were selected from many letters in the Ogilvie-Forbes of Boyndlie Manuscripts at the University of Aberdeen Library. The Ogilvie family lived in the northeastern part of Aberdeenshire, about two miles south of Fraserburgh, at the estate of Auchiries, established by James Ogilvie in 1715. Alexander Ogilvie (1723–1791), the oldest son of James Ogilvie and Margaret Strachan, was heir to his father's estate. But, his younger brothers had to find careers elsewhere, and several of them went to America to "try their fortunes." Only one of them, Charles (1731–1788), succeeded in his Carolina ventures. He became a merchant in Charleston, but then moved to London in 1761 to handle his firm's business from there. He sent his nephew George (Alexander's son) to South Carolina to superintend his plantations there, and it is George's letters about his experiences in South Carolina that are included here.

The Cumines were neighbors and friends of the Ogilvies and fought beside them in the Jacobite Rebellion of 1745. In addition, Alexander Ogilvie, the recipient of three of the Alexander Cumine letters included here, was married to Mary Cumine, daughter of George Cumine of Pitullie, and hence it seems likely that the correspondents were related by marriage.[2]

---

[1] *Source:* Ogilvie-Forbes of Boyndlie Papers, MS 2740/10/4–5, Aberdeen University Library, King's College, Aberdeen. *Courtesy* obtained through Aberdeen University Library. The letters are all retained copies.

[2] Ogilvie-Forbes of Boyndlie Papers (hereafter Ogilvie-Forbes Papers); Alistair Tayler and Henrietta Tayler, *Jacobites of Aberdeenshire & Banffshire in the Forty-Five* (Aberdeen, 1928), 367.

Alexander Cumine decided to leave Scotland in October 1762 to try his fortune in Charleston, South Carolina, and he arrived on the *Nightengale* in the spring of 1763. He worked for a merchant for awhile, because he wanted to learn the business so that he could start his own firm, but when trade declined, Cumine took a job in February 1769 as a Latin schoolteacher in Beaufort, South Carolina. He taught 20 boys for £14.6s sterling each, and 4 girls for £7.3 each. Because he remained loyal to Britain, he was forced to leave South Carolina in October 1777, and went to Jamaica.[3]

George Ogilvie (1748–1801) was the only son of Alexander Ogilvie of Auchiries and Mary Cumine Ogilvie. During the 1760s, he lived in London with his uncle, Charles Ogilvie, and family while he was in school there. In 1767 Charles wrote his brother Alexander (George's father) that he had no place for George in his business, and thought he was "too young & inexperienced to enter upon Bussiness by himself." George was then only 19. However, six years later, Charles employed his nephew to manage his plantations in South Carolina, and offered him 50% of the profits.[4] George proved to be very industrious; in a short time he earned enough money to buy his own plantation on Crow Island near Camden as well as property in Georgia.[5]

George Ogilvie's letters, written from his uncle's plantation, Myrtle Grove, are curiosities in themselves. They describe, as no other letters in this collection do, the wildness of the back parts of America and the isolation. His experience in Georgia was completely new to him. Not only was he in a strange, remote country, but he had to take uncultivated wilderness and turn it into working, and profitable, plantations – something for which his training in Britain had not prepared him. No such estates existed in Britain, where private property had been under cultivation for centuries. He was often lonely and took up writing poetry. One of his poems, *Carolina; or, The Planter*, composed in 1776, is an account of his building a plantation

[3] Gregory Palmer, *Biographical Sketches of Loyalists of the American Revolution* (Westport, CT, 1984), 193; Alexander Cumine to Alexander Ogilvie, March 17, 1770, Ogilvie-Forbes Papers, MS 2740/10/4/13. In this letter, Cumine writes that he was then teaching 15 boys for £1200 currency or £171.8.7 sterling per year. He would use £70 sterling for his maintenance and save £100 sterling to help him get ahead.

[4] Tayler and Tayler, *Jacobites of Aberdeenshire*, 367; Ogilvie-Forbes Papers, MS 2740/10/3/13; Edmund Berkeley and Dorothy Smith Berkeley, *Dr. Alexander Garden of Charles Town* (Chapel Hill, NC, 1969), 255–256.

[5] Berkeley and Berkeley, *Alexander Garden*, 256.

from scratch, beginning with digging up roots and forming mounds to restrain the "tide-stem'd river."

The troubles with Great Britain soon put an end to George's life as a South Carolina planter. He refused to take the Oath of Abjuration required by the revolutionary government, and was banished. He returned to Scotland, arriving in 1779, and later that year married his cousin Rebecca Irvine of Dumfries. They had 11 children. George inherited Auchiries in 1791, and stayed in Scotland until his death in 1801. He returned to South Carolina only briefly in 1785/6 to try to recover some of his confiscated property.[6] He had lost quite a lot in his adventure in America; he estimated that he would have made 2000 guineas a year or more if he had been able to keep his plantations. Shortly after he inherited Auchiries, he became comptroller of customs in Aberdeen – a job that must have seemed very far removed from digging up roots and building mounds to restrain the "tide-stem'd river."[7]

Alexander Cumine to Mary Ogilvie,[8] Charleston, South Carolina, April 1, 1763

Dr Madam   Charlestown April 1st 1763

I wrote Mr Ogilvie[9] of the 21st of March[10] in which I told him I think fully of my Agreement with Mr Hetherington I can say no more on that subject, only that I'm oblidgd to stay but two Years the first for 6 or Seven pound and the Second for 20 pound with one Suit of Cloaths and Bed and

[6] Berkeley and Berkeley, *Alexander Garden*, 275, 276, 316; David S. Shields, "George Ogilvie's *Carolina; Or, The Planter* (1776)," *The Southern Literary Journal* (Special Issue, 1986), 6–7.

[7] George Ogilvie to Alexander Ogilvie, April 25, 1778, Ogilvie-Forbes Papers, MS 2740/10/5/3; Palmer, *Biographical Sketches of Loyalists*, 656; Shields, "George Ogilvie's *Carolina*," [27] (p. 7 of *Carolina; or, The Planter*).

[8] Mary Ogilvie was the wife of Alexander Ogilvie of Auchiries.

[9] Alexander Ogilvie of Auchiries.

[10] In this letter Cumine writes of his arrival in South Carolina and his regrets at not having studied "Physic." He took a job with John Hetherington, who was a Charleston merchant in partnership with Alexander Kynock until October 1763, when the partnership was dissolved. Philip M. Hamer, et al., eds., *The Papers of Henry Laurens*, (Columbia, SC, 1968), 4: 195n (hereafter *Laurens Papers*).

Board equall with himself; I have been offerd the Ushership of the School here which is now made worth [70?] £ sterling a Year which I have Rejected by the Advice of my friends here; for setting aside the danger of being rejected after the severest Examination, the name of a Scotsman being almost enough for that; I would make little more than bare bread by it and that with the greatest trouble and vexation eternaly confind and ever out of the way of preferment, for as to my making a Stock by it and then commence Merchant it would Require a number of Years, as I could not save more than 20 or at most 30 pound a Year which would be long in procuring me a sufficient Stock to trade with whereas said they as soon as you are acquainted with business Mr Ogilvie[11] will procure you Credit in London and if you get a substantiall Partner you will do very well & instead of making 30 £ you have a Chance of making 3 or 400 pound a Year. When You write me give me your Sentiments of the Matter, and if Mr Charles & his Lady make you a Visit this Summer You might brotch the subject and I wish I was introducd to Mrs Ogilvie's[12] Relations here as they are people of Consequence in the place –

I write George[13] by this Opportunity and wont miss one in writing some of my friends or other. I expect you are as good as your promise in taking Notice of My Mother. As to my Shirts you mentiond to me in your last Letter and which my Mother wrote me You would make for me I could wish some of them were ruffled for there is not a Person here but wears their Ruffled Shirts, and it's necessary for one to be gentilly drest when they go into Company or they make but a poor figure for the People are very gay here.[14] I'm much oblidgd to you Madam for being so kinde as to provide

11 Charles Ogilvie. Charles Ogilvie was a younger son of James Ogilvie of Auchiries. Charles lived in Charleston, South Carolina, for about ten years, from 1751–1761, during which time he was a shipowner and partner in the merchant firm of Ogilvie & Ward, and later Ogilvie & Forbes. In 1761, he returned to London to carry on the firm's business there, while his partners, John Forbes and William Michie, stayed in Charleston. Lewis Namier and John Brooke, eds., *The House of Commons, 1754–1790*, 3 vols. (London, 1964), III: 223–224; *Laurens Papers*, 2: 133n.

12 Mary Ogilvie, Charles Ogilvie's wife. In 1762, Charles married Mary Michie, daughter of James and Martha Michie of Charleston, South Carolina. James Michie was a landholder, lawyer, chief justice, member of the Royal Council, and judge of the Vice-Admiralty Court, and was therefore a person of "Consequence in the place." *Laurens Papers*, 2: 203n.

13 George Ogilvie was 15 at this time. See George Ogilvie's letters later in this section.

14 One other observer, writing in 1774, noted of Charleston that "It is upon the whole rather a gay place, there being public dancing assemblies and plays acted in it, with horse racing about a mile off." "Charleston, S.C., in 1774, as Described by an English Traveller," *Historical Magazine*, 9(1865), 343.

me some Shirts which is a necessary Article here, it being necessary to Shift [e]very day in Summer, and it is already as warm as Summer wt you

I do know but next year, if life Remain, when I have got a little Cash I may send for two or three dozen of thread and Cotton hose as they could be dispos'd of to advantage and some pieces of Linnen and I could by this means lay out any money I had to advantage. Give my Compliments to Mr Ogilvie and Miss Peggie[15] to your Friends at Auchiries, I would be glade to know if L – P[16] was still alive or not if he is Mind me to him in the kindes[t] manner I was extreamly sorry I was so stupid as come away with out seeing him but was then in Confusion & never reflected. Remember me to all that family, Ill write the Master of Pitsligo[17] next Opportunity; Charlie is very well and writes you by this occasion Give my Compliments to Johnie Perie, Ill be glade to hear from You as often as possible, for it will be great Cordial to me at such a distance to hear from your family & my Mother, whom when you write me you will acquaint oft I have wrote Mr Charles and design to keep a close correspondence wt him & George. I have keept my health perfectly as yet. Ill conclude wishing you & your family all happiness & Am Madam Your Most Obdt humble Servant

Alexr Cumine

Alexander Cumine to Alexander Ogilvie, Charleston, South Carolina, April 22, 1763

Sir   Charlestown So Carolina Aprile 22 1763

I hope you Receiv'd my Letters of the 21st of March and first of Aprile, the one to you and the other to Mrs Ogilvie; in which I told you of my Agreement with the Merchant I stay with, I'm to stay with him only two Years [certain?] & to have next Year 20 £ sterling if not more for We are

---

[15] Margaret Ogilvie was Alexander and Mary Ogilvie's daughter. She later married William Urquhart of Craigston. Tayler and Tayler, *Jacobites of Aberdeenshire*, 368.

[16] Lord Pitsligo, 1678–1762 (Alexander Forbes, 4th Lord Forbes of Pitsligo). Lord Pitsligo, a Stuart supporter, was influential in rallying many of his neighbors in Buchan to support the Jacobite Rebellion. After Culloden, he was sought after by Hanoverian troops for his treasonous behavior, and spent his time in disguise, hiding out in caves and in the dwellings of some of his tenants. Lord Pitsligo eventually settled at Auchiries, where his son, John, Master of Pitsligo, was living. John's wife was Alexander Ogilvie's sister, Rebecca. In 1741, when Alexander Ogilvie's father died, Lord Pitsligo served as his guardian. Lord Pitsligo died in December 1762. Tayler and Tayler, *Jacobites of Aberdeenshire*, 367, 379–385.

[17] John Forbes, son of Lord Pitsligo. Tayler and Tayler, *Jacobites of Aberdeenshire*, 380.

not finally agreed yet, we have spoke only in General terms, but we will make a finall agreement presently when Mr Forbes[18] is once at leasure & Mr Keith[19] comes to Town; and by the time the two years are gone I will be perfectly acquainted with business, and capable of entring into business; and if your Brother[20] would be so good & kinde as intrust me with 2 or 300 £ sterling worth of Goods which would enable me to enter into partnership with some Merchant here, I might make perhaps a pretty good fortune for myself in a short time; and this is the way all the Merchants here have begun viz by Credit, & if One be diligent & industrious & make proper Remittances the Merchants [at home?] will trust him more & more, and so enable him to extend his trade further; there is plenty of money to be got here if One was once in the way of making it, they think no more of laying out a Guinea on coming into a Shop here, than some will at home of laying out a Shilling. Mr Forbes is very kinde to me & desir'd me the other day, if I should want money to come to him and he would supply me, and I'm sure he would assist me to sett up for myself, for he is a very kinde [sort?] of Man & very National I'm told with regard to his Countray men, they viz your Brother Mr Forbes & Meckie[21] are deeply engagd in business. their House is one of the Greatest in Town & frequented by the best of Company; & they go under the denomination of Ogilvie Forbes & Company; I like this place very well as yet, its very pleasant just now every thing is green and beautifull & as Virgil says, nunc formosissimus annus.[22] We had green pease two Weeks ago, but by & [by?] every thing will be dried up by the violent heat of the Sun it is already exceeding hott; A good number of people have gone home from this Province in the last Ships for London every one of whom have made fine Fortunes here carrying with them as was said in the news papers one hundred thousand Dollars in Specie besides [Gold?], and among the rest is one Mr Henderson[23] from Aberdeen who has been Schoolmaster here for 14 or 15 Years & has made a pretty little Fortune for himself

[18] John Forbes, partner of Charles Ogilvie in the merchant firm of Ogilvie and Forbes.

[19] William Keith, the son of Dr. William Keith, who lived at Keithfield in St. John's Parish, Berkeley County. *Laurens Papers*, 4: 203n.

[20] Charles Ogilvie.

[21] William Michie, Charles Ogilvie's co-partner and co-owner (with John Forbes) in the 120-ton ship *Carey*. *Laurens Papers*, 7: 278n; "Ship Registers in the South Carolina Archives, 1734–1780," *South Carolina Historical Magazine*, 74(1973), 207.

[22] "Now is the year most fair." Virgil, *Eclogues*, 3.56.

[23] William Henderson had been a schoolmaster at the Charleston Free School from March 25, 1753 to March 25, 1763, after serving as usher (assistant) of the free school from October 1750 to March 1753. Henry Laurens wrote a favorable letter of recommendation for Hen-

& family which enables him now to return to his Countray; by him I send this Letter, along wt him goes a Young Lad to Aberdeen for his Education one Mr Keith a Son of Doctor William Keith's of Keithfield some where about [ ], he is married to an Aunt of [Ben Eugee's?] by whom he got 1000 Guineas & is a Gentleman of a fine fortune & he sends his Son to Aberdeen to compleat his Education he is to stay wt Mr Skeen; and there is another Scotsman among the passengers one [Monson Parson?] of the Scots [Meeting?] who has made a fine Fortune here by a marriage and is gone for St Andrews from whence he came the Scots generally do well, which is the Reason the Natives dislike them, and bear them [so?] much Envy. Yester night was married the Right honorable Lord William Cambel,[24] Commander of his Majesties Ship Nightingale, who convoyd us here, to one Miss Isard a fine Young Lady & One of the greatest Fortunes in the Province, he carries her home with him they say She has a fortune of 14,000 £ Sterling, and was Just on the point of being married to a Gentleman of Fortune here, but the Duke of Argyl's Son & a Scotsman too soon defeat his Antagonist & gaind the prize from a Carolinian such things as these procure us their hatred. this night My Lord & his Lady sup wt Mr Forbes who does honor to his Countray in countenancing & entertaining his Countray men the Officers of the Army & Men of War are always wt him, which is no small advantage to him in the end as they take every thing they need from his Store.

Charlie is very well but has neglected to write his friends so soon as he ought. he does not seem to feel for the anxiety his friends may be in, tho I told him to write when I did yet he has senslesly put his Letters, even now on board [the?] Man of War, and She maynt now sail for some time. My Lord has got married, & so his friends wont [hear?] from himself for some-time I desird him just now to [write?] afresh but does not seem disposd to it; as for me it gives me pleasure to write my Friends, & Receive word from them and I hope you'll favour me with as [close?] a Corespondence as possible I am Sir Yours &c

Alexr Cumine

derson to Monkhouse Davison in London, saying that Henderson's reasons for leaving South Carolina were his failing health and the severity of the climate for his children. *Laurens Papers*, 4: 77n; 3: 416, 416n. See also 8: 130n.

24 Lord William Campbell, son of the 4th Duke of Argyll and the Honorable Mary Bellenden. In 1762 he became a captain in the navy, and as commander of the *Nightingale*, he sailed to South Carolina in 1763, where he met and married Sarah Izard, daughter of Ralph Izard and Rebecca Blake Izard. In 1766 he was appointed governor of Nova Scotia, and in 1773, he accepted the governorship of South Carolina.

Alexander Cumine to Alexander Ogilvie,
Charleston, South Carolina, June 17, 1763

Dr Sir　　　　　　　　　　　　　　　　　Charlestown 17th June 1763

I was much disapointed in my expectation of some Letters by the Vessel from London the other day; I expected a Letter from George as his Uncle[25] wrote his Partner by the Vessel and he might have known of it if he had askd his Uncle. I long prodigiously to hear from some of you if I dont by the next opportunity Ill think you are all dead or have [forgot?] I'm anxious to hear from my Mother how she is doing and expect to hear from your family and [you?] at the same time as I have ordred her to write when you do & only then.

I'm still in perfect health myself thanks to Heaven, and the Countray seems to agree wt me very well, only the heat is very troublesome and keeps me in a Continual sweat all day long But we endeavour to keep up the Spirits wt Cooling draughts of punch and such like as much as possible; I like the Countray very well, its a Countray very good for a poor man for any person who will be industrious & carefull will get his Bread here. The people who are reckond poor here are not in the condition they are wt you difficulted to get a Subsistance; but eat and drink well who tho they have not plantations and Negroes yet have houses and small pieces of Land where they bring up Horses & Cattle & Fowls and such like wt Rice & Corn by which means they live very happily and what they spare of their produce they bring to market here and sell to advantage, whereas the poor att home very oft cann't get where with to Cloath & keep themselves alive another Beauty in this Countray is that all white people are on an equall footing, excepting the Dutch & foreign Settlers, who are not much regarded. But among the British every one is a Companion to another equally affable & [free?] no distinction att all and young Beginners are encouragd and supported if they behave well and are industrious and carefull and [if] one [once?] gets a good name he's sure to thrive; and here fine advantageous marriages may be and are often made, if a Man is in Business he will get [a?] Lady wt £1000 or £2000 as soon as ask her its his own fault if [he?] dont and her Fortune & Relations establish him [presently?], Mr Hetherington wt whom I live is going to be married next week to a very pretty young Lady one Miss Miller wt a handsome Fortune of £3000 str which wt her numerous Friends will establish him effectually in his business, but

[25] Charles Ogilvie.

will detain him in this Countray longer than he designd as he dont like it very well And I'm told more matrimonial happiness subsists in this place than perhaps in any part of the [World?]; the Women are pretty and beautifull & [   ] and [   ] surprisinly are quite easy [kind and affable?], they see but little of the World here and have not the advantage of the Education the Ladys at home have[26] or they would be very clever for they as well as the Men have very strong natural [   ], But the Ladys are very expert at the needle and sew extreamly well, they are very fond of Foreigners & especially our Countray men; they seem to have gaind the affections of the fair here some how or other, for not one who is inclind that way but makes fine Marriages, for the Scots are very numerous and are extreamly industrious & sober by which means they are become the principall Merchants in the place there being three Scotch Merchants here to one of any other Nation and they have been extreamly lucky in trade & making Connections and generaly make good Husbands which makes the Ladys like them so. Thus I have given you a Charecter of the people here as far as I can yet know I have been in the Countray for some time at a Store we have there and have seen the manners of the people there as well as in Town.

I'm to have from Mr Hetherington 16 £ str and to stay wt him from year to year as I think proper We agree very well, But he must give me a good deal more next year else I wont stay wt him; I wrote George & his Uncle to send me a suit of Cloaths, which I have now contermanded as I have been oblidgd to get a Suit for Mr Hetheringtons wedding, and am not sure but I may get my Cloaths for prime Cost. that is Cloath Cloaths, but am not sure, and have no occasion to pay them till the years End

---

[26] Education in South Carolina before the Revolution suffered in comparison not only to that in England but to that in some of the other colonies as well. Planters commonly hired tutors for their children, but free schools also existed. Many families paid tuition for their children to attend these "free" schools, but the poorer children were supported by benefactors. South Carolina had no college before the war, so educational opportunities beyond grammar school (equivalent to the modern high school) were available only to those families who could send their children to a college in another colony or abroad. Few colonial women were well educated. They received little formal education, as they were expected to prepare themselves for the domestic life. Robert M. Weir, *Colonial South Carolina: A History* (Millwood, NY, 1983), 248–252. As Ebenezer Hazard observed of the opportunities for women's education in South Carolina in 1778: "The young ladies are generally kept in the country till they are 15 or 16 years old, and then brought to town and put to a boarding school for a year. I am told *their* education in particular is scandalously neglected." H. Roy Merrens, "A View of Coastal South Carolina in 1778: The Journal of Ebenezer Hazard," *South Carolina Historical Magazine*, 73(1972), 184.

when We Reckon every thing else I will send home for such as Linnen & hose & Shoes all which are excessive dear here I would pay [20/?] sterling for a pair Shoes here & from London I will gett them for half that – I will write Mrs Ogilvie in a week or two for I have occasions now every week this Comes by Mr Rose[27] your friend who is gone home in his New Ship. Give my kinde Compliments to Mrs Ogilvie Miss Peggie & your Friends at Auchiries & the Coast side Charles is well my Compliments to his Sister & Johnie [Pirie?] I am Sir [Your very?] humble Sertt & hearty well Wisher

Alexr Cumine

Alexander Cumine to Alexander Ogilvie, Port Royal, South Carolina, February 15, 1766

Sir   Portroyal South Carolina 15th Feby 1766

Your much esteemd Favour of 12th Jany 1765 I duely received, and wrote you soon after since which I am favoured with none of yours, I long much to hear from you, and my Mother

I was lately favoured with a letter from George accquainting me of his going down to Scotland; since then I have not heard from him; As to myself I still Continue here with Mr Francis Stuart,[28] and keep my health extremly well, I have not had a fitt of sickness since I came into the Country – Your Brother has never wrote me since my arrivall in this Country.

I designd by this Conveyance to have sent my Mother four Guineas, but as it is uncertain whether the Ship will go for London or not, being

---

[27] John Rose, owner of the *Heart of Oak*, registered in Charleston on April 27, 1763. The ship was cleared to sail on June 14 for Cowes, England. The ship's London registry (November 11) listed Henry Laurens as one of the owners. *Laurens Papers*, 4: 77n.

[28] In a letter dated January 26, 1765, Cumine wrote Alexander Ogilvie that he had moved to Port Royal, South Carolina, and now lived with Francis Stuart. Stuart was a younger brother of John Stuart, superintendent of Indian affairs for the southern district of North America. John Stuart and Patrick Reid established a merchant firm in Charleston in 1748, the year John Stuart arrived in America. They put Francis in charge of managing the firm's store at Beaufort, Port Royal. When the firm went bankrupt, Francis started his own firm in Beaufort (Francis Stuart & Co.), where he remained until his death in 1766. Francis, having started out with no more than £50, made a fortune of £10,000 sterling. John R. Alden, *John Stuart and the Southern Colonial Frontier* (London, 1944), 161–164, 174; Alexander Cumine to Alexander Ogilvie, Port Royal, March 4, 1766, Ogilvie-Forbes Papers, MS 2740/10/4/12.

bound to [Cowes?] for Orders have declin'd it but another Opportunity which will be soon, meantime must entreat you to supply my Mother any small thing she may want such as a Boll or two of meal, and I shall take care to reimburse you; this will be adding to the many Favours already received.

I have no Occasion by this time to inform you of the Opposition the Stamp Act has met with in this part of the British Dominions, you will see a full detail of the American transactions on this Occasion in the publick papers, and shall only observe to you that tho no person here approves of this Odious Act so disagreeable to the people as being imposd on them by a Legislative Body where they have no proper representation, yet the sober thinking allow that improper steps have been taken, and that they have gone the wrong way to work to obtain redress; the disputing the authority of Parliment to tax Ameria to be sure is very daring yet I cannt help thinking the people of America hav[e] [no?] reason to complain; and no Inhabitant or [   ] of America can think otherwise, America is of the utmost importance to great Britain, & I think it is no good Policy in the Ministry to alienate the minds of the Colonists from their Mother Country and awaken in them a Spirit of Industry and Economy, for the richer and more luxurious the Inhabitants grow the more of the British Manufactures will they consume, and the less will they think of rivalling Great Britain, in short the people here think themselves highly injured by this Act and are determined never to admitt of it till compelld by Force and if the Government at home persist God knows what may be the Consequence Our Ports have been shut up for some months and the Vessells are now permitted to sail yet are they & their Cargoes subject to Seizure as their Clearances are not stamped. I have sent by the Vessell that Carries this a half barrell rice for my Mother which George will send down, I shall be glad to hear from you Give my kindest Compliments to all your Friends at Auchiries and Pittendrum, and Mr Cumine of Pittulie;[29] and please remember me to Miss Peggy I beg you would present my Compliments to your Lady having nothing more to add will Conclude wishing you and your Family all happiness & Felicity & I am my Dr Sir Your most Obedient hble Servt

Alexander Ogilvie Esqr   Alexander Cumine

---

[29] William Cumine of Pitullie (1721–1767) fought with Lord Pitsligo and Alexander Ogilvie in the rebellion of 1745. Tayler and Tayler, *Jacobites of Aberdeenshire*, 138–140.

George Ogilvie to Margaret Ogilvie, Myrtle Grove Plantation, Santee River, South Carolina, June 25, 1774[30]

My Dearest Pegie   MyrtleGrove Santee Saturday 25th June 1774

I have a huge mind to begin this letter with assuring you that this is the first hour I have been perfectly at leisure since we parted – It is not reasonable to expect youl believe me – I can hardly believe myself – let us see, how has this brother of yours been employed? what has he been doing since he left London? there I'l admit he had some [show?] of business! I must answer, Nothing! or next to nothing – at Sea, I expected to do a world of things – and a World of things had I to do when I embarkd – but at sea with a Number of troublesome Passengers there is no settling to bussiness – well said I, there will be plenty of time in Carolina – the warm weather will oblige me to keep the house and I may as well write as be Idle The first three days after my arrival were employd in renewing old and making New acquaintances – the fourth I set out to meet my Uncle at Indian Land[31] – was gone about a week about another week passd in resting from one and prepairing for another Journey – about a fortnight was spent here, at George-town and other Places to the Northward – then Back to Charlestown rest a few days and off again about 150 Miles right Inland for Camden and other parts on the Waterie River from whence we returnd this day Week – My Uncle accompanyd me in the above expeditions but that is a pleasure I can no longer hope for as he is now bussie prepairing for his return to England and will I expect carry this Letter – I left him very well in town yesterday for I only arrivd here late last night and propose returning to Charlestown on Friday so you see I am not yet settled – indeed I expect to lead a kind of Vagabond life looking after my own and My Uncles bussiness – For our Plantations lay almost at the Oposite Corners of the Province – This of Myrtle Grove being about 50 or 60 Miles North our other new settlement Calld Belmont is within 4 Miles of Camden about 126 Miles West and my

---

[30] Margaret Ogilvie, whom George addresses affectionately as "My Dearest Pegie," was George Ogilvie's sister (see p. 191, n. 15). George Ogilvie's letters have been printed in David S. Shields, "The Letters of George Ogilvie," *The Southern Literary Journal* (Special Issue, 1986), 117–125. Shields has included two letters written by Ogilvie that are not in this volume: April 25, 1778, and February 1779, ibid., 125–132.

[31] George's uncle, Charles Ogilvie, owned three plantations in South Carolina: Belmont (near Camden); Myrtle Grove on the Santee River; and Indian Land, 70 miles south of Charleston.

Uncles own Plantation at Indian Land about 70 Miles South from Charles-town – and youl observe that partly the Situation of the places but chiefly the Badness of the Roads and accommodation in Crossing from one Country Place to another renders it necessary to go and come allways thro the Me-tropolis of the Province – so that I cannot visit these three places and return again under 500 Miles were I to pay no visits off the Road which may be computed at least 100 Miles more but this I do not at present consider as any disadvantage having allways found traveling agree with both my health & inclination besides I hope it may Check the Growth of laisiness, a weed that vegitates most luxuriently in this Climate – It is not worth mentioning – but having no overseer here just now, I slept last night (for the first time in my life) *at least* four miles distant from any white Person – like the Tyrant of some Asiatick Isle the only free Man in an Island of Slaves –

Ever since I arrivd I have intended giving you and my other friends some Idea of the Situation and occupation of a Carolina Planter – particularly of myself – but as I know of no Book to which I can refer you for information I find that to be understood it is necessary to give too long a detail for the Compass of one letter besides the Subject will stand me in good sted when-ever Im disposd to plague you with a long Epistle and in order to spin it out the longer I shall begin with some observations upon the province in General of which Ive already seen more than nine tenths of the white natives for it is but very lately that the Low Country people ever thought of visiting the Back woods which are principally inhabited by Northern stragglers and Irish Emigrants – but you must make allowance for remarks made on so superficial a view and I shall acknowledge my mistakes as I discover them on being better acquainted or informd – You have probably heard that all the Sea Coast of this and the Nieghbouring Provinces is one Continued dead Plain intirely coverd with wood except small spots where Plantations are settled – which is so near a literal truth that I know of no hills within less than Eighty miles of the Sea so high as to give a prospect over trees that grow on the Lowest swamps – indeed the trees in the swamps generally Grow so much taller than the trees upon high land as to be all equal atop & the places labord for plantations are so small in Comparison with the immence woods that the Eye does not perceive the least inequality nor any kind of opening when it surveys the Boundless forrest either from the sea or the Top of any building, of which there are very few of sufficient height to give a view over the woods – From those that are the prospect is only bounded by the Horizon & only varigated by the different Shades, that distinguish the high land & swamp trees – I said this plain Extends at least Eighty miles from the Sea – but if we except a Small ridge of Hills calld

the High hills of Santee about 14 Miles long & scarce two broad with a few
stragling hills in that neighbourhood it extends in this province at least thirty
miles further Back – at which distance the Country begins and continues
rising till it forms Part of the vast Chain of Mountains calld Apalaches which
intersect North America from N.E. to S.W. at the Distance of about 200
or 250 Miles from the Sea – the Southern extremity of them terminating
about the same distance from the Gulph of Florida – I am uncertain how
far they extend to the Northward – Behind these Mountains the Country
again sinks into fertile & I may say boundless valleys waterd by the Noble
Rivers Ohio and Mississippi – the Northwestern Branches of which last
seem to set Limits to our still imperfect knowledge of North America except
the trifling discoverys made on the Western Shores of California – For near
a hundred miles from the Sea one may say of this Province without much
exaggeration or exception that the *high* Lands are the poorest and *the Low*
the Richest in the world when I say high you must understand me to mean
every foot of Land that is not naturally coverd with water the greatest part
of the year either by stagnate Rain Water Overflowing of Rivers or the
diurnal flux of the Tides which you may imagine in so low and flat a Country
rise a great way from the Sea in the large Rivers with which this Province
abounds – by far the largest proportion of the high Land is what we call
Pine Barren *here*; being nothing but white Sand intermixd in some places
with a little sour Red Clay and such land produces nothing but Pine trees
& a Poor scrubbie Oak only fit for firewood – and early in the Spring or
after violent Rains a Little sour Stringie grass such as even Buchan Cowes
would turn up thier Noses at – tho custom here reconsiles the Cattle to it –
there is to be sure some high Land of better Quality where the soil is a
grayish Clay with blackish sand which produces Oak of various kinds Walnut
& Hickery, both of which have a great resemblance to the English Walnut
with a variety of other Forest trees which tho many of them bear English
Names are widely different from their Namesakes with you – Such Land is
esteemd good for Indigo Indian Corn Oats Wheat &ca. but is soon Exhausted whereas the LowLands calld Swamps are so exceedingly Rich that
many of them which have been planted above Sixty years without rest or
Mannure of any kind produce as Good Crops as at the first settling and are
deemd inexhaustible – The Swamp Lands are distinguishd by Inland and
River Swamp The Inland Swamps are Islands or lakes, which you will, of
Bog formd by stagnation of Brooks and Rain Water and enrichd with the
spoils of the surrounding high Lands – when these Swamps are Cultivated
they are *draind*, tho seldom so dry, if intended for Rice, as to be passible in
all places with dry feet – besides there is allways a Dam or reserve of water

at the upper end (if there is an upper end, but in general these swamps are dead Levels however they have all these Dams) for the purpose of Laying the Rice fields underwater which is generally done in this Month & the Next a little earlier or Later as the Season Requires – and should the season prove so Extreamly dry as to make these Dams or Reserves fail then the Planter loses his Crop which renders the Inland Swamp Plantations more precarious than the Tide Swamps, which when situated far enough from the sea to be clear of salt water and near enough to have the tides strong and regular are reckond the best Plantations of any for every kind of produce as there is always water for the Rice and all their fields are surrounded with high and strong Banks that keep the Corn and Indigo dry The River Swamps above the Tide are generally so liable to be overflowd at improper seasons by the sudden rising of the Rivers that tho the Quality of the soil is rich beyond Conception, much superiour to the Inland and equal to the Tide Swamps, yet their value is lessend prodigiously by that consideration as our Rivers sometimes Rise thirty nay forty foot in one Night but these floods or freshes, as theyr calld here, never do any damage where the Tide rises – which renders these Tide Lands by far the most valuable – when properly in order, they last forever but puting them in Complete order is both Tedious and expensive & generally reckond worth Seven pounds Sterling an acre – being all coverd with trees of a prodigious size which must be cut down, split up and burnd but the most laborious articles are the Banks and drains which must be of vast Size and Strength to withstand the force of the Tides – but a Graceless Neighbour of mine swears that when all these things are properly done we can mak good Crops in spite of G-ds teeth – however I believe he finds himself mistaken for once as the Grasshoppers have eat up his Indigo and the Crayfish damagd his Rice – This Island is Tide swamp such as I have been describing and My other Place calld Belmont, *high River swamp* – and *So high* that it has not been touchd with the freshes above once these twenty years – indeed it is reckond the highest piece of Swamp in the Province – being in some places from 30 to 40 foot above the Common level of the River Waterse which joining, about 30 Miles below Belmont, another large River calld Congerie – near the small Ridge of hills mentiond above & takes as well as the hills the name of Santee from an Indian nation now extinct – is reckond the finest in the province – about twenty miles from the Sea it again divides, forming a Chain of Islands of which this is one and about Seven Miles below me it emptys itself into the Sea by, for ought I know, as many Mouths as the Nile – but all of them impassible for ships of burthen by reason of Bars of sand at the Entrances – You perhaps lookd for a more particular discription of Both Myrtle Grove and Belmont – but you must excuse me 'till next time – For I can no longer resist the temptation of a Plate of wild Cherries which has just made its appearance – after dispatching them I shall treat myself with a dry shirt and a dry pair of Breeches for those I have on are driping with my mornings tea – nay do not laugh, I have not bep----d myself but when the Thermometer is at 92 water finds more ways than one out of our leakie Casks – Thank G-d here comes a Black Cloud – betokening a Thunder Squall – so I shall eat my broild Chicken Coolly, and as comfortably as a broild Chicken can be eaten in State

If my Uncle does not go very soon I shall most probably write some of my other friends with you – but if I should not have time pray make one of your best Sunday apologys for me – and you may venture to answer for the Sincerity of my affection and good wishes – you need not be afraid of saying more than my heart feels for you all I long very much to hear from you having no letters from Scotland later than February – Your affectionate

Geo Ogilvie

George Ogilvie to Margaret Ogilvie, Myrtle Grove Plantation, South Carolina, November 22, 1774[32]

A few days before I left Charlestown I receivd a Couple of most agreeable and welcome letters [one from?] you the other from my Father which last I acknowledgd before I left town and would have done the same to you had I not been hurryd hither on Account of some misunderstanding betwixt my Negroes & overseer (a very common and the most disagreeable circumstance) attending Planting when I got here no less than ten of the Best (say most useful hands) were run away but they all returnd to their duty on hearing that I was at home which induced me to pardon them much more easily than they deservd as runing away is one of the faults I am angriest at of any that Negroes have and I do not find that the Overseer had requird any thing unreasonable of them – The very strong terms [wt?] which you describe the Attachment of my dear friends and relations to your unworthy Brother made me for a moment forget that the Immence [Waters?] of the Atlantick di-

[32] This copy of the letter has no addressee, no date, and no place of writing. However, a docket on the back of the letter says that it is a copy of one written to his sister from Myrtle Grove on November 22, 1774.

vided me from a family whose very looks your letter seemd to present to my view judge of my gratitude by what yourself would feel in my situation and do the like justice to it in your discription to these best of people – I ask no more

Myrtle Grove a terrestial Paradize! let me see, what Paradizial objects would present themselves to your mere Corporial View (not that of your fertile fancy) A few Rough boards naild together so nicely as to admitt the wind and the light thro every seam – placed on the top of a sandy hillock about five feet above the level of the water forms what we call a House of 26 by 14 feet which divided into two rooms contain last night My Overseer his wife two Children John Smith two Gentlemen, who came to see me, and your most humble Servant in all Seven Whites besides two or three Negros how do you like my accommodation within doors? Without I believe I told you already that except a few sandy Hillocks making all together about four or almost five Acres the water coverd the whole Island as well as the banks on each side the River and all the neighbouring Islands once every twelve hours and the whole coverd with thick woods so matted with Briars and shrubs of the Creeping or vine Kind that there was no passing thro them without a Hatchet and the ground so soft that every step was up to the knees in Mud whilst swarms of Mosketoes are drawing blood at every Pore . . . Charming walks, but with your good leave I think they resemble the Paths *to* the Heavenly more than the walks *of* the earthly Garden of Eden

After this description which on my honour is not exaggerated in the smallest circumstance you will smile when I say I think Myrtle Grove will in a few years be both pretty and pleasant, at least at the time of Year when the Musketoes are Quiet I have already got about a Hundred Acres cleard of Trees and great part of it under sufficient Banks – and as the House stands near the N.E. Corner of the Island – I have already a view of the River to the North and East – and to the south of a Large Creek which nearly divides the Island as the River is very bold and the Banks coverd with stately trees the prospect in a Country where wood is scarce would be esteemd very fine – but here we think an open field the finest in the universe – however I have not forgot my old friendship for trees so far as not to leave a few of the old Inhabitants standing here & there –

I forget if I mentiond in my last letter that this Island is divided equally betwixt my Uncle & Mr David Deas[33] Whose daughters you may have

---

[33] David Deas came to South Carolina from Leith, Scotland, in 1738, and with his brother

seen or heard of [in?] Edinburgh – the upper or West end belongs to him & the Eastern End to my Uncle on a late Survey of it, it is found to Contain above 3000 Acres and is reckond worth at least Six pounds Sterling P Acre in its uncultivated State bringing such land into Complete order is reckond worth six or seven pounds more P Acre but I should think it may be done for less unless people are so unlucky as to lose many Slaves. Out of upwards of 50 belonging to my Uncle & me now on this Island & have gone thro greater hardships than any they will meet with in future only one Sickly Woman [has?] died which is much less than the Common Calculation for the Healthiest Parrish in England This is to be sure better luck than we could well expect & we were so much afraid of its being Sickly at first that we sent all the New Negroes intended for this Place to be seasond at my Uncles old Plantations but I expect them here in a few days now – I have also some reason to hope that this place will continue to be full as healthy as any in the Neighbourhood for by standing in the Middle of so large a River there is a constant Circulation of air indeed all last summer it blowd a very brisk Gale every day from 11 till betwixt 3 & 4 oClock which made it appear Cooler here when the Mercury stood at 94 $\frac{1}{2}$ than in some other places when it was not above 80 or at most 84 so much more do our feelings of heat or cold depend on the agitation or Stagnation of our Atmosphere than on the [ac]tual temprature of the air indeed nothing is more easily accounted for as the Current of air being constantly passing has [not?] time to receive any additional heat from our breath and Efluvia of our body whereas the same stagnate Atmosphere continuing a long time in Contact with our bodys & instead of refreshing us acquires in a short time a degree of heat equal to our skin which it touches and the heated air which we expire – Besides the free Circulation of air this place derives another advantage from being situated so near the Mouth of the River that at high Tides the Water is almost salt at least far from fresh now we reckon that the Sea air is much healthier than the inland, untill we get a great way back out of the Swamps – but if the free Circulation of Air Contributes to make this Milenium pleasant in Hot weather you may judge by Cortes[34] that in [w]inter it has a Contrary effect – for an elevation of 4 or 5 feet in a level of 6 or Seven Mile wide and 150 Long exposes us as much to the wind as the highest knoll at Cortes does in a Country like Buchan – and when I tell you that we have Ice this morning upwards of an Inch thick on Water standing in

John set up a merchant firm in Charleston. David Deas died in 1775. *Laurens Papers*, 1: 61n, 94n.

[34] Cortes is a hamlet in northeast Aberdeenshire five miles south of Fraserburgh.

the Kitchen and remind you of the Craziness of my Mansion you will readily believe that I sufferd almost as much with cold last night as I did with heat any night during the Summer – my two Guests tho cramd into a bed scarce three feet wide & coverd over head and Ears with more Blankets than ever Person Largue & has Rib sweated under, did nothing but Grumble, Laugh and Scold all night and the Cook Wench having turnd a parcell of Young Negroes out of the Kitchen they are all laying round the hearth so thick that I have very little benefit from the fire one of them John Wilkes has got his whole Wardrobe on his Back consisting of a Couple of shirts 2 pair Breeches two Coats & two WasteCoats whilst the Overseers eldest son a boy of three year old is runing about in his Shirt rejoicing that the frost has [kild?] the Musketoes which no longer since than yesterday morning were as bad as at any time in the Summer – for altho we have had several slight frosts before – none of them had been severe enough to destroy these devils in Minature – Who for six Months in the year would make this Country a Hell upon earth especially at Night [were it not?] for Pavilions of Gauze which [only differ from?] Courtains in having no divisions being all of one piece and Long enough to trail on the Ground to prevent musketoes from [getting?] under which they frequently do notwithstanding all our precautions to prevent them and then, Like McBeath, "they Murther Sleep."[35]

I had not been long in this Province before the Poverty and sandiness of the high Land and the flatness, [richness?] and want of solid consistence in the Lowlands made me imagine that all on this side the Mountains of this and the neighbouring Provinces of Virginia No Carolina Georgia and the Floridas have been gaind from the Sea – and very lately too in Comparison of the rest of the World – The high Lands which run in continued Ridges for a great length in proportion to their Breadth may without any extraordinary Latitude of reasoning be supposd to have been thrown up by force of such a prodigious body of Water when agitated with the violent tempests that often prevail in these parts – the High banks once formed the Swamps follow of course Betwixt these banks the Hollows receive and retain not only the lime from the mountains but also the vegetable & Animal productions of the [Sea?] – which mixing and fermenting together became in a short time capable of nourishing the seeds of Plants and trees whose leaves Roots & stems have Servd in tim[e] to augment the Growing soil in time other banks are formd and other swamps generated and hence it seems most natural to account for the Ridges being poorer and the Swamps Lower

---

[35] The rest of the letter has been crossed out on George Ogilvie's copy.

and softer the nearer the[y] are to the Sea especially towards the Gulph of Florida and I cannot help thinking that had vegetation and fermentation been promoted in our [Mosses?] with the same Genial warmth of the Sun they would have bore a still nearer resemblance than they now do to the Inland swamps in this Province I have mentiond the above conjecture to two very ingenious Gentlemen who both think it very probable and mentiond several thing[s] that seemd to corroborate it one was that a few years [ago?] a Person diging for a Well near a hundred miles up Pedee River found thirty feet under the Surface the Skeleton of a Whale the Back bone of which is kept as a Curiosity to this day – The small ridge of Hills mentiond in my last on the upper part of this River (to pursue the Idea) may be presumd to have been small Islands – as they are full of Stones which seem entirely composed of Petrifyd [Shells?] – but having no aquafortis with me I had not an opportunity of [trying?] if they still retaind the Efervescent Quality – but if they do not there are stones in many other places as far from the Sea which produce as good Lime as fresh sea Shells – The greater objection is what [became?] of the Waters that formerly coverd so many [large?] Provinces at first I thought of the floods recorded by both Sacred and profane writers to have happened in the Old world but I can scarce allow this Country so old an Existance neither is it probable that it was gaind from the Ocean all at once but may we not suppose that the vast body of Waters to the south of the Equator where our late discoverys prove that no [large?] Continent doth now exist may have formerly been dry Land – which may it is possible have been coverd by, as gradually as this has been gaind from[,] the Sea

Letters of Thomas Taylor, Georgia, 1776, and Baikia Harvey, South Carolina, 1775

BUSINESS enterprise on the eve of the American Revolution took many forms, one of which was the transportation of large groups of indentured servants to plantations owned by two or more partners, where the labor and skills of the servants created profits from the production of crops, clothing, iron goods, and other commodities. Two such schemes were attempted in the newly ceded lands of the Georgia backcountry before the Revolution. One involved the plantation of Friendsborough, founded by William Manson, a Quaker ship captain, and his Newcastle, England, partners, William and John

Chapman. The other was the adjacent settlement of Brownsborough, organized by Jonas Brown of Whitby, Yorkshire, and his son Thomas, together with their friend James Gordon. Both settlements flourished until the outbreak of war in the backcountry forced the settlers to disband and the plantation business to break up. The Thomas Taylor letter concerns the immediate arrival of the 100 servants indented to Manson, and some early problems that the war caused for their settlement plans. Baikia Harvey, a servant bound to the Browns and Gordon, relates in his unique letter the emigrant experience from the perspective of an indentured servant.[36]

Thomas Taylor to the Rev. Dr. Percy, Wrightsborough, Georgia, January 13, 1776[37]

Thomas Taylor, a 22-year-old surgeon and friend of the Mansons, went to Georgia with William Manson and his family, and 100 indentured servants that Manson had recruited to help build Friendsborough, his Quaker settlement near Wrightsborough, Georgia. At first, Taylor lived near his friends, but later joined the royal militia as a surgeon. He became "more deeply interested in the Fate of this Country" when he married Bellamy Johnston of Augusta in 1781. However, in 1782 he was banished from the state and his property was confiscated. He and his family went to Florida until Taylor was pardoned by the Georgia legislature, when they returned to Georgia.[38]

[36] For a detailed history of this enterprise, see Bernard Bailyn, *Voyagers to the West: A Passage in the Peopling of America on the Eve of the Revolution* (New York, 1986), chap. 15; Edward J. Cashin, *The King's Ranger: Thomas Brown and the American Revolution on the Southern Frontier* (Athens, GA, 1989), 17–18.

[37] *Source:* Miscellaneous Collection, William L. Clements Library, The University of Michigan, Ann Arbor, MI. *Courtesy:* William L. Clements Library. The letter was addressed "To The Revd. Dr. Percy, Northumberland House, London." The letter is a recipient copy.

Thomas Percy (1729–1811), as chaplain to the Duke of Northumberland, lived at Northumberland House in the Strand in London. In 1769 he had been chaplain to the king, and in 1782, became bishop of Dromore in Ireland. A. F. Falconer, ed., *The Correspondence of Thomas Percy & David Dalrymple, Lord Hailes* (Baton Rouge, LA, 1954), xviii, n. 30; 98.

[38] T47/10/153–155, Public Record Office, London (hereafter PRO); Palmer, *Biographical Sketches of Loyalists*, 850; Cashin, *King's Ranger*, 133, 145, 191; quote from Thomas Taylor to the Rev. Mr. John Wesley, February 28, 1782, Shelburne Papers, 66: 665, William L. Clements Library, The University of Michigan.

Revd. Sir/   Wrightsburgh in Georgia Jany. 13.1776

The very great Obligations which I lie under to your Kindness render me desirous of making all the Return in my Powr, that of acknowledging it.

After a tedious Passage of near fourteen Weeks we arrivd at Savannah Decr. 12th having lost only four children in the Small-Pox, out of ten who were infected altho at one Time during the Passage upwards of half our People were down in a Fever.[39]

As we brought no Goods for Sale the Committee at Savannah made no Objection to our Landing.[40] After staying there a few Days I came forward with about half our Poeple (between forty & fifty) The Distance hither is about 160 Miles. We were eight Nights upon the Road, five of which we encamp'd out, part of the Time in Rain, Frost & Snow. The Country for ye first hundred Miles is a mere sandy Plain with frequent Swamps all coverd with the long leav'd Pine. As you approach this Settlement the Land is much richer & diversified with Hills & Dales. The Country too is more populous, most of the Settlers having arriv'd within this eight Years from the back Parts of Pensylvania & Virginia. The Land here bears pretty good Wheat, Rye, Oats, Pease, Indian Corn, Indigo, Cotton &c. Peaches are pretty plen-

---

[39] A similar account was written by William Manson and published in the *Newcastle Journal. Or, General Advertiser*, February 17, 1776:

NEWCASTLE

"Extract of a letter from Capt. Manson, of the Georgia Packet, who sailed from hence in Sep. last[,] SAVANNAH, Dec. 16, 1775 'We arrived safe here on the 12th inst. after a long passage of 82 days from the Orkneys. In the fore part of the voyage the small-pox broke out amongst us, and carried off four children, but as all appearances of the infection had ceased seven weeks before we had arrived, we were excused from performing quarantine. – Three children, likely to live, were born in the passage. – On affirming we had no goods on board but for plantation use, we were permitted to land our stores, and will be allowed to pass peaceably to our plantation in the back settlements, two hundred miles up the country. The Marlbro' belonging to Mr Brown of Whitby, from the Orkneys with emigrants, arrived here five weeks before us, and having brought some coals for sale, was obliged, by the committee of safety, to throw them overboard before she could enter. The congress have shut the ports of Georgia against all exportation, from this day to the first of March next, but with permission for such ships as have entered and cleared outwards before to complete their loading. We accordingly cleared outwards yesterday for London, and took in six barrels of rice, by way of beginning, at 3l. per ton, which is a very high freight, owing to so few ships being here.' "

[40] See previous note.

tifull but no other Sort of Fruit, merely (I believe) for Want of Culture. The Woods hereabouts consist of short leav'd Pine, Oak, & Hiccory.

Altho' this Province has acceded to the Resolutions of the Congress[41] yet the Majority of the Poeple are Friends to Government. Indeed they are all amazingly ignorant of the true State of Affairs. few will believe but there are as many Liberty-Men in Arms in England as in America, & they are mostly perswaded, the Dutch mean to assist them. Not one in fifty has every heard of Lord North's conciliatory Motion,[42] but they are taught to believe that ye Ministry have vowd Death & Destruction to the whole Continent. Some of the Committee Men for this District with whom I have convers'd are mightily cool'd in their Zeal of late. At their last Sitting only five out of thirteen could be got to act.

The Bulk of the Poeple grumble mightily at the *Patriotism* of the Merchants who when they had got in a large Stock of Goods consented to the Non-Importation that they might get their own Price for them.

Some Time ago two Gentlemen in the back Parts of the Province of South-Carolina rais'd a Body of about 1200 Men to oppose the Congress, these after some Skirmishes have [   ] [. . . pers'd] by the Militia of that Province, about 150 have been taken Prisoners who after being cruelly use[d] were sent down to Charles Town. The rest dare not return to their Habitations so that the Country around is pillag['d] & desolate. I beg my Respects when Oppertunity offers to my good Friend Dr. Berkeley & remain with the most unfeign'd Esteem Revd. Sir Yr. most obedt. Servant

Thos. Taylor

P.S. We have just heard that Canada is reduc'd & the Governor taken Prisoner.

Four of our Poeple were debauch'd into the Provincial Service at Savannah, but upon Application to the Council of Safety, they have promis'd that the Officer shall be disgrac'd & the Men restor'd, they being all indented Servants[43]

---

41 The First Continental Congress that met in Philadelphia in September 1774 passed certain resolutions against Great Britain, among which was one to stop the importation of goods from Britain, Ireland, and the British West Indies. When the Georgia provincial congress met in Savannah on January 17, 1775, it adopted these measures with some alterations. Kenneth Coleman, *The American Revolution in Georgia, 1763–1789* (Athens, GA, 1958), 44–47.

42 In February 1775 Parliament passed a proposal that the prime minister, Lord North, called his conciliatory measure, which waived parliamentary taxes from any colony that contributed its fair share toward the financing of the common defense.

43 The four servants, William Budge, Francis Wallace, Thomas Purdy, and John Douglass,

Baikia Harvey to Thomas Baikie, Snowhill, South Carolina, December 30, 1775[44]

Baikia Harvey, a 16-year-old indentured servant from Kirkwall, Orkney, Scotland, bound himself to Messrs. Browns and Gordon to work on their new Georgia settlement, Brownsborough.[45] He went to America with a shipload of Thomas Brown's indentured servants on board the *Marlborough*, which arrived in Savannah in mid-November 1774. He told the Scottish customs officers that his reason for going to America was to "seek a better way of living."[46] However, Harvey was not happy at Brownsborough. He was "us'd . . . vere ill" by Thomas Brown, so he ran away and joined Colonel Richard Richardson's expedition of rebel soldiers, who were looking for Tories in the backcountry of South Carolina. This was where he probably met LeRoy Hammond, who was helping William Henry Drayton and William Tennent in their effort to rout out the loyalists. When he returned, the well-to-do Hammond bought Harvey's remaining servant time from James Gordon, and Harvey went to work for Hammond, whom he liked very well. He rejoined the army and in 1777 was a private in Lt. William Caldwell's company. However, Harvey was never able to realize his plans of finding a "better way of living" by learning a trade in America and by making good wages; he was killed on October 11, 1779 during the assault on the British redoubt at Spring Hill.[47]

were enlisted by a recruiting officer, John Spencer, who was acting under the authority of the Council of Safety. Manson petitioned the Board of the Council on January 2, 1776, saying that Spencer and other recruits had "attacked his house, pulled down his fence, and would have proceeded to further violence if not prevented by people in the house . . ." and he had enlisted his servants. The Board ordered Spencer to "surrender the men so enlisted, receiving back their enlisting money, or pay the expenses of indenting and bringing them to America." When Spencer replied that he could not "surrender up" the servants, the Board ordered two lieutenants to rescue them. Allen D. Candler, comp., *The Revolutionary Records of the State of Georgia*, 3 vols. (1908; reprint, New York, 1972), I: 82–84.

[44] *Source:* Watt of Breckness MSS, D3/385, Orkney Islands Area Archives, Orkney County Library, Kirkwall, Orkney, Scotland. *Courtesy:* Orkney County Library. Addressed to "Thomas Baikie, Esq., in Burnass in the Parish of Firth the Orkineys North Britin." The letter is a recipient copy.

Harvey is writing to his godfather, Thomas Baikie of Burness (1724–1782).

[45] James Gordon and Thomas Brown went to Georgia, and Jonas Brown stayed in Whitby, England, to manage his other business affairs there. See Bailyn, *Voyagers to the West*, 545–555.

[46] T47/12/56, PRO; *Georgia Gazette*, November 23, 1774.

[47] Cashin, *King's Ranger*, 36–37, 100–101; N. Louise Bailey, et al., eds., *Biographical Directory*

Dear Godfather

I am vere sorry that I did not take your Advise and stay at home with you as I have found to my sad Experence that I ought not to have slightig your Advise Mr Gordon was vere good to me but Mr Brown us'd me vere ill and I Runaway from them & wint to the Armey that was mar[c]hing up to the Back parts of South Carolina against a sett of people they call Torrys in this Country and when I came back I went to One Mr LeRoy Hammond[48] a Merchant in So. Carolina & he Bought my time which I am vere glad of for he & his Lady uses me vere will & gives me Cloaths & I Ride with my Master & Loves them Both You'l Please to send me all the Money you can Colect that is my Due by the first safe oppertunity that I may be enabled to Buy my time & Put myself to some Tradesman to Learn his calling for a Tradsman has good Wages in this Country I beg that none of my Relation[s] may come to this Country Except they are able to pay their passage thir Selves and then they may come as soon as they like this is a good poor mans Country when a man once getts into a way of Liveing but our Country people knows Nothing when they come hear the Americans are Smart Industours hardy people & fears Nothing our people is only Like the New Negros that comes out of the ships at first whin they come amongst them[.] I am Just Returnd from the Back parts Where I seed Eight Thousand Men in Arms all with Riffel'd Barrill Guns which they can kill the

of the South Carolina Senate, 1776–1985, 3 vols. (Columbia, SC, 1986), 1: 649; American Revolutionary Roster Fort Sullivan (later Fort Moultrie) 1776–1780: Battle of Fort Sullivan (Charleston, SC, 1976), 107, 174.

[48] LeRoy Hammond and his wife, Mary Ann Tyler Hammond, moved from Virginia to Augusta, Georgia, in 1765, where Hammond set up a mercantile business (LeRoy Hammond & Co.), became an Indian trader, and operated a ferry. He soon bought 600 acres in South Carolina across the Savannah River and about five miles up the river from Augusta, where he built his New Richmond plantation in 1771. Snow Hill, Hammond's summer residence, was about a mile below New Richmond. He became a colonel in the rebel army during the Revolutionary War and represented the Ninety Six District in the Provincial Congresses, the General Assembly, and the Legislative Council. N. Louise Bailey and Elizabeth I. Cooper, Biographical Directory of the South Carolina House of Representatives, Volume III, 1775–1790 (Columbia, SC, 1981), 301–302; Ted Ruddock, ed., Travels in the Colonies in 1773–1775 Described in the Letters of William Mylne (Athens, GA, 1993), 114; Cashin, King's Ranger, 20.

Bigness of a Dollar Betwixt Two & three hundreds yards Distance the Little Boys not Bigger then my self has all their Guns & marshes with their Fathers & all thir Cry is Liberty or Death Dear Godfather tell all my Country people not to come hear for the Americans will Kill them Like Deer in the Woods & they will never see them they can lie on their Backs & Load & fire & every time they Draw sight at any thing they are sure to kill or Criple & they Run in the Woods Like Horses I seed the Liberty Boys take Between Two & three hundred Torrys & one Liberty man would take & Drive four or five before him Just as the Shepards do the sheep in our Country & they have taken all their Arms from them and putt the Headmen in Gail – so that they will never be able to make head against them any more – Pray Remember me to my Dear freind Mr James Riddoh Mrs. Gordon Madam Allin Madam Young My Uncle & Aunt & all their Femily & in perticular Mr. John Gordon – I am Dear Godfather Your Most Obident and Huml. Godson

Snowhill Near Augusta in Georgia   Baikia Harvey
Decemr. 30th 1775

P.S. Please to write me the first Oppertunity to the Care of Mr. John Houston in Savannah Georgia Province &C –

Hester Wylly to Mrs. Helen Lawrence, Savannah, Georgia, December 14, 1768[49]

H ESTER Wylly emigrated to Georgia from Coleraine, County Londonderry, Ireland, in the latter part of 1768, after having received a letter from her brother Alexander requesting that she come

[49] *Source:* D 955/11, Public Record Office of Northern Ireland, Belfast; *Courtesy:* Messrs Martin, King, French, and Ingram, Limavady and the Deputy Keeper of the Records, Public Record Office of Northern Ireland. The letter is a recipient copy. The Public Record Office of Northern Ireland holds approximately 3000 emigrant letters, "very few of which were written by women." Only a small number of these letters were written before the nineteenth century. (*Guide to Sources for Women's History*, Department of the Environment for Northern Ireland [Public Record Office of Northern Ireland, 1993].) Of about 6000 letters written by Irish emigrants, only about 10% were written by men and women who emigrated between 1670 and 1814. Kerby A. Miller and Bruce D. Boling, "Golden Streets, Bitter Tears: The Irish Image of America During the Era of Mass Migration," *Journal of American Ethnic History*, 10(1990–1991), 33, n. 26.

to Georgia to be with him. Many of her relations had already migrated to America, including four brothers (Alexander, Samuel, Richard, and William), an uncle (Francis Macartan), and an aunt who lived in Charleston, South Carolina. She left her sister, Helen Lawrence, behind in Coleraine. The Georgia Wyllys were prominent members of the Savannah elite. Her brothers were representatives in the Commons House of Assembly and were well connected with the planter and business community in Savannah. Probably as a result of her brothers' connections, she met, and in 1769 married, James Habersham, Jr., son of the well-known Georgia merchant James Habersham, who was acting governor of Georgia in the early 1770s. They had five children, four of whom were still living at the time of Hester's death c. 1812.[50]

Hester's letter does not contain as much information about discoveries as the other letters do, but her experience represents that of most women who came to pre-Revolutionary America as free emigrants. Most either came with their families, or were sent for by their husbands, fiancées, fathers, or brothers, who prepared their way and made the necessary arrangements. Hester's brother Alexander wrote her in June 1768 that he had made plans for her to come to Savannah to be with him, if she wanted to come. For the first leg of her journey, he proposed that she find "Reputable & Safe Company" for her trip from Ireland to London, where she was to contact "one Miss Isabell Mossman," a relative of Alexander's wife, whom she could locate through the merchant Ralph Young. Alexander had sent Young £25 sterling for his sister's expenses and instructed Hester to travel to Georgia in the company of Miss Mossman. He regretted that their brother Richard could not return to England in order to accompany her "Cross the Atlantick," but he was too busy. He hoped, however, that Miss Mossman's "Good Company" would "prove a Sufficient Shield to Guard Her dear Innocence from Insult or Injury."[51] Alexander had also made arrangements for Hester to stay with him when she arrived in Georgia.

Hester's emigration was paid for in advance and was relatively risk-

---

[50] Alexander Wylly to Hester Wylly, Savannah, June 17, 1768, D 955/10, Public Record Office of Northern Ireland (hereafter PRONI); Allen D. Candler, ed., *The Colonial Records of the State of Georgia* (Atlanta, 1907), 15: 303–304; Jack P. Greene, *The Quest for Power: The Lower Houses of Assembly in the Southern Royal Colonies, 1689–1776* (Chapel Hill, NC, 1963), 495; D 955/57, PRONI; Kenneth Coleman, *Dictionary of Georgia Biography* (Athens, GA, 1983), 378; Alexander Wylly, Jr., to Rev. Mr. Sampson, February 26, 1816, D 955/50, PRONI; Cashin, *King's Ranger*, 17, 240.

[51] Alexander Wylly to Hester Wylly, Savannah, June 17, 1768, D 955/10, PRONI.

free, except for the potential hazards that she might encounter on the ocean voyage. She, like most women at the time, was dependent on the decision making of male relatives. Those men who could afford it left their wives and families in Britain, and came to America to find land or opportunity, and perhaps get established before returning to collect their families or sending for them. Metcalf's fiancée,[52] Ann Gill, promised to marry him, but she stayed in Yorkshire until he had started his farm building in Nova Scotia. Eventually, when he was ready, Metcalf sent her instructions on how to come and where to engage passage at Liverpool. This was common. Thomas Feilde came to Virginia without his family, as did the first laborers of the settlement at Ryegate.[53]

What Hester's experience does not show is the extent to which women could influence the decisions of their male relatives. Hester wanted to emigrate to Georgia, so she dutifully followed her brother's instructions. However, some women were able to prevent or delay their husbands' emigration plans. Hector McAllister's wife Mary refused to leave her home on the island of Arran, even though her husband owned land in North Carolina, where many of their friends and relatives had already settled.[54] Hector could get only so far in his attempt to join his brother in Carolina; he chartered a ship, organized a large group of emigrants, and wrote inquiries to the Governor of North Carolina. But that was as far as he could get; his wife remained adamant. Hector's brother called her the "only Hindrance" to their leaving Arran. So, too, was John Witherspoon's wife Elizabeth reluctant to leave. She eventually acquiesced, but her objections delayed their departure. Witherspoon explained his wife's "Melancholy thoughts" in a letter to Benjamin Rush: "It is not easy for one in her Situation after being retired and at Leisure to think without Concern on having left Relations & all the friends of early Life for Ever at least while in the body – ".[55]

Hester's experiences when she arrived in Georgia also do not reflect those of most women who came with their families as free emigrants. She lived in the household of her brother, a prominent

---

[52] See letter of James Metcalf, this volume.
[53] For example, John Waddle and David Ferry, see p. 102, this volume; see also p. 117.
[54] See p. 173, n. 13, this volume.
[55] John Witherspoon to Benjamin Rush, October 8, 1768, John Witherspoon Manuscripts, Princeton University Library, Princeton, New Jersey.

planter, landholder, and slaveowner, where she did not have to cook, clean, churn butter, sew her own clothes, or milk the cows. She could afford to spend her time at one of the "Constant assemblys & Many other amusements," such as riding her horse, or visiting friends in a horse-drawn chaise. However, most women who emigrated to America had to work hard, doing the kinds of household duties described earlier in this volume for the women who settled in Nova Scotia.[56] Female spinners, weavers, and seamstresses were always in demand. When Whitelaw was lamenting the lack of female "helps meet" at Ryegate, he said "a parcel of good spinners would be the very making of the place."[57] Women's work did not, in general, include heavy agricultural labor, but in some places, women did help to plow, drive horses, and chop away bushes and shrubs.[58] Their employment was not only needed, it was essential. As Metcalf wrote to his fiancée: "I must Marry for I Cannot Live well as I am."

Hester was certainly not needed in the fields, but soon after her arrival she got married and had her own household to run, where she, too, probably performed her share of work, especially in caring for five children.

My Dr Hellen[59]   Savanna in Georgia december 14 1768

I with pleasure Imbrace this oppery of writing you by Captn. Anderson who Sails for London in a few days – I wrote you Some time after I arrived here giveing you an account of what happened me while I was on Sea[60] – & of the affectinate reception I met with from all my freinds in this plase – & as I hope you have received that Letter it is unnesecary for to write further on that Subiect – I wrote to My Uncle Mccarten[61] Immediately after I Came

---

56 See p. 49, this volume.

57 See p. 102, n. 36, this volume.

58 "Journal of Colonel Alexander Harvey of Scotland and Barnet, Vermont," *Proceedings of the Vermont Historical Society for the Years 1921, 1922, and 1923* (Montpelier, VT, 1924), 228; Roland E. Chardon, "The Cape Florida Society of 1773," *Tequesta*, 35(1975), Appendix A: "Information and recommendations to the Cape Florida Society, by William Gerard De Brahm; with cover letter to Lord Dartmouth, dated May 4th, 1773," p. 34.

59 Helen Lawrence, Hester Wylly's sister who lived in Coleraine, Ireland.

60 This letter is not in the collection.

61 Francis Macartan and Martin Campbell were partners in a deerskin exporting business from

& of my Intention to pay him a visit – I recived from him a very affectinate
Letter & desired me to go up as Soon as possible – but unluckeily for me
my Brother Could not go to the end of the month as the assembly was to
Sit – my Uncle was taken Suddenly Ill & he was so desirous to See me that
he attempted to Come by water to my Brothers as he knew he was a dying
& wanted to See me – but as his disorder was an Impostume[62] in his breast
it broke & he died before my brother Could See him – he made his will
the day before he died – & as I have not yet Seen it – I Can not give you
the full perticulers I Can only Let you know he Left to alleck[63] 6 hundred
pounds to his thiree Children a hundred a peise to Selly a hundred & fifty
pound & a Gold Watch – & to me three hundred pounds Sterling & his
own Gold Chasced Watch and trinkets – to Sam[64] and Dick[65] a hundred
pounds each & his wearing apparrall – & I am Sorry for My Dr Little John
Sake to Inform you he only Left you twenty pounds to put you in mourning
as you had never wrote him he thought you did not want his help – I hear
he has Left Some Legesies to people in Coleraine & belfast but who I Cant
tell – the remainder is Left to My Couzin Cortin Campell – I believe he
died worth about eight Thousand pounds he is greatly Limented by every
person that know him as he was the most Charitable Man I ever heard of
– I have received three Letters from aunt Campell – With a pressing In-
vatation to go to Charls town – I Intend to go there after Chrismas to Stay

the 1740s to the 1760s. Macartan's will was dated October 29, 1768, and proved November
10, 1769. *Laurens Papers*, 3: 32n, 165n.

[62] Absess.

[63] Alexander Wylly was Hester's brother with whom she lived in Georgia. He was a leading
planter who owned a substantial amount of property, including lands in Christ Church, St.
Matthew's, and St. George's parishes, as well as a town lot in Savannah. He served as a
representative in the Commons House of Assembly from 1760 to 1764 and was speaker of
the Commons House from 1764 to 1768. He died in 1781. Betty Wood, *Slavery in Colonial
Georgia, 1730–1775* (Athens, GA, 1984), 234n; Pat Bryant, *English Crown Grants in St. George
Parish in Georgia 1755–1775* (Atlanta, GA, 1974), 233; Marion R. Hemperley, *English Crown
Grants in Christ Church Parish in Georgia, 1755–1775* (Atlanta, GA, 1973), 205; Greene, *Quest
for Power*, 461; Peter Coldham, *American Loyalist Claims* (Washington, D.C., 1980), 1: 540.

[64] Hester's brother in Jamaica.

[65] Richard Wylly, Hester's brother, was a planter/businessman who had business connections
with Hester's future husband, James Habersham, Jr. He married twice; his first wife was
Mary Bryan, and his second was Mary Morrell (maiden name also Bryan). He represented
Vernonburgh in Christ Church parish in the Commons House of Assembly. *The Letters of
Hon. James Habersham, 1756–1775*, Collections of the Georgia Historical Society, vol. VI
(Savannah, GA, 1904), 120; D 955/57, PRONI; Candler, ed., *Colonial Records of . . . Georgia*,
15: 303–304.

Some time She wrote me the Shocking account of what happend poor Mrs Lewis whish I Suppose you heard of before this – I am exeadingly Sorry on my Dear Brother Lawrences[66] account as it Must Certainly be a very great Loss to him – poor Creatures the were in great disstress for 9 days on Sea in an open boat & no more then a gill a water a day – & Lost every thing but what was on them I wonder what Could tempt Mrs Lewis to Come in the providence – my aunt Informs me the Intend Staying in Charls Town to Spring if that is the Case I Shall be very happy with Mrs Lewis – I wrote her & at the Same time my Aunt to take notice of them Whish I find She has done – My Dear Hillen I am Sure it will give you pleasure to hear that this place agres with me as well as Ireland – I have not as yet found any difference – its true in the heat of Sumner the people that is exposed to the Sun is Subject to What the Call fever & egue [ague] – but it Soon Leaves them & is Seldom dangerous – the Weather at this time of year is mush the Same as our Winter only a Little Uncertain – the provisions is the Same plenty of good Beef & Mutten – & fowlls – fish – & every thing – the princepel produce is rice & deer Scins – as for the people here the are extremly polite & Socible – We form a wrong notion of the Women for I assure you I never Saw finer Wemen in any part of the World – nor finer Complexions in My Life – the are very gay and Spritely – We have Constant assemblys & Many other amusements to Make the place agreeable, – the dress in the Same Manner as the do in London & tho every thing is Sold at at Least a hundred per Cent yet the dress very fine – My Brother alleck Live in the Sumer time about eight Mils from Savanna & in the winter in town his wife is a very agreaabl Little woman – he has three fine Children – to boys & a girl – My Brothe[r] William[67] Lives a quarter of a mile from allecks he has one girl & a boy – Sam Stays in Jamecia & is in a very good way – as for dick he is Just gone out to the West Indies Super Cargo – but will Set up for him Self When he returns – I Live always with alleck who is very fond of me he has made me Several presents – billy tother day bought me a hansome hors & Saddle as [the?] Ladies [   ] was amaced when I first Came here to [   ] of their houses made of wood – & none [   ] paved but all Covered with Sand every [   ] two or three Singl hors Chairs & We [   ] but in them the think nothing of going [   ] mils to pay

[66] Probably refers to her brother-in-law, Helen's husband.

[67] William Wylly served as representative to the Commons House of Assembly for Halifax and the Parish of St. George. He died before the Revolution. Candler, ed., *Colonial Records of . . . Georgia*, 15: 304; Alexander Wylly, Jr., to Rev. Mr. Sampson, February 26, 1816, D 955/51, PRONI.

a visit it is a hundred [   ] Charl[s] Town by Water & hundred &
[fif . . .] [   ] My Dr Hellen I expected Letters from [you?] [   ] their
was a Ship Came here tother [   ] great number of people from bel[fast?][68]
[   ] Miss no oppertunity of writin[g] [   ] know What pleasure it
mus[t] [   ] know you all are – My Letters [yo . . .] [   ] I Come here
Whish Will return [   ] next May – So I beg you may wri[te] [   ]
Letters directed to Mr Joseph Gaylord on [Lime?] Street London & you
may be assured the will Come Safe I have Sent mrs gaylord Some green
oranges Whish is the produse of this Country – as for [these?] kind of things
it would be a folly to Send them to you as you Could never recive the[m] I
Shall write you by one Captn. Sullavan who will Sail for Cork in aprill and
if I Can get any thing Worth Sending will – My Love to My Dr brother
Lawrence and am my Der Hellen your ever Loveing Sister

Hester Wylly

I am affraid I have tired you with my Scrall My Brothers & Sister[69] Send
their Love to you [al?] I beg You will find a Spare hour to write to my Sister
as She very well [deserves?] that peise of respect from you my Love to all
my good freinds in Colerain My Dr Hellen Since I wrote the above I have
ben in Company with a Mrs Crosby a Lady from Armagh who has been
here about too years & as the Climate dont agre with her She returs in
Captn. Andersons So I Send my Letters by her ones more ad[ieu?]
My Dr [   ] Hellen

[68] This ship arrival was probably the *Prince George*, which left Belfast at the end of September
1768, and arrived in Savannah on December 2 with 107 emigrants. These emigrants had
been recruited for the new Georgia township of Queensborough. See E. R. R. Green,
"Queensborough Township: Scotch-Irish Emigration and the Expansion of Georgia, 1763–
1776," *William and Mary Quarterly*, 17(1960), 183–199.

[69] Hester is probably referring to her sister-in-law, Susanna Wylly, Alexander's wife. Hester
lived with them before she married James Habersham, Jr.

INDEX